AFTER *the* ROMANOVS

Also by Helen Rappaport

Joseph Stalin

Encyclopedia of Women Social Reformers

Queen Victoria

No Place for Ladies

The Last Days of the Romanovs

Conspirator

Beautiful For Ever

A Magnificent Obsession

The Romanov Sisters

The Victoria Letters

Caught in the Revolution

The Race to Save the Romanovs

In Search of Mary Seacole: The Making of a Cultural Icon

WITH WILLIAM HORWOOD
Dark Hearts of Chicago

WITH ROGER WATSON
Capturing the Light

AFTER *the* ROMANOVS

RUSSIAN EXILES IN PARIS FROM THE BELLE ÉPOQUE THROUGH REVOLUTION AND WAR

◆◆◆

HELEN RAPPAPORT

ST. MARTIN'S PRESS
NEW YORK

Library of Congress Cataloging-in-Publication Data

Names: Rappaport, Helen, author.
Title: After the Romanovs : Russian exiles in Paris from the Belle Époque through
    revolution and war / Helen Rappaport.
Description: First edition. | New York : St. Martin's Press, 2022. | Includes
    bibliographical references and index. |
Identifiers: LCCN 2021044046 | ISBN 9781250273109 (hardcover) |
    ISBN 9781250273116 (ebook)
Subjects: LCSH: Russians—France—Paris—Social life and customs—20th
    century. | Russians—France—Paris—Intellectual life—20th century. | Russians—
    France—Paris—Social conditions—20th century. | Political refugees—France—
    Paris—History—20th century. | Exiles—France—Paris—History—20th
    century. | Russians—France—Paris—History—20th century. | Paris (France)—
    Intellectual life—20th century.
Classification: LCC DC718.R8 R37 2022 | DDC 944/.3610049171—dc23
LC record available at https://lccn.loc.gov/2021044046

For Sue Woolmans, a good companion
on many of my Russian literary journeys

I have packed my Russia in my bag,
And take her with me anywhere I go.
—VLADISLAV KHODASEVICH, POEM READ TO NINA BERBEROVA
AS THEY LEFT RUSSIA BY TRAIN, 1922

There is no sweeter destiny than to lose everything.
There is no happier fate than to become a vagabond.
And you've never been closer to heaven
Than here, tired of boredom
Tired of breathing,
Without strength, without money,
Without love,
In Paris
—GEORGIY ADAMOVICH,
"THANK YOU FOR EVERYTHING," 1931

They do not know us. They do not know the Russian emigration. For
most people, the émigrés are nothing but down-at-heel aristocrats,
dragging their nostalgia and fatalism around the bars. . . . You only
need to add balalaikas, sonorous songs of the Volga, a disorderly
dance and there you have it—the Russian emigration.
—COUNT VLADIMIR KOKOVTSOV,
IN JEAN DELAGE, *La Russie en exil*, 1930

Contents

Russians in Paris: Cast of Characters

The list below comprises the most frequently cited Russian names in the text.

Akhmatova, Anna (1889–1966) one of Russia's most revered poets; in Paris before World War I

Antonina Nesterovskaya (1890–1950) morganatic wife of Prince Gavriil; in Paris granted title Princess Romanovskaya-Strelninskaya

Bakst, Léon (1866–1924) painter and costume and set designer, famous for his work in Ballets Russes with Diaghilev

Benois, Alexandre (1870–1960) artist and critic, close collaborator in Ballets Russes with Diaghilev and Bakst

Berberova, Nina (1901–93) leading writer of the Russian Paris emigration; after 1951 enjoyed distinguished academic career in United States; partner of Khodasevich

Bunin, Ivan (1870–1953) much admired short story writer; leader of Paris literary emigration; Nobel laureate in 1933; husband of Vera Muromtseva

Chagall, Marc (1887–1985) Belarusian Jew, born Moishe Shagal; leading modernist painter in Paris; emigrated to the United States in 1941

Chaliapin, Feodor (1873–1938) opera singer who performed with Diaghilev and the Saisons Russes in Paris and toured Europe extensively

Countess von Hohenfelsen (see *Princess Paley*)

Diaghilev, Sergey (1872–1929) influential art critic, patron, and ballet impresario; founder of the Ballets Russes; associate of Bakst, Benois, Nijinsky, and Stravinsky

Don-Aminado (1888–1957) pen name of Aminodav Shpolyansky; journalist and satirist noted for his humorous short stories

Egorova, Lyubov (1880–1972) ballet dancer from St. Petersburg Imperial Theater; danced with Nijinsky for Diaghilev's Ballets Russes

Ehrenburg, Ilya (1891–1967) pro-Soviet journalist, essayist, and writer who commuted between USSR and France and associated with many of the Paris literary émigrés

Fokine, Michel (1880–1942) born Mikhail Fokin, choreographer and ballet dancer, collaborator with Diaghilev

Gazdanov, Gaito (1903–1971) writer who supported himself in Paris driving a taxi from 1928 through 1952; member of French Resistance during World War II

General Alexander Kutepov (1882–1930) White Russian leader; commander of ROVS; in exile in Paris from 1928; abducted and murdered by OGPU in 1930

General Yevgeny Miller (1867–1939) succeeded Kutepov as head of ROVS in Paris; abducted in Paris 1937 by the NKVD; tortured and shot in Moscow

Gippius, Zinaida (1882–1945) poet, critic, and religious thinker; founder of Paris literary group the Green Lamp with her husband, Dmitri Merezhkovsky

Gorgulov (Gorguloff), Pavel (1895–1932) émigré who assassinated French president Paul Doumer in 1932

Grand Duchess Maria Pavlovna (1890–1958) daughter of Grand Duke Paul; sister of Grand Duke Dmitri; daughter-in-law of Princess Poutiatine

Grand Duchess Vladimir (1854–1920) born Marie Alexandrine of Mecklenburg-Schwerin; became Maria Pavlovna on her marriage to Grand Duke Vladimir in 1874; mother of Grand Dukes Kirill, Boris, and Andrey and Grand Duchess Elena, Princess of Greece

Grand Duke Alexander Mikhailovich (see *Sandro*)

Grand Duke Alexis Alexandrovich (1850–1908) son of Tsar Alexander II; brother of Grand Dukes Vladimir and Paul

Grand Duke Andrey Vladimirovich (1879–1956) son of Grand Duke Vladimir, husband of Kschessinska

Grand Duke Boris Vladimirovich (1877–1943) son of Grand Duke Vladimir

Grand Duke Dmitri Pavlovich (1891–1942) eldest son of Grand Duke Paul, brother of Grand Duchess Maria; lover in Paris of Coco Chanel

Grand Duke Kirill (Cyril) Vladimirovich (1876–1938) curator of the Romanov throne in exile; proclaimed himself Emperor in Exile; husband of Victoria Melita

Grand Duke Mikhail Alexandrovich (1878–1918) brother of Tsar Nicholas II; not to be confused with Grand Duke Mikhail Mikhailovich (1861–1929), who was known as Miche-Miche

Grand Duke Nikolay Nikolaevich (see *Nikolasha*)

Grand Duke Paul Alexandrovich (1860–1919) son of Tsar Alexander II and brother of Grand Dukes Vladimir and Alexis; father of Grand Duke Dmitri and Grand Duchess Maria; husband of Princess Paley

Grand Duke Vladimir Alexandrovich (1847–1909) brother of Grand Duke Paul and husband of Grand Duchess Vladimir

Gul, Roman (1896–1986) writer and critic

Karsavina, Tamara (1885–1978) prima ballerina who danced with Diaghilev's Ballets Russes in Paris

Kerensky, Alexander (1881–1970) minister of war, then prime minister of the Provisional Government in 1917; in Paris, editor of émigré journal *Dni*

Khodasevich, Vladislav (1886–1939) leading poet and literary critic of the Paris emigration; partner of Nina Berberova

Knorring, Irina (1906–43) underrated poet of the emigration who died tragically young of diabetes

Kschessinska, Mathilde (1872–1971) Russian prima ballerina of Polish parentage; formerly mistress of Nicholas II when he was tsarevich; wife of Grand Duke Andrey

Kuprin, Alexander (1870–1938) short story writer; returned to Soviet Union in 1937

Lenin, Vladimir Ilyich Ulyanov (1870–1924) Bolshevik revolutionary; head of the first government of the Soviet Union from October 1917 through 1924

Lifar, Serge (Sergey) (1905–86) ballet dancer and choreographer; danced with Karsavina for Diaghilev's Ballets Russes in Paris

Merezhkovsky, Dmitri (1865–1941) influential poet, philosopher, and religious thinker; with his wife, Zinaida Gippius, founder of the Green Lamp literary society in Paris

Milyukov, Pavel (1859–1943) foreign minister in Russian Provisional Government in 1917; in Paris, editor of major Russian language newspaper *Poslednie novosti* (Latest News) (1920–40)

Mother Maria Skobtsova (1891–1945) née Elizaveta Pilenko, poet and nun who set up a food kitchen and refuge for Russian émigrés in Paris

Muromtseva, Vera (1881–1961) diarist and long-term partner of Ivan Bunin; from 1922, his second wife

Nabokov, Vladimir (1899–1977) émigré novelist and poet in Berlin 1922–37; after briefly fleeing Hitler's Germany for Paris, emigrated to the United States in 1940

Nijinsky, Vaslav (1889–1950) ballet dancer and choreographer who created a sensation in Paris when he debuted with Diaghilev's Ballets Russes

Nikolasha, Grand Duke Nikolay Nikolaevich (1856–1929) World War I general; leader of monarchists in Paris from 1919 till his death

Odoevtseva, Irina (1895–1990) novelist and poet who returned to Soviet Union in 1987 to considerable acclaim and published bestselling memoirs

Poplavsky, Boris (1903–35) one of the most promising young poets of the Paris emigration who destroyed himself through drug taking

Prince Felix Yusupov (1887–1967) leading aristocrat and socialite of the Paris community; with his wife, Irina, founded the fashion house Irfé

Prince Gavriil Konstantinovich (1887–1955) great-grandson of Tsar Nicholas I; contracted morganatic marriage to Antonina Nesterovskaya in 1917; elevated to grand duke in 1939

Prince Vladimir Paley (1897–1918) son of Grand Duke Paul and Princess Paley

Princess Paley (1865–1929) née Olga von Pistohlkors; from 1904 Countess von Hohenfelsen; wife of Grand Duke Paul, granted title Princess Paley in 1915

Princess Poutiatine (Sofya Putyatina) (1866–1940) mother of Sergey Poutiatine, second husband of Grand Duchess Maria

Princess Vera Meshcherskaya (1876–1949) founder of the Russia House, a home for indigent elderly Russian émigrés at Sainte-Geneviève-des-Bois

Princess Zinaida Shakhovskaya (1906–2001) writer and literary critic

Remizov, Alexey (1877–1957) prolific writer, illustrator, and folklorist who struggled to find an audience in emigration

Sandro, Grand Duke Alexander Mikhailovich (1866–1933) husband of Nicholas II's sister Grand Duchess Xenia

Sedykh, Andrey (1902–94) pen name of Yakov Tsvibak; writer and journalist; emigrated to New York in 1942

Soutine, Chaim (Chaim Sutin) (1893–1943) Jewish expressionist painter, friend of Chagall

Stravinsky, Igor (1882–1971) composer, collaborator with Diaghilev and Nijinsky on the groundbreaking Ballets Russes production of *The Rite of Spring*

Teffi (1872–1952) pen name of Nadezhda Lokhvitskaya; popular short story writer in prerevolutionary Russia; leading figure in Paris literary emigration

Tsvetaeva, Marina (1892–1941) outstanding poet of the Paris emigration who struggled with loneliness and poverty; returned to Soviet Union in 1939

Troyat, Henri (1911–2007) pen name of Lev Tarasov; wrote in French and took citizenship in 1933; earned numerous honors, including the Prix Goncourt

Vertinsky, Alexander (1889–1997) popular singer and cabaret performer who enjoyed success in Europe and after his return to Soviet Union in 1943

Victoria Melita, Grand Duchess Victoria Feodorovna of Russia (1876–1936) daughter of Prince Alfred of Great Britain and Grand Duchess Maria Alexandrovna; wife of Grand Duke Kirill

Yanovsky, Vasily (1906–89) writer and memoirist; emigrated to the United States in 1942

——>··<——

CHAPTER I

La Tournée des Grands Ducs

I n Paris during the summer of 1900, there was no more select place for *Le Tout-Paris* (a popular expression referring to those in fashionable French high society) to be than the Hôtel Ritz on place Vendôme, where they could be seen taking afternoon tea amid the elegant statues, urns, and fountains of its shady gardens. During a season when Paris was packed with tourists for the Exposition Universelle and the Second Olympiad, this quaint English tradition for "le five-o-clock," as the French called it, was a magical ritual hour in the social round enjoyed by the superwealthy upper crust of Paris.

Afternoon tea at the Hôtel Ritz was also de rigueur for any well-heeled foreign visitor. In the Ritz garden you would see the best-dressed women in Paris in their fine gowns and enormous picture hats, presenting an image of "a large aviary full of multicolored birds."[1] The hats might obscure the view somewhat, but if you looked hard enough you would soon be sure to pick out a Russian grand duke or grand duchess, a prince or princess, a count or countess, among the chosen few. For the French-speaking Russian aristocracy, Paris for the last forty years or more had been a home away from home, a safe haven in winter from the bitter cold of the northern Russian climate and the rising threat of revolution that was increasingly targeting their class. So much so that by the beginning of the new twentieth century, Paris was fast becoming "the capital of Russia out of Russia"—for those with plenty of money.[2]

The Russian discovery of the French capital in fact goes back to the time of the modernizing tsar, Peter the Great, who made a visit to Paris in 1717 and fell in love with Versailles. He had favored all things French in the construction of his own "window on the West"—the Russian capital St. Petersburg. Catherine the Great— the wife of Peter's grandson—and herself an avowed Francophile, was, during her reign from 1762 to 1796, the most vigorous promoter of Franco-Russian cultural links. She ordained that French be the official language at court and entered into an extensive correspondence with the writers Voltaire and Diderot. Her patronage of French arts and crafts was everywhere to be seen in her palaces in St. Petersburg and Tsarskoe Selo.

The beginning of the nineteenth century had brought a downturn in political relations between the two countries, with the French and Russians on opposing sides during the Napoleonic Wars, culminating in the ignominy for the French of Tsar Alexander I riding in triumph into Paris on March 31, 1814, after the rout of the Grande Armée from Russia. The two countries were at odds again during the Crimean War of 1853–56. But as relations recovered in the 1860s, the Russian aristocracy and moneyed classes returned to Paris in droves. Many made Paris their home, such as the writer Ivan Turgenev—familiar to Parisians since the mid-1850s in frenchified transliterated form as Tourgenieff. He had become an almost permanent resident in Paris after 1847, having left Russia in pursuit of his obsessive love for the married French opera singer Pauline Viardot. Turgenev lived for many years in an apartment in the same building as Viardot and her husband on the rue de Douai, till his death in

1883. So beloved was he by the French that he had by then become an unofficial cultural ambassador for Russia in Paris and a friend of some of its leading contemporary writers—Dumas, Zola, Maupassant, Flaubert, and George Sand.

The Exposition Universelle of 1867 brought a huge influx of twenty thousand Russian visitors into Paris. So many were now traveling to Paris on a regular basis that Tsar Alexander II donated 200,000 francs to help build a new and dedicated place of worship for them—the Alexander Nevsky Cathedral, which opened on the rue Daru in the 8th arrondissement in 1861. After the disruptions in Europe caused by the Franco-Prussian War of 1870–71 and Russia's estrangement from Germany and Austria-Hungary after the Russo-Turkish War of 1877–78, the first seeds of a new golden age of rapprochement with France were sown. By then the French were showing an increasing interest in Russian literature and culture, thanks to their promotion in French journals by the diplomat and critic Eugène-Melchior de Vogüé.[3] But during the reign of the authoritarian and straitlaced Alexander III, who came to the throne after his father's assassination in 1881, reaction set in. For the pleasure-seeking Romanov grand dukes (including Alexander's own brothers: Vladimir, Alexis, and Paul) the temptation to self-indulgence in the pleasure domes of Paris became even greater, along with trips to the luxurious hotels and casinos of Biarritz on the Atlantic coast and the French Riviera.[4]

In France expatriate Russians could now bask in the burgeoning Franco-Russian friendship, which reached its pinnacle with a series of political alliances in the 1890s, much to the annoyance of Kaiser Wilhelm, who had tried hard to drive a wedge between the two countries. This newfound relationship was sealed by the hugely popular five-day state visit of Tsar Nicholas II and his wife, Alexandra, along with their ten-month-old baby daughter, Olga, to Cherbourg and Paris in October 1896. The family had sailed to France from Scotland after a visit to Queen Victoria at Balmoral. According to the tsaritsa's close personal friend Baroness Buxhoeveden, "The Russian Sovereigns, from the moment they set foot on French soil, were the objects of an unceasing ovation"; on entering Paris, their reception "became positively delirious."[5] Cries of "*Vive le bébé et la nounou*" greeted even little Olga and her nanny as they drove in an open carriage down a Champs-Élysées festooned with decorations and artificial blooms in the chestnut trees. During that hectic "Russian Week," Paris's population, then 2 million, swelled with 930,000 visitors. President Fauré accompanied Nicholas and Alexandra on a whistle-stop tour of the Paris Opera, the Louvre, and Notre Dame, the mint, and the Sèvres factory. Nicholas also laid the foundation stone of a bridge—Le Pont Alexandre III—in his father Alexander III's honor.

Throughout the visit security was very tight, for the tsar was the number one target of Russian revolutionaries and anarchists. There was no time for a shopping walkabout as Alexandra had hoped. But she and her husband were at least able to thrill, in splendid isolation, at the beauties of Versailles and be entertained in style at a sumptuous banquet followed by a theatrical performance from the French actress Sarah Bernhardt. Throughout the tour the Romanov couple's every move was closely followed and described in detail in the French press; Alexandra's fashion sense and beauty were widely commended. Everything Russian or pseudo-Russian was snapped up in the shops: commemorative china, "Le Tsar" soap, Russian flags and emblems, portraits of the Romanov family, Russian bear toys, and cabinet-card photographs of Nicholas, Alexandra, and baby Olga. A special Franco-Russian cheese was created; Russian-style clothes were labeled as a "Gift from the Tsars."[6] In the wake of the imperial visit, "Paris went joyously Rooski" as one contemporary observed.[7] The French birth registrars were soon recording increasing numbers of little Ivans, Dimitris, Olgas, and Serges.

Of all the expatriate Russians who haunted Paris during the season at this time, none reveled more in all that the capital had to offer than the colorful, if not notorious, Russian grand dukes. Such had been their predilection, since the 1860s, for visiting under cover of darkness all that the Parisian underworld of eroticism, not to say vice, had to offer that the concept of La Tournée des Grands Ducs (The Grand Dukes' Tour) had become a feature of the off-the-map Paris tourist trail. The tour — taken after midnight, when the theaters turned out — provided paying customers with the frisson of experiencing the red-light district's fashionable brothels; the gambling dens and bars of Belville, Montmartre, and Les Halles; and the cabarets of La Butte. It became part of the Belle Époque mystique.[8] There was even a novel on the subject, *La Tournée des grands ducs: Moeurs parisiennes,* published in 1901 by Jean-Louis Dubut de Laforest, a prolific French author and publisher of erotica who had been prosecuted for obscenity in 1885.

It is said that the catchphrase had originated with two particular Russian grand dukes — Vladimir and Alexis, sons of Tsar Alexander II — who had, since their youth, been regular visitors to Paris in search of its darker pleasures and the gourmet food that they both so enjoyed. Grand Duke Vladimir, Nicholas II's most senior uncle (and, until the birth of the tsarevich in 1904, third in line to the throne), had been the focal point of an "avuncular oligarchy" that dominated court in the years up to the 1917 revolution.[9] Darkly handsome, with his "immense height . . . piercing eyes and beetling brows," Vladimir was the most powerful of the grand dukes. He was a most imposing if not frightening figure, as was his worldly and equally formidable German-born wife, Maria Pavlovna (originally, Marie of Mecklenburg-Schwerin).* Vladimir never quite came to terms with

---

* As Maria Pavlovna bore the same name as Grand Duke Paul's daughter, they were referred to as "the elder" and "the younger" respectively — though to make matters simpler, Vladimir's

the fact that he was not emperor himself (though his wife certainly nurtured that hope for their sons after his death). If he couldn't be tsar in Russia, then at least he could play the *grand seigneur* to the hilt during his regular biannual visits to Paris, traveling there from St. Petersburg via Berlin in his own lavishly upholstered wagon-lit complete with a full-size bed.[10] Once installed at his favorite Hôtel Continental on rue Castiglione opposite the Tuileries, Vladimir would indulge his libidinous and sometimes violent behavior, his colossal appetite for gourmet food and wines, and his extravagant spending habit (a trait that rubbed off on his son Boris). His wife, "who only demanded of life that it should amuse her," could, when she accompanied him, quietly feed her own passion for shopping and (when in Monte Carlo) a flutter on the gaming tables.[11] It is hard to comprehend today the prodigious wealth Vladimir enjoyed, thanks to an income from the imperial treasury of $350,000 (equaling something like $10 million in 2022) that was further bolstered by his personal fortune, his lands, forests, and mines, as well as salaries from various military and other sinecures. It was indeed fair to say at the time that Vladimir's wealth was equal to that "of several of the Great Powers."[12] At his 360-room palace in St. Petersburg, he kept volumes of recipes he had obtained from the best chefs in Russia, France, and Austria. He reputedly had the finest wine cellar in the city and thought nothing of ordering prime sturgeons from beyond the Urals and the best black caviar by the barrel. So well known was he in Paris as a hard drinker and gastronome that Vladimir was nicknamed "Le Grand Duc Bon Vivant" and you could find *filet de sole Grand Duke Vladimir* on most menus there.[13]

Even though Vladimir's cupidity went before him, he was redeemed by his exemplary good taste. He was keenly intelligent and

---

wife was more often referred to as Grand Duchess Vladimir. She will be referred to in this latter form throughout this book to avoid confusion.

cultured, a man whose refinement thus raised him above the level of merely an "old buck about town."[14] He was extremely erudite— history and art being his passions—an amateur painter of some talent, and a collector of icons. In St. Petersburg he served from 1876 to his death as president of the Imperial Fine Arts Academy and enjoyed an extremely influential position in the art world. Russian money was always welcome in Paris and, as British ambassador's daughter Meriel Buchanan recalled, Grand Duke Vladimir "did not *merely* engage in reckless extravagance" when in Paris, "*but . . .* spent many hours at museums and art galleries, collecting paintings and antiques."[15]

The Russian aristocracy fitted in perfectly with *Le Tout-Paris* of the Belle Époque, which operated as one large private club with its own rules. The French press regularly titillated readers with stories of the vices and eccentricities of the grand dukes, particularly tales of their behavior at Maxim's restaurant, "where everybody except the *épouse légitime* [legitimate spouse] went" for a rollicking night out. Here you could just as easily rub shoulders with "Prince Galitzine, Prince Karageorgevitch, Prince George of Greece, and, of course, Vladimir and his sons."[16] A tale was also told of a cousin of Vladimir's, Grand Duke Sergey Mikhailovich, who was well known for gambling for high stakes in Cannes. At Maxim's one evening, Grand Duke Sergey presented his mistress, Augustine de Lierre—one of Paris's *grandes cocottes* (high-class prostitutes)—"with a 20-million franc necklace of pearls tastefully served on a platter of oysters."[17] Other grand dukes vied over the favors of her fellow courtesan, the Spanish dancer La Belle Otero, who on one occasion returned from a trip to St. Petersburg with a traveling case full of diamonds, emeralds, and rubies.

Grand Duke Vladimir was as lavish in his tips as his spending, even "adding a number of unmounted gems to the gold coin tossing" at Maxim's on one occasion. As his cousin Grand Duke Alexander—

better known as Sandro*—later recalled, Vladimir's visits to Paris "meant a red-letter day for the chefs and maîtres-d'hotel of the Ville Lumière, where, after making a terrific row about the 'inadequacy' of the menus he would invariably finish the evening by putting a lavish tip in every hand capable of being stretched out."[18]

By the late nineteenth century, so popular were the wealthy Russians in Paris that they were nicknamed "the Boyars." At his famous cabaret in Montmartre, the singer Aristide Bruant would yell out "Here come the Cossacks" whenever the Russians descended for an evening's carousing.[19] On such occasions the Russian grand dukes tended to favor the private rooms—or *cabinets particuliers*—in which to enjoy the charms of French courtesans. But sometimes when the Boyars were out for a whirl, their behavior got out of hand: one particular count was "partial to making pincushion designs with a sharp-pronged fork on a woman's bare bosom," and a group of Russian officers "played an interesting little game with loaded revolvers. They'd turn off all the lights, then fire in every direction. The extent of the human damage was hushed up but the material damage was stupendous, and their equerries paid royally for the frolic."[20]

Not all grand dukes came away unscathed, however. One such unnamed but very wealthy one had spent the night at a restaurant with a couple of ladies of the night, only to be overcome by tiredness. While their victim slumbered, his companions had helped themselves to all his personal possessions, including his clothes, leaving him only his white tie, which they tied round his neck before departing. When the *maître d'hôtel* went to the room a couple of hours later to check on his guest and present his bill, he discovered "a stark naked figure snoring heavily on the sofa." On being

---

* Everyone knew Grand Duke Alexander as Sandro. In order to spare the reader from an endless litany of grand duke this and grand duke that, he will be referred to as Sandro throughout.

aroused, the grand duke was presented with a bill for five hundred francs, but had no means of paying. The police were sent for and, wrapping the grand duke in a tablecloth, put him in a cab to take him to the police station. It took some persuasion for them to relent and take the grand duke instead to the Russian embassy.[21]

Another grand duke who was a regular patron of Paris nightlife was Vladimir's bachelor brother Grand Duke Alexis,* who in 1897 had bought a luxurious apartment at 38 rue Gabriel on the Seine's Right Bank. Good-looking, and fairer than Vladimir, Alexis was remembered by Queen Marie of Romania as "a type of the Vikings who would have made a perfect Lohengrin, as Wagner would have dreamed of him."[22] Tall, like all the Romanov grand dukes, Alexis was, however, heavily built and prone to being overweight, with a loud voice and larger-than-life manner to match his size. Like his brother Vladimir, he was an uninhibited pleasure-seeker. He made no bones about his love of wine, women, and carousing with gypsies, his unrepentant motto being "you must experience everything in life."[23] His cousin Sandro dubbed him "The Beau Brummell of the Imperial Family."[24] He certainly was the archetypal man-about-town; in fact, the burly Alexis bore no little resemblance to his hedonistic fellow royal, King Edward VII, who had also taken the sexual and culinary delights of Paris to his heart as Prince of Wales. Alexis was no intellectual or aesthete like his brother Vladimir, but rather a plain-speaking, good-natured navy man who could be an interminable bore on the subject of his glorious past days in sailing ships (equally, he would draw a veil over his incompetence as an admiral of the fleet during the naval battles of the Russo-Japanese War of 1904–05). As Sandro quipped, "His was a case of fast women and slow ships." Alexis made frequent extravagant trips to Paris with

---

* Actually Alexey, but he was better known by the French form of his name as he spent so much time in Paris.

Vladimir—so much so that it was a common joke in St. Petersburg that "the ladies of Paris cost Russia at least a battleship a year."[25] There was much gossip about money destined to fund the construction of new battleships and cruisers for the Imperial Navy making its way into Alexis's pockets during his tenure as commander in chief of the Imperial Fleet—but he was not alone in his brazen siphoning off of money from the treasury; this was but one of many "gigantic swindles" that helped boost the revenues of the unscrupulous Russian grand dukes.[26]

Alexis's comfortable life in Paris went some way in consoling him for the loss of the love of his life—Zina, Countess Beauharnais, who was married to his first cousin and friend, the Duke of Leuchtenberg—and with whom Alexis had conducted an unhappy *ménage royal à trois*.[27] When Zina died of throat cancer, Alexis comforted himself for his loss with a string of actresses and dancers; on one occasion, he arrived at the legendary Moulin Rouge with his suite, surrounded by police protection agents, demanding whether any of the dancing girls could dance the *"russkaya"* (presumably he meant the Cossack dance the *lezginka*). His request was derided with howls of laughter by the clientele. Instead, the resident star dancer, La Goulue (immortalized in the paintings of Toulouse-Lautrec), danced a cancan for him, after which Alexis is said to have literally covered her body with banknotes. He invited her to a tête-à-tête dinner later at Maxim's, where they ate Beluga caviar and celebrated the Franco-Russian alliance in style.[28]

Eventually, Alexis transferred his affections and his money to a French-Jewish actress, Elizabeth Balletta, who was popular with the French theater company in St. Petersburg. He lavished her with jewelry from elite Parisian establishments such as Cartier, thanks to his generous naval sinecure. But after Russia's catastrophic naval defeats by the Japanese, the imperial court was outraged to see La Balletta parade a new diamond and ruby cross that had set Alexis back

$22,600 (the equivalent of more than $700,000 now)—and promptly nicknamed it "The Pacific Fleet." La Balletta had, they complained, "cost the Russian people more than the Battle of Tsushima"—a naval debacle that had forced Alexis's resignation.[29]

During those final years of the Belle Époque, when Paris served the idle rich as a place to indulge themselves and be rejuvenated, it was a boom time for the luxury trades; for jewelers such as Boucheron, Chaumet, and especially Cartier, who could rival the best of Fabergé in St. Petersburg. The French couturier Charles Worth was a special favorite of the Russian grand duchesses, patronized for many years by the dowager empress Maria Feodorovna. Everywhere in Paris, the tills of the exclusive *parfumiers*, furriers, fine art dealers, and antiques emporiums rang to lavish amounts of Russian money. The Royal Suite at the Hôtel Ritz, with its empire-style decor "combining with the necessary pomp the maximum degree of comfort" was frequently used as a Paris headquarters by the Russians when they arrived on shopping trips.

Aside from Grand Dukes Vladimir and Alexis, Grand Duke Mikhail (Mikhailovich)* visited regularly with his wife, the Countess Torby; Grand Duke Nikolay Nikolaevich came in 1900 and demanded guards be posted throughout the hotel for his protection. Thanks to him, the Ritz was turned into "a veritable royal fortress."[30] It regularly staged brilliant gatherings in its private reception rooms in honor of the visits Grand Duke Vladimir made with his wife. Head Chef Monsieur Gimon, who had previously worked at the Russian embassy in Madrid, was more than able to cater to the quirks of Russian taste in food and wine: "He could

---

* Known in the family as Miche-Miche, he was banished from Russia—by Alexander III in 1891—for contracting a morganatic marriage. The couple settled in England in 1900, and for a while lived at Kenwood House on Hampstead Heath.

turn out such things as borscht, blinis, bitokes, and lobster aspics as masterfully as any chef at the Russian court."[31]

From 1902, however, there was one Russian grand duke who rose to the fore in Paris and, with his wife, became the focus of expatriate Romanov Russia in Paris during the pre–World War I years. Grand Duke Paul Alexandrovich, the youngest of the four sons of Alexander II, was by far the most modest and democratic of the Russian grand dukes; his beautiful home at Boulogne-sur-Seine would become, thanks to the charm and social skills of his wife, Olga, Countess von Hohenfelsen, not just a magnet for the most cultured and influential on the French literary, musical, and political circuit but also effectively an "annex" to the Russian embassy in Paris.

Tall "like a column of marble,"[32] slim and elegant in his uniform of commander of the Horse Guards—for he was a military man like his cousin Grand Duke Nikolay Nikolaevich—Grand Duke Paul was quietly handsome with a neat but large bushy mustache and gentle brown eyes that stared out of an austere, oblong face. The eyes bore a hint of seriousness and melancholy that was inherited by his son Dmitri Pavlovich. While his older brothers had achieved a notoriety at home and abroad with their libidinous behavior, Paul was far more restrained and private; as Romanovs went, he seemed uncharacteristically "high-minded, upright and loyal." He disliked self-indulgence and excess and had a reputation for being kind, polite, and dignified.[33]

Paul was, however, a sad figure for many years, having lost his young wife, Princess Alexandra of Greece, in 1891 after only three years of marriage, leaving him with two young children, Maria and Dmitri. He had remained utterly inconsolable until he met and fell in love with a notable beauty at the Russian court—Olga von Pistohlkors. But she was already married—to a captain in the Horse Guards—and had three surviving children by him. Paul and Olga's subsequent affair resulted in an illegitimate son, Vladimir, born in

1897, and an enormous scandal at the Russian court. Despite the fact that Tsar Nicholas was deeply fond of Paul, he had had no option but to follow the strict protocols then in force, and immediately ordered the couple from court. Olga, herself a most forceful personality, urged Paul to save her from the disaster of social ostracization, and with his brother Vladimir's help, he managed to persuade Nicholas II to agree to granting Olga a divorce. Nicholas did so on the understanding that Paul would not marry her. But shortly afterward, he had defied that order, left Russia secretly, and like Grand Duke Mikhail before him, contracted a morganatic marriage with Olga, in Livorno, Italy. Nicholas's predictable response was the same as that for Mikhail. Paul was stripped of his military honors, his assets were confiscated, and in 1902 he was banished from Russia. Far worse than this was that Paul's children by his first wife were placed under the guardianship of his brother Grand Duke Sergey and his wife Ella (the tsaritsa's sister). Nicholas had been firm about setting an example; as he told his mother, "In the end I fear, a whole colony of members of the Russian Imperial Family will be established in Paris with their semi-legitimate and illegitimate wives."[34]

By 1903, having spent some time in Italy, Paul and Olga decided to make a base for themselves in Paris. It was an opportune time, for Russophilia still ruled in the city in the wake of the Franco-Russian alliance. Anxious to protect his assets, and anticipating the outcome of their forbidden marriage, Paul had deposited money in foreign banks and is said to have fled Russia with two suitcases containing three million in gold rubles (the equivalent of thirty million dollars at the time).[35] In St. Petersburg his wife might be a shamed woman, a persona non grata, but in Paris Olga would become the meteoric star of French high society. Initially, the couple lived in a grand apartment at 11 avenue d'Iéna, a lovely tree-lined avenue in the 16th arrondissement, where their daughters Irina and Nataliya were born in 1903 and 1905 and where they held their first salons and receptions.

But in order to achieve their desired position in Paris society, there was a pressing need for Olga, denied the use of the title grand duchess, to acquire a title suitable to her new station in life. For her difficult position as the morganatic wife of a senior Romanov created all kinds of problems of protocol and precedence at official functions. Thanks to the Prince Regent of Bavaria, she was invested with the title Countess von Hohenfelsen in 1904. This more lowly title still did not solve all the precedence issues, however, and Olga's status remained a subject about which Paul was highly sensitive.

Events in Russia in 1905 caused both Grand Duke Paul and Countess von Hohenfelsen a great deal of anxiety. The slaughter in January 1905 by Cossack troops of innocent and unarmed protesters on a peaceful protest march for better wages and living conditions had brought shame and ignominy on the Russian tsarist system—both at home and abroad. Paul and Olga were horrified by the events of what became known as Bloody Sunday. Over dinner at their apartment on rue d'Iéna with French diplomat Maurice Paléologue (a future ambassador to St. Petersburg from 1915 until the revolution), they spoke candidly of their fears for their home country. All three were privy to the intense political gossip then swirling around the salons in St. Petersburg and Paris and aware of German intrigues to try to force Russia into an alliance against Britain. Olga and Paul were both convinced that the protests in St. Petersburg would be the downfall of the old Russia: "Well! We're lost aren't we?" Paul told Paléologue. "You can see for yourself: within and without, everything's crumbling."[36]

The assassination by an anarchist of Paul's brother Sergey in Moscow barely a month later seemed to him a clear act of retaliation, and it confirmed how dangerous life in Russia was becoming for the Romanov family. Nicholas II had immediately commanded that Paul return to Russia for Sergey's state funeral. But he crossed the border from Germany alone; Olga was turned back as an "undesirable alien"—a fact much reported by the British and French press.[37] Despite his refusal to make concessions to Paul's morganatic wife, Nicholas, in a private meeting with Paul after the funeral, informed his uncle that he had pardoned him and that he himself could return to Russia whenever he chose. His state appanage—worth several million francs a year—and his honors would be restored to him. But Paul was not allowed to reclaim his children from his widowed sister-in-law Ella, and Olga was not welcome. The scandal of her adultery had found its fiercest critic in Nicholas's highly moral wife Alexandra, who insisted that the countess should not be welcomed back at the Russian court for several more years.[38]

It was now painfully clear that Paul and Olga must make their home permanently in Paris; but they needed a far more imposing residence and initially looked for somewhere near Versailles. Finally, they found the perfect home at L'Hôtel Youssoupoff* at 2 avenue Victor Hugo, Boulogne-sur-Seine, in the 16th arrondissement.[39] It had been built in 1860–61 for Princess Zinaida Naryshkina, widow of Prince Boris Yusupov, when she had remarried to Comte Charles de Chaveau and settled in Paris. When the princess died in 1893, Prince Nikolay Yusupov in St. Petersburg inherited the mansion, but it had been empty for more than ten years when Paul and Olga found it.[40]

Olga at last had a project into which she could throw all her energies and bring to life the rarefied style of Belle Époque living and entertaining to which she aspired. In many ways the couple were archetypal Proustian figures: and indeed the Countess von Hohenfelsen gets a passing mention in the great French classic *À la recherche du temps perdu* (*In Search of Lost Time*), in which Marcel

---

* The use of "Hôtel" to describe grand residences in Paris is misleading, for they were private homes, not hotels. The Hôtel Youssoupoff is now the home of the École et College Dupanloup, a private Catholic school. Avenue Victor Hugo has since been renamed avenue Robert Schuman.

Proust's fictional character Madame de Guermantes is described as having offended Grand Duchess Vladimir by making the social faux pas of wrongly referring to Countess von Hohenfelsen as "Grande-Duchesse Paul."[41] Paul gets a mention too, as the "good Grand Duke," as do the high society personalities with whom he and Olga regularly associated: Prince and Princess Murat, the Comtesse de Portales, Lady de Gray, Vera de Talleyrand-Perigord, Prince and Princess Baryatinsky, Madame de Chevigné, the Comtesse de Greffulhe, and the poet Robert de Montesquiou—who appears in Proust as the "Baron de Charlus."

Despite the pain of separation from Russia and Paul's children, as well as their son Vladimir—who had returned to St. Petersburg to train at the elite military school the Corps des Pages—Paul and Olga enjoyed a gilded exile with their two daughters, in a home created together that was "worthy of a Pompadour or a Du Barry."[42] In achieving it they sought only the very best craftsmen that Paris then had to offer. By 1905 Olga had commissioned extensive redecoration and improvements by the celebrated interior designer Georges Hoentschel, who filled the house with her favorite furnishings of the eighteenth century: fine art and antiques, Gobelins tapestries, Louis XV furniture, sculptures, miniatures, bronzes, marbles, and fine paintings. Olga scoured the Parisian art salerooms and expositions for new acquisitions—particularly ceramics and glass, as well as jade and gemstones and oriental porcelains, in what would be a constantly evolving collection of art and antiques that was the envy of Paris.[43]

In this sumptuous, glittering environment, serviced by a staff of sixteen, Olga was the consummate hostess, while the more retiring Paul enjoyed nothing better than his daily walks with Irina and Nataliya in the nearby Bois de Boulogne. He and Olga held very select dinners for intimate friends—and visiting Romanovs too, who, when in Paris, consented to receive Olga despite her being banned

from the St. Petersburg court.[44] Sundays were her receiving day, between 4 and 7 P.M.

Over the next few years, the French press—in particular *Le Figaro*—always a little starstruck by Romanov royals, was regularly announcing this or that salon or reception or ball hosted by the re-fined and charming Grand Duke Paul and the countess, his wife, "one of the most beautiful people in Paris, a great lady of spirit and heart as much as by situation, affable with all and admired by all."[45]

When Olga wasn't busy arranging her latest soirée, she would be in hot pursuit of French luxury goods at the finest shops on the rue de la Paix. When she and Paul had first married, he had bought her numerous jewels there suitable to her new position. Patronage of Cartier had become something of a Romanov habit, with Grand Duke Alexis buying jewels there for his mistress La Balletta and Grand Duchess Vladimir also being a regular. Between 1905 and 1915, Olga was spending something in the region of 5,500 francs a month just on jewelry—in all 56,000 francs at Cartier alone (and not counting the money Paul had also spent on her there).[46]

Olga's diaries, which survive in the state archives in Moscow, are an endless catalog of self-indulgence, of her expenditure on dress fittings and hairdos several times a week, on perfume from Roger & Gallet and Houbigant, on beauty products from Guerlain. She had already become acquainted with the best shops on the rue de la Paix before she met Paul—from accompanying her first husband, Erich von Pistohlkors, on trips abroad. She was a regular patron of Paquin, whose gowns cost 5,000–6,000 francs each, and had be-come a devoted customer of Charles Worth—a few doors down from Cartier. Olga dreaded getting fat and not being able to squeeze into her gorgeous, expensive gowns, so avoided eating at table, in-stead having snacks in private between meals.[47] It was worth it for the moment of triumph she enjoyed at Madame Yturbe's Hungar-ian costume ball in 1912, where she arrived dripping in luxury: a dress by Worth encrusted with rows of pearls and a Cartier tiara of pear-shaped diamonds on the bodice, an imposing hussar-style fur hat bearing a Cartier diamond and pearl corsage, and a matching fur cape. Olga's coiffure for the occasion cost 99.50 francs (around $700) at the hairdresser Savary. A photograph of her in full rig by fashionable photographer Boissonas & Taponier and widely circulated in the press marked the high point of Belle Époque fashion.

On a typical day in May 1904, Olga had noted in her diary a trip to jeweler André Falize to inspect Princess Mathilde's jewels* and "then to Cartier to look at different objects and buy some." After lunch she ordered a hat at Meyer's establishment, and then went to the Austrian patissier Anton Rumpelmayer on rue de Rivoli for tea and gateau, then once more back to Cartier. Such shopping expeditions, she wrote in her diary, were all "terribly exhausting," as were the never-ending stack of invitations that demanded her and Paul's attendance at charity fetes, baptisms, marriages, garden parties, balls, and trips to the opera and theater. When it all got too much, they would head off with their children to Biarritz, the South of France, or Italy, or go to Germany to "take the cure."[48]

But when they *were* in Paris, Paul and Olga committed a great deal of their time and money to the support of the arts. Paul was now the most important figure in the Russian colony in Paris and he "triumphed seeing his wife obtain a marked place in this . . . glittering society." As one regular guest, the diplomat Charles de Chambrun, mistily recalled of such golden evenings chez Paul and Olga: "All these memories have been lost in the mists of the Seine. Oh! To make those times in Boulogne live again!"[49] By the mid-1900s the house at Boulogne was renowned for its sumptuous dinners and superb cuisine; it had become a magnet for writers, politicians, dip-

---

* Napoleon III's sister Mathilde had died in January 1904 and her jewels were up for sale at Galeries Georges Petit.

lomats, artists, and musicians, as well as visiting Russians of distinction.[50]

It was through her passion for music that Olga had met and become great friends with one of the leading Parisian music patrons: the American-born Winnaretta Singer, long a resident of Paris, where she was known by her married name the Princesse de Polignac. Winnaretta had been heiress, in 1875, of the lion's share of her father Isaac Singer's $13 million sewing machine fortune* and had invested much of it in the arts—especially music. After a brief unsuccessful marriage in 1893, she had married the much older Prince Edmond de Polignac, a charming but rather ineffectual man whose "one tradeable asset [was] his princeliness": a classic tale of American new money coming to the rescue of failing penniless aristocracy.[51] The couple, who were both talented musicians, conducted an affectionate but asexual relationship—they were both gay—based on shared cultural interests, until Polignac's death in 1901. By this time, the desired French aristocratic connection had won Winnaretta (affectionately known as "Aunt Winnie" by her friends) a much-sought-after place at the apex of Proustian Paris society. The music and literature salon she had established in the imposing neoclassical citadel she had built at the junction of rue Cortambert and rue Henri-Martin was the venue to which all new and aspiring composers flocked in search of patronage. Its main reception room was large enough to accommodate a full chamber orchestra, and Grand Duke Paul and Countess von Hohenfelsen, as regular guests, enjoyed the music of Fauré, Ravel, Debussy, Poulenc, and Satie, among others.

Grand Duke Paul and his wife frequently returned the compliment; it was at a dinner party they held at their home in Boulogne-sur-Seine in December 1906 that they first introduced Winnaretta to

---

* This is the equivalent of nearly $315 million now. Singer had sixteen children by three common-law wives. Winnaretta was the eldest of his six legitimate children.

"a tall, energetic young man with a white lock in the midst of thick black hair" who was currently visiting from Russia.[52] At the time, he was one of the most dynamic and influential Russians in the arts in St. Petersburg. As a music and ballet impresario of consuming ambition, he was soon to take Paris by storm with an incomparable ensemble of singers, dancers, choreographers, and set designers. Winnaretta Singer would be one of many to fall under his spell. His name was Sergey Diaghilev.

CHAPTER 2

"We Really Did Stagger the World"

The name Sergey Diaghilev has become synonymous with Paris in the 1900s and with the storming of this citadel of high culture at that time by his extraordinary, magnetic dance company, the Ballets Russes. In Russia, by the age of only twenty-three, he had already envisioned his future path as a mover and shaker in the world of European culture. "I am first a great charlatan, though with brio," he confidently announced to his stepmother in a letter of 1895, "secondly, a great *charmeur*; thirdly I have any amount of cheek; fourthly I am a man with a great quality of logic, but with very few principles; fifthly I think I have no real gifts." Gifted or not, he was confident even then that he had found his "true vocation" as a patron of the arts. "Being a Maecenas I have all that is necessary save the money—*mais ça viendra*," he predicted.[1] The success would come, certainly, but the money side of his ambitious ventures would be a perennial problem.

Although he had originally trained in the law, Diaghilev had wanted to be a musician and had taken lessons with the composer Rimsky-Korsakov. The Russian visual arts had been an equal passion, and in 1898 he became cofounder in St. Petersburg of an artistic group named the Mir Iskusstva (World of Art), its objective being to challenge the old and, in their view, outmoded order in Russian painting and promote a dynamic new modernism. From 1899 leading members of this loosely affiliated group included Diaghilev's key future collaborators: the artists Alexandre Benois and Léon Bakst. Under Diaghilev's editorship they produced their own lavishly illustrated, eclectic art journal, *Mir Iskusstva*; but although partially funded by Nicholas II, the magazine's circulation remained low—fewer than fifteen hundred copies per issue. Between 1898 and 1904 the group staged six art exhibitions in Russia and championed neo-Russian art moderne—their version of Austrian Jugendstil and French art nouveau—favoring in particular Russian folk art and traditional Slavic design. But the magazine proved an extremely difficult enterprise to keep afloat, having as it did many contributors with differing interests and artistic ambitions, and it soon lost its financial backing and folded.

Diaghilev had started out with the ambition of becoming director of the six Russian imperial theaters, including the Mariinsky, famed for its opera and ballet, but had been sadly stymied by his colorful private life (he was openly gay) and the lack of an influential position at court.[2] This did not deter him; as a natural mover and shaker whose heart lay with promoting the best in Russian music and art to a wider audience, he decided to create a shop window for Russian artistic excellence abroad. It was time to show the world the art that it had been missing. And where better than Paris, the artistic capital of the world, where there already was a burgeoning Russian colony? Diaghilev knew the city well and had been a regular visitor since the 1890s; as he wrote to his collaborator, Benois: "The French would be fools not to agree. I'll show them the real Russia."[3]

In November 1906, when he dined with Winnaretta Singer chez Grand Duke Paul and his wife, Diaghilev was in Paris to promote an Exposition de L'Art Russe as part of that year's annual Salon d'Automne. His major financial backer in the venture, which ran from October 6 to November 15, had been the art-loving Grand Duke Vladimir, with further support coming from the influential Parisian society hostess, the Comtesse de Greffulhe.

Till now, Russian art beyond icon painting was little known outside Russia. With Benois, Diaghilev pulled together an unprecedented cross-section of their country's best art since the eighteenth century: 750 works that included examples by Bryulov, Bakst, Kustodiev, Levitan, Levitsky, Roerich, Serov, Somov, and Vrubel. Many of these priceless works of art and sculpture came from the collections of the imperial palaces; in a considerable coup, Diaghilev succeeded in persuading Tsar Nicholas of the "state importance" of Russian art being exhibited abroad, and obtained his permission for it to be seen in Paris for the first time.[4] His success in this was thanks in the main to the personal influence over the tsar of Grand Duke Vladimir (whose children had been taught drawing by Bakst) as chair of the Committee of Recommendation. The exhibition, which filled twelve halls of the Salon d'Automne, proved to be "of exceptional interest and brilliance," according to Benois. With the decor of the rooms designed by Bakst and a beautiful souvenir catalog illustrated by Benois, it went a long way to acquainting Parisians with the work of the Mir Iskusstva group. More important, as Benois recalled, "in this way we formed connections with a number of people who became our friends." But these were not just friends and aficionados, they were the all-important wealthy and culturally connected *Le Tout-Paris*, who would become Diaghilev's crucial future patrons.[5]

The 1906 exhibition was the first step in the Mir Iskusstva group's "export campaign of Russian art," spearheaded by Diaghilev. Russian literature was already well appreciated in France, but he knew that Russian music and the Russian theater were almost unknown. Having come to the conclusion that "nothing could be achieved in Russia and therefore it was indispensable to transfer his activity beyond her borders," Diaghilev turned his attention to music for his next venture.[6] In the Concerts Historiques Russes that he planned for 1907 at the Paris Opera, Diaghilev set out to enlighten his audience on innovative new Russian music beyond the world of Tchaikovsky, who till then was almost the only Russian composer with whom they were familiar. In order to best engage his French audience's interest, Diaghilev hired two of the most talented contemporary Russian artists to front a season of five concerts: the opera singer Feodor Chaliapin and Diaghilev's old music teacher, Rimsky-Korsakov, who was to conduct his own work and a potpourri of work by the Russian composers Glinka, Borodin, Rachmaninov, Tchaikovsky, and Glazunov. But, as ever, there was the crucial problem of funding. Diaghilev was obliged to exploit his best sycophantic charms to persuade Grand Duke Vladimir that "our enterprise is beneficial from a national point of view," Vladimir having a crucial influence over his nephew Tsar Nicholas in gaining essential court subsidies. But extracting the money was hard work: government ministers also had to be assured of the benefits to the crown of the cost of sending an unknown troupe of Russian performers to Paris.[7] In the end, a Dutch rubber merchant and galoshes manufacturer residing in St. Petersburg came up with a substantial donation. In Paris subscription lists for the concert series were raised and published in *Le Figaro,* the daily newspaper read by *Le Tout-Paris,* Grand Duke Paul and the Russian ambassador Alexander Nelidov being notable among them. The crucial financial support of the Comtesse de Greffulhe to this and the following season had been won after Diaghilev had sat at the piano and played her excerpts from the Russian music he loved and wished to promote.[8]

On May 16, 1907, *Le Tout-Paris* came together for the first Russian concert. Included among them were Grand Duke Paul and Countess von Hohenfelsen; Paul's brother Alexis; their sister-in-law Grand Duchess Vladimir (her diamond tiara "glittering over the spectators," as the press noted); the grand duchess's sons Boris and Kirill; and Kirill's wife, Victoria.[9] The highlight of the evening was undoubtedly the imposing figure of Russian bass baritone Chaliapin, singing an aria from *Prince Igor*, an opera by Borodin based on a twelfth-century epic poem. The son of poor peasants from the Volga, Chaliapin had already scored successes with the Bolshoy Theater in Moscow and had toured in Milan and Berlin but was appearing in Paris for the first time. The French gave him an ecstatic response, repeated at the four succeeding full houses of May 19, 23, 26, and 30. On May 29 Grand Duke Paul and Countess von Hohenfelsen hosted a musical evening at their Boulogne-sur-Seine mansion. Here Chaliapin had further delighted his entranced listeners and ensured more funding for Diaghilev from French patrons, for although the season had been a critical success, it had lost money.[10] In order to keep his artistic mission afloat, Diaghilev managed to secure the invaluable assistance of French concert agent Gabriel Astruc in staging more Russian opera the following year. In 1908 selected scenes from Mussorgsky's *Boris Godunov*—once more starring Chaliapin—were chosen for the Paris Opera, Diaghilev opting to think big with a large cast. For this production, which was repeated for six more performances, he was determined to present an image of old medieval Russia that was arresting and new, "so that the French are staggered by the grandeur of it all."[11]

Diaghilev had insisted on obtaining authentic costumes from the late sixteenth and early seventeenth centuries and had "despoiled all the Eastern shops in St. Petersburg" for peasant costumes, embroidery, and fabrics of the period. Léon Bakst re-created those costumes that could not be bought in elaborate detail, with sets designed by the painter Alexander Golovine.[12] This epic opera with its large chorus and orchestra from Moscow's Bolshoy Theater was unlike anything Paris had ever seen before; the performance in itself was a logistical feat that Diaghilev pulled off with his usual flair. Once more, Chaliapin stunned Paris with a bravura performance. Diaghilev had cleverly chosen the most theatrical moments from the opera, including the impressive coronation scene, with its massed chorus and procession of boyars and priests, and the psychodrama of Boris's death scene, which the great singer milked to full dramatic effect.[13] The French press was ecstatic—one critic, in an overload of praise, likening the commanding power of *Boris Godunov* to Shakespeare, for conveying "an intense awareness of the past, an all-embracing universality, realism, richness, profundity, a mercilessly disturbing quality, artistry and that same unity of the tragic and the comic, that same supreme humanity."[14]

After the triumph of the opening night, Chaliapin telegraphed a witty note to a St. Petersburg friend: "Alps crossed. Paris taken."[15] Once again, the Saison Russe had electrified Paris, and once again the enterprise had lost money. Diaghilev's Paris patrons rallied round: on June 2, 1908, following the penultimate performance of *Boris Godunov*, Winnaretta Singer held a soirée to celebrate the season, during which this captive group of admirers—including Grand Duke Vladimir, his sons Kirill and Andrey, and Grand Duke Paul, with their wives, were solicited for pledges of financial support for the 1909 season.[16] But just as Diaghilev was planning an ambitious program with which to stun *Le Tout-Paris*, disaster struck. On February 17 of the following year, his primary backer, Grand Duke Vladimir, died suddenly in St. Petersburg.

This death came hard on the heels of that of another Romanov supporter of Diaghilev in the Paris Russian colony—Grand Duke Alexis, on November 14, 1908. Both brothers had died before their time, Alexis at fifty-eight of pneumonia and Vladimir at sixty-two of a cerebral hemorrhage. In Paris Alexis's solemn funeral procession was an impressive sight: cavalry and a military band accompanied the elaborate hearse, drawn by six horses wearing black ostrich plumes, the coffin draped in the Russian naval ensign and decorated with a wreath of orchids and roses sent by the President of the Republic. Grand Duke Paul and Countess von Hohenfelsen headed the family mourners at the Russian Orthodox funeral service at the Alexander Nevsky Cathedral on rue Daru. Afterward Paul—accompanied by Olga, thanks to a special dispensation from Nicholas II—traveled with the coffin back to St. Petersburg for burial in the Grand Ducal Vault at the Peter and Paul Fortress. Alexis's brother Vladimir's coffin joined his there barely four months later.

Despite the inevitable financial difficulties brought by Vladimir's death, and the loss also of his subsidy from Nicholas II soon afterward, Diaghilev was able to persuade Gabriel Astruc to provide the funding to save his 1909 Saison Russe in Paris.[17] This time he set out to dazzle audiences with yet more fantastical, fairy-tale images of old Russia. It had been his original intention that the emphasis should again be on opera, but Diaghilev came under considerable pressure this time to include the new Russian ballet in the bill.[18] It is perhaps the greatest irony that, according to his collaborators Benois and choreographer Serge Lifar, ballet had in fact never been Diaghilev's primary interest, and Benois certainly felt that he did not understand it.[19] Yet the stunning ensemble of dancers that Diaghilev brought to Paris in the years leading up to World War I would make the careers of a whole generation of unforgettable Russian dancers. As prima ballerina Tamara Karsavina remarked: "Many are the names which Diaghilev wrote, with his own hand, in the book of fame"—her own included.[20]

But how would the discerning, cultured audiences of Paris respond? When Diaghilev's patron, the Comtesse de Greffulhe, first met the Russian dancers after they arrived in Paris in 1909, she thought them wild, "barbarians" even. To her refined tastes they seemed "drably provincial and uncultivated." But that all changed the moment she saw their dress rehearsal on May 18, when she "completely fell under their sway." That day Greffulhe had no doubt that she had witnessed something exceptional, the "miracle of Russian art."[21]

The six-week 1909 Saison Russe, premiered the following day, was staged at a new venue, the Théâtre du Châtelet. Its stage was far from ideal and had to be rapidly upgraded and adapted to accommodate the dancers, who found themselves having to rehearse against a constant cacophony of hammering and banging.[22]

Witnessing the prodigious physicality of the Russian dancers, the stagehands thought them all "lunatics." Tamara Karsavina recalled their horror: "*Ces Russes, oh, là là, tous un peu maboule*" ("These Russians, oh la la! They are all a bit crazy"), they would say.[23] "Crazy" and "mad" would become the operative words of many who witnessed the Russian dancers in those early years.

On stage, their talents were fully exploited by a new member of the team, whom Diaghilev had recruited as resident choreographer for the Paris season—Michel Fokine. A teacher at the Imperial Ballet School, Fokine would, over the next four years of his collaboration with Diaghilev, create some of the seminal work of the Ballets Russes in the period up to World War I. Five short pieces choreographed by him were taken from the repertory of St. Petersburg's Mariinsky Theater, drawing on the creative talent of the best in Russian music and design. The intention was clear: to break away from the old French and Italian courtly forms of ballet that had barely changed in two hundred years. Their domination of classical ballet and its now stale images of pretty ballerinas dressed like wax dolls in cotton-candy tutus performing traditional story ballets was about to be overturned.[24] "We were frankly opposed to everything obsolete and to whatever was too much hampered by tradition," wrote Benois. Their ballet programs were to be "nothing short of revolutions in art."[25]

To keep traditionally minded balletomanes happy, the 1909 season included the more ethereal and romantic *Les Sylphides*—an homage by Fokine to the early nineteenth-century ballet, danced to the music of Chopin—starring prima ballerina Anna Pavlova. She was, of course, much admired and applauded for her exquisite technique, but it was the Polovtsian dances from act 2 of Borodin's opera *Prince Igor* that captivated the Paris audiences. It featured the leading male dancer from the Imperial Ballet, Adolf Bolm, as the Chief Warrior, backed up by an ensemble of dancers in exotic Tatar costumes, who thrilled with their ferocious, unrestrained athleticism. "The Russian savages," remarked Benois, had brought to Paris for judgment, "the best of art that then existed in the world."[26] They took six curtain calls at the premiere on May 19, 1909, at the end of which, recalled Fokine, "the audience rushed forward and actually tore off the orchestra rail in the Châtelet Theater."[27] This performance, with its wild, insistent rhythm and physicality, marked a turning point in ballet history: for the first time, the music was of equal importance, dictating the thrust and tempo of the dance rather than being merely an adjunct to it. It "provided ballet with its center of gravity," explained Benois: "the moment had arrived when one listened to the music and, in listening to it derived an additional pleasure from seeing it."[28] This, he explained, was the "mission of ballet"; from now on, Diaghilev's Saisons Russes in Paris would be a "general offensive" aimed at introducing audiences to music featuring new Russian composers.[29]

With this in mind, the May 19 program included music by the unknown Russian composer Nikolay Tcherepnin, who provided the score for the one-act ballet *Le Pavillon d'Armide*, choreographed by Fokine. With French baroque-style sets and costumes by Benois—a clever piece of flattery that greatly pleased Parisian aesthetic taste—it featured a pas de trois in which a meteoric new talent first took to the Paris stage: Vaslav Nijinsky. Another product of the Imperial Ballet School, Nijinsky seemed quite plain and unprepossessing offstage;

but when he put on his costume and danced, recalled Benois, his timidity vanished and he took on "an exceptionally attractive and poetical personality." Ballerina Tamara Karsavina noticed this transformation too: when dancing, Nijinsky became "a creature exotic, feline, elfin," who "completely eclipsed the respectable comeliness, the dignified commonplace of conventional virility."[30] There was no doubt in Benois's mind that "Paris felt the presence of a genius" when watching Nijinsky in the role of Armida's slave.[31] Even more significant in the history of ballet, at a stroke he transformed the way in which the male dancer would hereafter be viewed. Prior to his arrival on the scene, "the male classical dancer, considered far inferior to the ballerina, was limited to supporting her and to dancing a few steps to give his partner a rest," as prima ballerina Mathilde Kschessinska recalled. Nijinsky, with his "soaring flights," elevated the male dancer to an equal footing, imparting "a new direction and style, which proved a veritable revolution in the art of ballet."[32]

His mercurial talents were again demonstrated on June 2 in the ballet *Cléopâtre*, choreographed by Fokine and featuring the music of seven different Russian composers. Audiences were stunned by the exotic, colorful sets and costumes by Léon Bakst, and Benois considered this ballet the "crowning glory" of the season.[33] But despite the appearance in it of three of Russia's best ballerinas—the seductively expressive Ida Rubinstein, in the title role, and Tamara Karsavina and Anna Pavlova—the star of the show was undoubtedly the charismatic twenty-year-old Nijinsky, as Cleopatra's favorite slave.

One of Diaghilev's patrons, the Comtesse de Noailles, summed up the excitement generated by that first night in May:

I realized at once that something miraculous was happening, that I was witnessing something absolutely unique. Everything that could strike the imagination, intoxicate, enchant, and win one over, seemed to have been assembled on that stage, to be luxuriating there as naturally, as beautifully, as vegetation responds to a beneficent climate.[34]

The Paris audience was entranced: "A sort of psychosis, a mass delirium, seemed to sweep over the spectators which the Press re-echoed the following and many a succeeding day."[35] *Cléopâtre* attracted the biggest audiences to the Châtelet and, according to Benois, its success "surpassed that of Chaliapin." Paris could not stop talking about Nijinsky; the posters for the season might have featured an image of Pavlova, but *he* was the talk of the town, a fact that made up Pavlova's mind not to return in another Diaghilev season. Paris didn't have room for two big stars, and she was in any event uncomfortable with Diaghilev's new style of modern ballet.[36]

With alarming inevitability, Diaghilev still failed to make money from his venture and, indeed, was left in considerable debt to Astruc, the financial losses of the 1909 season being in the region of $500,000 today. But at least he now had "a circle of fanatical worshippers" in Paris—*les ferventes des russes*—who appreciated that he had opened up new vistas on dance for them.[37] And after this season, a new force entered Diaghilev's creative world, who would at last transform his fortunes: the composer Igor Stravinsky. The exotic setting of *Cléopâtre* had been such a huge success that Diaghilev decided to repeat it in the 1910 season with two fantasy ballets, one, *The Firebird*, based on a traditional Russian fairy story, and the other, *Schéhérazade*, taken from the *Tales of the Arabian Nights*.

The Paris Opera was the venue for this season, when *Schéhérazade*, with a ravishing score by Rimsky-Korsakov and voluptuous sets and costumes by Bakst, was premiered on June 4, 1910. It featured highly charged performances from Nijinsky and Ida Rubinstein that shocked some balletgoers with their eroticism and that brought accusations of degeneracy—all of which considerably boosted ticket sales.[38] This time, it wasn't just the dancers who were a sensation; Bakst's spectacular oriental-inspired designs, which anticipated the later fashion for art deco, made him an overnight star and triggered a fashion frenzy. More than any other designer, Bakst set his stamp on the Ballets Russes, and this production above all others came to epitomize the company's exotic style. French couturiers adopted Bakst's designs and advertised gowns in *étoffes Schéhérasades* (Scheherazade fabrics). The couturier Paul Poiret offered him twelve thousand francs for "twelve drawings of fashionable outfits."[39] His new collections, dominated by harem pants, turbans, Russian-style embroidery, and beads, certainly drew on Bakst.[40] In 1912 Bakst collaborated with Paquin on a collection of "street dresses" inspired by Ballets Russes productions, as too would Coco Chanel later. Callot Soeurs, another exclusive couturier, based a whole collection on Ballets Russes style featuring Bakst's favorite saffron yellow.[41] But this was just the beginning: Bakst's innovative designs were echoed in a plethora of oriental-style fabrics, draperies, carpets, lampshades, divans, and other furniture. They even infiltrated the embryonic silent film industry's costume and makeup styles.[42] Russian ballerinas were now überchic and in demand as models, with Pavlova and Karsavina both asked to pose in clothes from the Paris fashion houses. In every part of Parisian cultural life, the influence of the Ballets Russes could be seen, and this in turn inspired a growing interest in Paris's Russian émigré culture, especially painting.

For *The Firebird*, Diaghilev had specially commissioned Stravinsky, a pupil of Rimsky-Korsakov, to write the music. He and Diaghilev envisaged the ballet as a "total work of art"—an integration of music, dance, and visual effects. So confident was Diaghilev in his new discovery that just prior to opening, he is said to have declared, "Mark him well. He is a man on the eve of celebrity."[43] For his part, Stravinsky looked on Diaghilev as "a kind of Oscar Wilde—very elegant, very chic, and very distant—like a dandy."[44]

Three weeks after *Schéhérazade*, *The Firebird* was premiered on June 25, with sets and most of the costumes by the artist Alexander Golovine and starring Tamara Karsavina as the Firebird. Diaghilev made sure word went out about his brilliant new composer Stravinsky: *Le Tout-Paris*—Marcel Proust, Debussy, Sarah Bernhardt among them—turned out in force to witness the debut of this stunning new talent. Stravinsky's dramatic score "was afire, burning brightly and sending off sparks," wrote Fokine, who danced in, as well as choreographed, the ballet.[45] "It expressed every moment of the tale and had an unheard-of, fantastic quality." Critics agreed: here was a "danced symphony," a perfect integration of ballet and music quite unlike the usual run-of-the-mill productions.[46]

But once more it was the sight of Nijinsky, in the pas de deux with Karsavina, that drove audiences into raptures: "You would have thought their seats were on fire."[47] People pressed around the dancers at the end of the performance and would not leave, interrogating Nijinsky on how he executed his tremendous *grandes assemblées*—those thrilling extended leaps. "Was it difficult to stay in the air?" they asked, 'No! No! Not difficult,' he replied, 'You have just to go up and then pause a little up there.'" The following day, Paris talked of nothing but the Saison Russe's "soaring angel."[48]

Buoyed by the stunning success of the 1910 season, when according to Karsavina "something akin to a miracle happened every night—the stage and audience trembled in a unison of emotion," the following year Diaghilev made a major decision.[49] The logistical challenge of managing his vast theatrical enterprise, involving "a traveling circus of dancers, musicians, composers, designers, scene painters, rehearsal pianists, wigmakers, and publicists," was hugely costly.[50] Till now the Paris seasons had consisted of an ensemble of dancers on holiday leave from the Russian Imperial Ballet in St. Petersburg. Diaghilev decided the time had come to create a permanent Russian dance company for touring in Europe. Now formally named the Ballets Russes, it would be based in Paris with Michel Fokine as the principal choreographer and Nijinsky, now released from the Imperial Ballet Company, as its *premier danseur*.

In 1911 the company took Paris by storm once more, with Nijinsky in Fokine's *Petrushka,* danced to a scintillating score by Stravinsky with set and costumes by Benois. Perhaps the most quintessentially Russian of all the Diaghilev productions, *Petrushka* was set in all the bustle and energy of a Shrovetide fair in St. Petersburg in 1830, with Nijinsky creating one of his immortal roles as the clown in a stylized puppet show. For composer Stravinsky, Nijinsky as Petrushka was "the most exciting human being" he had ever seen on stage. "To call him a dancer is not enough, . . . he was an even greater dramatic actor."[51]

In that same year, Winnaretta Singer had taken the gifted Russian composer Stravinsky to her bosom. She was drawn to his slim, dandyish figure and invited him to dine at her Paris mansion and visited him in Rome when he was working on the score of *Petrushka.* "From the first," she wrote in her memoirs, "it seemed to me impossible not to recognize the importance of this new genius."[52] Her friendship with Stravinsky was an entrée into Diaghilev's inner circle, and by 1911 she had taken on the role of "discreet power broker" for the Ballets Russes. After another successful season in 1912, during which the company performed also in Berlin, Vienna, and Budapest and Nijinsky once more stunned audiences with a subtly erotic performance in *L'Après midi d'un faune* to Debussy's ravishing music, people began to wonder: Was there anything more to come from Diaghilev and Ballets Russes? They had already astonished Paris and were now dominating Europe with their dramatic flair, their balletic technique and artistic and musical inventiveness. Never one to mark time, Diaghilev already had plans for the future. Eager to push the boundaries further, he had come to the conclusion that Fokine's style was outmoded. He wanted to launch his protégé—and now lover—Nijinsky, whom he considered as more alive to "modern influences," as a choreographer. It would be an enormous gamble.

The genesis of a ballet based around "a solemn pagan rite" that would explode on the Paris stage in 1913 as *Le Sacre du printemps*—popularly known as *The Rite of Spring*—goes back to a story told by Stravinsky. He was in St. Petersburg, finishing off the score of *Firebird* in March 1909, when he "had a fleeting vision" that he said was "a complete surprise, my mind at the moment being full of other things." In it he saw a group of "sage elders, seated in a circle [watching] a young girl dance herself to death. They were sacrificing her to propitiate the god of spring." Stravinsky's claim to being the originator of the idea was disputed by artist Nicholas Roerich, set designer for the subsequent production, who said he too had posited the idea for a Slavic ritual as a possible ballet subject.[53] Either way, Diaghilev was eager to create original projects for his exciting new discovery Stravinsky, and in the winter of 1911–12 the composer shut himself away in Switzerland to write the score in time for the 1912 Ballets Russes season. In the event, however, *The Rite of Spring* was postponed till 1913.

When Stravinsky first played the opening of the piece to Diaghilev, the music's complex chords and repetitive rhythms, one of which in the opening "Spring Divination" sequence was repeated fifty-nine times, left him stunned and confused. Not wishing to offend, Diaghilev nevertheless had to ask: "And is this going on for long?" "Right to the end, my dear chap!" was the reply.[54] Stravinsky was deadly serious. Later, in April 1912 in Monte Carlo, he revealed more of the score to Diaghilev and Pierre Monteux, the French conductor whom Diaghilev was hoping would conduct the orchestra.

As Stravinsky thundered away frenetically on an upright piano, Monteux was struck by his "dynamism and his sort of ruthless impetuosity."[55] As Monteux recollected,

> *Before he got very far I was convinced he was raving mad. Heard this way, without the color of the orchestra, which is one of its greatest distinctions, the crudity of the rhythm was emphasized, its stark primitiveness underlined. The very walls resounded as Stravinsky pounded away occasionally stamping his feet and jumping up and down to accentuate the force of the music. Not that it needed much emphasis. . . . My only comment at the end was that such music would surely cause a scandal.*[56]

Monteux was so shocked by what he heard that he had wanted to run out of the room "and find a quiet corner in which to rest my aching head." Diaghilev, however, was delighted; he loved challenging audiences and wasn't afraid to take risks. A scandal would be great for ticket sales. "This is a masterpiece, Monteux," he said, "which will completely revolutionize music and make you famous."[57] When he heard a playthrough in Paris in May, the composer Debussy endorsed the sense of excitement at what was to come: "It haunts me like a beautiful nightmare," he said, "and I try in vain to retrieve the terrifying impression it made."[58]

"It seems that Diaghilev is stunned by my 'Sacrificial' inspirations," Stravinsky confidently informed his wife. As he worked on the score, the company set about planning something truly daring: a "primitive ballet with no romantic subject in a Russian setting."[59] The eventual blending of Dionysian rites, erotic dance, and pagan folklore would be Diaghilev's most ambitious production yet, involving forty-six dancers and an unprecedented ninety-nine-strong orchestra, with a running time of about thirty-five minutes. It would also receive far more rehearsals—around 120—than any other Diaghilev ballet. The cost was crippling for a return of only eight performances: five in Paris and three in London.

The task of choreographing such a trailblazing production fell on the young shoulders of Diaghilev's protégé Nijinsky, a fact that greatly disconcerted Benois, who rightly thought him too inexperienced. Stravinsky too, while admiring Nijinsky as a dancer, was horrified to find he was completely ignorant of the first principles of music, which he had to teach him in order for them to be able to work together. The choreography was undoubtedly an extraordinary feat of imagination, but Nijinsky's dance movements often bore little relation rhythmically to Stravinsky's music. He could not cope with the technicalities of musical timing and in some cases imposed difficult moves that even the dancers' sinuous bodies found hard to cope with.[60] But eventually, thanks to a lot of behind-the-scenes help from Diaghilev in the choreography, combined with a great deal of collective pain and anguish, the ballet gelled into a dynamic and thrilling synchronization with Stravinsky's jagged and dissonant score. It was clear to everyone that this would overturn every existing rule of conventional ballet. No tutus and dancing en pointe here; the female dancers would perform flat-footed, knees bent and turned in, arms and elbows at awkward angles, in defiance of every classical posture they had ever been taught. In order to assist the dancers in coping with the complicated meters and rhythms of the ballet, a Russian-Polish dance teacher, Miriam Ramberg (later familiar in Britain as Marie Rambert), was hired to coach them in the movement techniques of eurythmics.

Rehearsals of the ballet, begun in Berlin in December 1912, continued in Monte Carlo in the new year. They were stressful and turbulent and often descended, as one member of the company, Lydia Sokolova, recalled, into "complete chaos."[61] The classically trained ballet dancers found themselves having to adapt without ceremony to dancing with this strange, primitive, prehistoric posture devised by Nijinsky; so much animalistic jumping and pounding must have been ruination to their joints. Monteux's orchestra also struggled with the complicated rhythms of the score, which seemed to them "absolutely crazy." During rehearsals, at one particularly "offending conglomeration," double bass player Henri Girard recalled that "the whole orchestra broke down laughing and stopped playing." An indignant Stravinsky had jumped up shouting, "Gentlemen, you do not have to laugh. I know what I wrote."[62]

As opening night approached, the whole Ballets Russes company knew that this modernist blending of innovative music and dance would be a major assault on ballet, and indeed art, as it was then known. As French artist Jean Cocteau—a witness to those first performances—observed: "art could no longer be a simple matter of pleasing according to the bourgeois rules of supply and demand. It needed to be . . . a great insult to habit," without which it would only stagnate. It needed to "ignite the volcanic explosion."[63] And ignite the volcano it most certainly did. When the Ballets Russes 1913 season opened at the larger, modern venue of the Théâtre des Champs-Élysées in May, Paris was primed to be shocked by *The Rite of Spring,* thanks to rumors circulating that it was "difficult, violent, incomprehensible."[64] All of *Le Tout-Paris* turned out, therefore, on the evening of May 29 for the premiere, resplendent in their "low-cut dresses, tricked out in pearls, egret and ostrich feathers; and side by side with tails and tulle, the sack suits, headbands, [and] showy rags." Couturiers Poiret and Chanel, leading socialites the Comtesse Greffulhe and Misia Sert (another new and highly influential Diaghilev patron), the poets Cocteau and Apollinaire, Marcel Proust, Pablo Picasso, and composers Ravel, Debussy, and Satie: "Everyone who counts in the aristocracy, in the haute bourgeoisie, in Industry, Finance, Letters and Arts" had taken their place in the auditorium, remarked *Femina* critic Nicole Audry.[65] "All the celebrities, all the glories not just of France but also of Europe" were there, including Stravinsky's devoted fan Winnaretta Singer and other American expatriates such as the salonista Gertrude Stein and the writer Edith Wharton.[66]

The dancers were filled with terror as they gathered on stage for curtain up. Although the public dress rehearsal the previous day had gone without incident, they were extremely uneasy at how their performance would be received by its fee-paying elite audience. One can only imagine their collective shock as the curtain went up and the ballet proceeded to "a group of knock-kneed and long braided Lolitas jumping up and down."[67] The description was Stravinsky's own sardonic one many years later in a TV interview. One thing is certain: the performance of *The Rite of Spring* that night propelled ballet, and music, across the threshold into modernism. The sight of the eccentric, baggy—rather than the traditional close-fitting—costumes by Nikolay Roerich (who also designed the set) and strange conical hats was unlike anything Paris had seen before. Up on stage this multicolored tribe of dancers offended many with their dramatic savagery and uncouth, if not ugly, postures, as did the violent and sexual undertones of the work. Soon the audience began voicing its discontent.

Winnaretta Singer described what ensued as a "real battle" broke in a cacophony of noise: "The howls of some, the applause of others, went on for an hour . . . here and there someone would rise and shout out his views at the top of his voice, each party abusing and insulting the other in the most violent way."[68] Once the shouts and cat-calls began, there was no stopping them, though it was never quite a "riot"—a description applied retrospectively that has become part of the *Rite*'s mythology.[69] In an attempt to quell the noise, Diaghilev ordered the electricians to turn the house lights on and off. An anxious Stravinsky meanwhile paced up and down backstage, as the titanic struggle between orchestra and dancers versus the howling and whistling audience prevailed.[70] Conductor Monteux had, through it all, remained imperturbable—eyes fixed on the score and keeping to the precise tempo.

During the interval the police were called and pleas made to the audience to calm down. But things were no better when the performance resumed. A frantic Nijinsky, standing on a chair and gesticulating furiously in the wings, was reduced to shouting out the timing to the bewildered dancers who could not hear the orchestra, as they continued to try to hold it all together. "We had to run about more or less *ad lib*," recalled Russian company member Lydia Lopokova, "and stamp to various rhythms . . . we generated heat like a furnace on stage in the hot flannel costumes which were a brilliant red in the first act and white in the second." By the end, everyone was "soaked with sweat" as the curtain came down on this "stampede of humanity" in the final cathartic scene.[71]

It is said that Diaghilev had contrived the uproar of that opening night by giving out lots of free tickets and deliberately placing his supporters close to the aisles between the boxes of the dress circle, thus ensuring that they would be in shouting distance of any detractors.[72] His only comment afterward had been that the performance and the response to it were "Exactly what I wanted." Stravinsky, Nijinsky, and the company took five curtain calls—a fact that runs counter to claims of an entirely negative response to the ballet. For his own part, Stravinsky was "excited, angry, disgusted and . . . happy." Twenty minutes later, Nijinsky was on stage dancing the lead in the *Spectre de la Rose*.[73]

Marie Rambert remembered the sense of euphoria the company shared after the premiere and how "a gang of us . . . went off and had a great supper at a restaurant called the Reine Pédauque . . . then in fiacres to the Bois de Boulogne and walked, and ran about, and played games on the grass and among the trees for most of the night." At 2 A.M. they went to another restaurant in the Bois de

Boulogne for another supper and carried on eating and drinking till morning, finally taking breakfast at a dairy in Marie Antoinette's Petit Trianon.[74]

In the reviews that followed, the critical response was in the main so savage that one writer described it as a "*Massacre du printemps.*"[75] Although some recognized the "epoch-making side of this news-worthy theatrical incident," the choreography was universally derided. It was Stravinsky who came out of it far better for his music. Paris embraced him as a man ahead of his time, "The Messiah we've been waiting for since Wagner."[76] His score for *The Rite of Spring* quickly developed a life of its own quite separate from the Ballets Russes production, and already the following year it was being performed as a stand-alone concert piece. Diaghilev, thanks to his incredible tenacity, artistic vision, and prodigious capacity for work, had become "the Conqueror of Paris."[77] His Ballets Russes was to ride high on a wave of international acclaim for the next sixteen years, confirming Benois's confident assertion during those heady first days in Paris that "We really did stagger the world."[78]

CHAPTER 3

"Paris Taught Me, Enriched Me, Beggared Me, Put Me on My Feet"

It was once said by the Abbé Galiani (secretary to the Neapolitan ambassador) that "Paris is the café of Europe."[1] In the 1750s when he made that observation, the Parisian café served not just as a coffeehouse but also as an important social club for literary and political discussion. By the 1900s it had become legendary as a cultural magnet: a meeting place for travelers, artists, and writers from across Europe. It also now served a new purpose: as a refuge—if not home—for many impoverished artists and political dissidents who had chosen or been forced to flee tsarist Russia.

Montparnasse, the heart of bohemian café society in Paris, was a far cry from the grand mansions of Boulogne-sur-Seine or the richer districts of Passy and Auteuil inhabited by the Russian denizens of Belle Époque Paris. Montparnasse was for the hoi polloi—for rebels and misfits and down-and-outs, for creative artists long on talent but short on money struggling to become established. Many Russian revolutionaries had left Russia for Paris and other European cities after the 1905 revolution. But economic migrants had preceded them: the Ashkenazi Jews of the Russian Empire's western borderlands had been on the move out of Russia since the vicious pogroms launched against them in the 1880s and 1890s. Some had settled in Berlin, but others had traveled on to Paris, often without passports or papers, where they had found work in the sweatshops of the city's garment district. They had settled largely in a neighborhood known as the Pletzel located in the Marais area of the 4th arrondissement, which had been the site of a thirteenth-century ghetto known as the Juiverie.[2]

Just before Christmas 1908, having fallen foul of the Okhrana (the tsarist secret police) and not long released from prison for his pro-Bolshevik activities, seventeen-year-old Ilya Ehrenburg had arrived by train at the Gare du Nord. He brought with him a heavy suitcase filled with his favorite books and little else. A Lithuanian Jew by birth, from a middle-class family, he came to Paris to avoid further arrest, intent on working for the Bolsheviks in exile, having joined them in 1906. His hero, the Bolshevik leader Vladimir Lenin, had arrived in Paris at around the same time from Geneva. He was now holed up in a flat in the 14th arrondissement near the Parc Montsouris, with his wife and mother-in-law.[3] Conditions were cramped, but it was quieter here than in central Paris—Lenin having a pathological intolerance of noise. He was a vigorous walker and enjoyed being near the park, which was a favorite haunt of Russian émigrés living nearby.

From his pokey little room on the avenue Denfert-Rochereau a few streets away, Ilya Ehrenburg went to pay court to Lenin. The first thing he noticed with fascination was the shape of Lenin's "amazing skull"; filled to bursting with erudition and ideas, it "made one think not of anatomy but of architecture."[4] He had been surprised too by the revolutionary leader's extremely respectable appearance in stiff wing collar and dark suit, and the neat and obsessively orderly state of his flat. Lenin seemed so unlike the disheveled, chaotic Russian revolutionaries with whom he was more familiar. Indeed, Ehrenburg's own appearance, as noted by French artist's model Marevna, was precisely that of the archetype: "He had very long hair, hanging on his shoulders and it was greasy. He was dressed very sloppily, and looked in every way like the nihilists about whom one reads in foreign novels." Lenin nicknamed him "Shaggy Ilya."[5]

This wasn't Lenin's first time in Paris; he had dropped in briefly in 1903, with his protégé Leon Trotsky, to give a lecture on agricultural reform in Russia at the Salle de l'Alcazar d'Italie. This was a public meeting hall on the avenue de Choisy frequented by socialists and trade unionists that was looked upon as an unofficial Marxist university. For the three and a half years he would now spend back in Paris, from January 1909 to June 1912, Lenin kept a low profile.[*] Paris wasn't for pleasure; Paris was for work, and work of the most cerebral kind. In November 1909 at the Society of Scientists, Lenin presented the product of his hours of labor: a lecture titled "The Ideology of Contra-Revolutionary Liberalism and Its Social Significance." Celebrating May Day at the society in 1911, he announced with certainty that the counterrevolution of tepid liberal reform in Russia had failed; "now is the time for something else: the Russian Revolution."[6]

When he wasn't studying and writing his endless political pamphlets in the sanctuary of the Bibliothèque Nationale, Lenin might occasionally be seen crossing Paris on his bicycle, playing chess at the Café du Lion, or sipping a German bock beer and reading the Russian newspapers fresh from St. Petersburg in one of the quieter Montparnasse cafés. But he avoided the dense, smoke-filled atmosphere of the always busy more popular cafés. Indeed, he despised the sloppy, bohemian lifestyle of some of his fellow political exiles:

---

[*] This was the longest period Lenin spent anywhere in Europe in the years after being released from Siberian exile in 1900.

"Putrefaction!" he would exclaim in disapproval, "scum of the revolution."[7] They allowed themselves to be too easily diverted from the cause. Nor did he have time to spare for the theater, concerts, or art, with one exception: he enjoyed seeing the French singer-songwriter and working-class hero Gaston Montéhus at a *café-chantant** known as Folies Bobino on the rue Gaieté in Montparnasse. He liked Montehus's fiery brand of French socialism and his songs celebrating the militancy of the French proletariat.[8]

More often than not, when he *did* tear himself away from his books (moaning always about the bad service at the Bibliothèque Nationale; the libraries of London and Geneva had been so much more efficient), Lenin's time was taken up with interminable political meetings. Paris was full of rival political groups and factions from Russia—Bolsheviks, Mensheviks, anarchists, socialist revolutionaries, and Jewish bundists (trade unionists). Russian émigré politics were notoriously volatile. Exiles with too much time on their hands, and frustrated by the impossibility of campaigning in Russia, turned quarreling into an art form. Much of this took place in the crowded rooms of cafés in Montparnasse, such as the Oriental at number 11 rue d'Orléans.[9] Informally known as the "Bolshevik café," it was located not far from Lenin's apartment on rue Marie Rose, and his faction met here in a room on the second floor.

Lenin's eager acolyte Ehrenburg had, however, quickly found such meetings stultifying; poetry was far more to his liking than the combative world of émigré infighting. The artistic life of Paris, in contrast, "electrified" him. To stave off thoughts of homesickness and hunger, he fed on books borrowed from the Russian émigré library that had been established at 63 rue des Gobelins in 1908 and was a home away from home for many impoverished émigrés. In the

---

* The Folies Bobino had been established in 1800 as a dance hall and functioned like the English music hall as a venue for songs, monologues, dances, short plays, and farces.

early 1900s, the first Russian writers to spend time in Paris in search of greater freedom of expression and inspiration had been the better off and more socially mobile poets and philosophers, such as the St. Petersburg couple Dmitri Merezhkovsky and Zinaida Gippius. Between 1906 and 1914, this most influential if highly esoteric Russian literary pair set up a salon at their spacious apartment on rue Théophile Gautier in Auteuil. Back home in the Russian capital, Merezhkovsky—a critic, poet, and philosopher—and his wife Gippius, the equally influential (and many said, better) poet, had held court as the guiding lights of the symbolist movement in Russian poetry. Two other symbolist poets—Andrey Bely and Konstantin Balmont—had also spent time in Paris during those years. The impressionable young Ilya Ehrenburg aspired to follow in their footsteps and in Paris started writing poetry of his own—"bad poetry," as he later admitted. It was filled with gloom: "I wrote about my despair, about having had a life and having one no more . . . about the strangeness and the cruelty of Paris, about love." A treat for him amounted to a cup of coffee and "five croissants at the zinc counter" of the Café de la Rotonde or a bag of hot chestnuts bought on the street: "they cost only two sous, warmed one's hands and were deceptively filling. I ate the chestnuts and thought about Russia."[10]

In the years after 1908, precisely at the time when the Saisons Russes were captivating *Le Tout-Paris* at the Châtelet and the opera on the upmarket side of town, a whole generation of Ehrenburg's fellow countrymen and women began congregating in a cluster of cafés around the junction of the boulevard du Montparnasse and the boulevard Raspail. The Café du Dôme (opened in 1898 and expanded with a billiards room in 1902) and the Rotonde (opened in 1903 and favored by Lenin's enemies the Mensheviks*) were the

---

* The Mensheviks had also usurped the Café d'Harcourt on the boulevard Saint Michel from the Bolsheviks as their Paris meeting place.

most popular venues for the louder, more gregarious bohemians—the artists especially. Victor Libion, the large mustachioed patron of the Rotonde, while making no bones about his indifference to art, was enormously tolerant of the perpetual impecuniousness of his customers and was known on occasion to accept a drawing in exchange for one of Modigliani's absinthes.[11] He also looked the other way when starving artists broke the ends off the baguettes in the bread baskets and allowed favored clients, with only miserable cold garrets to go back to, to lie low in the dimly lit café long after the regulation closing time of 2 A.M. and huddle round its large cast-iron stove. After all, he later acknowledged, all these starving writers and artists "made my café famous."[12]

The intimate, tavern-like Closerie des Lilas, farther down at the junction with the avenue de l'Observatoire, was rather more upmarket. Preferred by the writers and poets, it became the favorite haunt in the 1920s of American writer Ernest Hemingway. All of these Paris cafés provided the prerequisite initiation for young émigrés—be they poets, painters, or revolutionaries—as "penny universities," places "that teach bohemian lifestyle, contempt for the bourgeois, sense of humor and heavy drinking." It was said at the time that the more "Bohemian" an artist looked, the more likely he was to be a Russian.[13]

Little by little, Ehrenburg was able to eke out a living from French translation and editorial work on magazines. He worked too as a guide showing visiting Russian teachers around Versailles, in between persisting with his poetry. Some of it was published back home in Russia; his first "undreamed-of success" was to receive six rubles for two poems published in a St. Petersburg magazine in 1911.[14] Ehrenburg lived the eternally hopeful life of the émigré on the precarious edge, much as he described his eponymous hero in the opening to his 1922 novel, *Julio Jurenito*: "sitting, as always, in a café on the boulevard Montparnasse in front of a cup of coffee,

emptied long before, waiting in vain for somebody to set me free by
paying the patient waiter six sous." His living conditions, he admitted, were "exceptionally squalid": his flat had no furniture beyond
a mattress; there was no stove, and he covered himself from the cold
at night with "newspapers on top of a thin blanket and a threadbare
overcoat."[15] The cold in winter there was so intolerable that he hung
out in heated cafés until late at night, reading and writing, and he
often did not eat for three or four days on end. So desperate was
he to see his work published that he took his poems to an émigré
Jewish printer—who normally ran off political posters and tracts
for the revolutionaries—begging him to do so on credit. But "Who
would have given me anything on credit in those days?" he asked.
"My shoes gaped, my trousers ended in a fringe; I was pale, thin and
my eyes often glittered with hunger." The printer said his poems
were bad; Ehrenburg agreed but scraped together enough francs to
publish a slim volume of them in a hundred-copies print run.[16]

During those first years in Paris there were many moments of intense loneliness; at other times, Ehrenburg shared the frustrations of
his life with equally struggling Russian poets, so obscure that their
names never became familiar enough to be forgotten. Whenever he
had a few sous, Ehrenburg headed for the welcoming ambiance of
a café, where he could rub shoulders with the French poet Guil-
laume Apollinaire (whom he admitted to imitating) and where he
might read his own less accomplished poetry to anyone who would
listen, especially émigré Marxist writer Anatoly Lunacharsky. Lunacharsky was then translating Marcel Proust into Russian, a writer
whose whole ethos ran totally counter to the Circle of Proletarian
Culture that Lunacharsky ran for politicized Russian workers in
Paris.

Eventually Ehrenburg found many sympathetic friends among
expatriate Russian painters. "Paris," for all of them, was their
school—"a good school but a harsh one," he later recalled.[17] Many

of them were Russian Jews for whom Paris was particularly liber-
ating, coming as they did from restricted lives in the Pale of Settlement. It was not just endemic tsarist anti-Semitism that hounded
them and placed constraints of travel and association that made it
hard for them to expand their artistic horizons. Jewish orthodoxy
also was highly censorious of artistic creativity—painting and
drawing were considered blasphemous, particularly any depiction
of the human form. Although the 1905 revolution, and the ensuing political clampdown that followed, had been the catalyst that
had prompted many politicized Jews to leave, others left for creative reasons, in order to seek out artistic inspiration and soak up
the explosion of new ideas then sweeping art, such as cubism. The
years 1908 to 1914 saw a whole generation of gifted Jewish (but
mainly nonobservant) artists decamp from the Pale of Settlement
and make the two-thousand-kilometer train journey to Paris and its
artistic heartland—Montparnasse. From Vitebsk came painter Marc
Chagall; from the Minsk area, Chaim Soutine, Michel Kikoine, and
sculptors Ossip Zadkine and Pinchus Krémègne all arrived. In Paris
they joined Ukrainian sculptors Alexander Archipenko and Chana
Orloff, Chaim Lipchitz from Lithuania, and the painter and Dadaist
poet Serge Charchoune.* For Chana Orloff, Montparnasse was "an
absolute paradise. Life was magnificent, free and cheap, but then we
were young. We put up with misery, with poverty. We lived very
simply, anywhere." Serge Charchoune felt an immediate sense of
belonging when he arrived in 1912: "I found myself in a kind of
Russian capital, I was very happy; I lived not just in a Russian colony,
but practically in Russia itself."[18]

Many of these Russian artists and sculptors at one time or another
lived in the extraordinary artists' community at La Ruche, a bizarre

---

* In order to spare the reader considerable confusion between the original Russian form of
the artists' names, the French spelling will be used in cases where people were better known
by the French version of their names that they adopted in emigration.

beehive-like construction of small studios in a circular formation. It was located on a plot of land at number 2 passage de Dantzig in the unfashionable Vaugirard district (a place where many of the impoverished Russian revolutionaries also found refuge). The building was created in 1902 from the vestiges of pavilions intended for artists during the Exposition Universelle of 1900. The site had been scheduled for demolition, but the La Chapelle pavilion had been saved, with rather grand caryatids salvaged from the British India pavilion placed at its front entrance.[19] Most of La Ruche's occupants were foreign artists, and few of them could endure La Ruche for long: the dark and pokey interior of 140 studios and flats had the most primitive amenities, and residents complained that the narrow studios were like coffins. La Ruche was dreadfully cold and drafty in winter; spartan, too uncomfortable, and rampant with vermin in summer. Archipenko described it as "like living inside a Gruyère cheese."[20] Zadkine extended the allusion: La Ruche, he said, was "a sinister Brie cheese, where every artist had a piece; a studio which began at a point and ended in a large window."[21]

Pinchus Krémègne spoke many years later of the sense of camaraderie at La Ruche: there was "a true brotherhood" among the Russian artists. Having made his way to the Russian-German border in 1912 without a passport, he had failed to get on a boat to the United States. And so he had taken a train to the Gare de l'Est with nothing but an address on a piece of paper—La Ruche. The city seemed so vast to him after the little villages of the Pale.[22] He and his fellow artists walked everywhere, most often from their digs at La Ruche to Montparnasse, in search of a friend and the loan of a few centimes for a meal. When they had money, which was rarely, they always shared it; they had known far worse poverty in Russia. "We ate little white rolls and drank tea like Russians are used to doing."[23] The Italian artist Amedeo Modigliani (a lovable but notorious drunk) often saved them from misery, recalled Krémègne. "He drew a portrait of someone, a sketch, and gave us the money [he got for it]."[24] Modigliani seemed always drawn to the Russians; in 1911 he had had a brief affair with the Russian poet Anna Akhmatova when she was in Paris, not long after she married fellow poet Niko-lay Gumilev. The romantic idyll with Modigliani was an instinctive meeting of hearts and minds between two then unknown creative artists who would set their stamp on the century. Akhmatova de-scribed it as being part of the "prehistory of our lives"—"his life being very short, and mine very long."[25] She never forgot those days in "beautiful Baudelarian Paris:"[26]

> *Whenever it rained (it often rained in Paris) Modigliani took with him a huge old black umbrella. We would sit together under this umbrella on a bench in the Jardin du Luxembourg in the warm summer rain. We would jointly recite Verlaine, whom we knew by heart, and we were glad we shared the same interests.*[27]

Together they would walk round the old parts of Paris, or visit the Louvre, the fine-boned, statuesque beauty Akhmatova tower-ing over Modigliani. In private he drew her naked many times; she remembered him always as "unlike anyone else in the world." He showed her the *real* Paris, but soon after, she returned to Russia and to Gumilev,* the man she had reluctantly married.[28] But Anna Akhmatova undoubtedly left something of herself behind in Paris with Modigliani: "Why, oh why, must you be better / Than the one I chose?" she asked in a poem about their affair. But she kept it private and most of the sixteen drawings Modigliani gave her were later lost.[29]

---

* Gumilev had met Modigliani when he and Akhmatova spent their honeymoon in Paris in 1910. He thought the painter a "drunken monster."

Much to the bafflement of everyone, the elegant and handsome Modigliani became great friends with one of the least physically appealing of the émigré Russian artists: the ragged and dirty Chaim Soutine. Indeed, Modigliani was one of the first to notice and admire Soutine's work. Somehow, they communicated, despite Soutine's having no other language than Yiddish when he first arrived. But tragically, in becoming virtually his only friend, Modigliani later sucked the already half-mad and lonely Russian into his spiraling world of absinthe and hashish addiction.[30] Few could fathom Soutine—this strange introvert, who looked like a hobo. Ehrenburg left a memorable pen portrait in *Julio Jurenito* of Soutine sitting in the dark corner of a café with his hat pulled down over his eyes—he hated being looked at—"scared and somnolent—as if he had woken up from his dreams, frightened, and leaving no time for washing or shaving. He had the eyes of a hunted deer—probably of starvation."[31]

Of all the Russian artists at La Ruche in the prewar years, the one who was to enjoy critical international success the soonest and pull himself out of poverty was Marc Chagall. He had arrived in search of Léon Bakst, who had taught him painting at the Zvantseva School of Drawing and Painting in St. Petersburg and was now at the height of his fame at the Ballets Russes. Like Chagall, Bakst was a Jew from the Pale of Settlement—born Leib-Chaim Rosenberg in Grodno—and it was at his St. Petersburg studio that Chagall had been first introduced to the sophistication and elegance that Bakst's Paris links exuded.[32] In 1910 Chagall had begged to go with him to Paris as an assistant but had been rejected because of his lack of expertise in scenery painting. Undaunted, Chagall vowed to follow him there, thanks to the sale of two paintings and an allowance of 125 francs a month from a lawyer patron. The four-day journey on hard third-class seats was worth it.[33] On arrival, Chagall immediately felt as though his creativity had been liberated: "My art needed Paris like a tree needs water," he declared.[34]

He spoke but a few words of French, yet Paris offered everything he craved and that the constraints of the shtetl of Vitebsk in northern Russia had not had: "light, color, freedom, the sun, the joy of living."[35] Here was a new, sophisticated artistic universe of the avant-garde. Chagall went to see Bakst backstage at the Ballets Russes during a performance of *Le Spectre de la rose* that Bakst had designed for Nijinsky.[36] Not long afterward, Bakst came to Chagall's studio to inspect his new paintings. He recognized a kindred spirit in his former student's vibrant canvases: "Now your colors sing," he told him. But the world of adulation by the *beau monde* now inhabited by Bakst and the Ballets Russes was a million miles from the collective struggles of the rabbit warren of yet-to-be-recognized talent at La Ruche. Chagall was one of the lucky ones—able to afford a studio on the top floor, which had far more light than the cheaper ones lower down the beehive, and with its own interior balcony, on which he slept. He paid 150 francs a year; his poorer compatriots could barely scrape the 50 francs for the cheapest ones, among them Soutine, who shared a tiny studio with Krémègne.[37]

La Ruche was a unique and unforgettable place in those years before the war, a melting pot of nationalities where the Russian and Polish Jews predominated in their own artistic ghetto within it, experimenting in the new avant-garde forms of cubism and expressionism. Chagall found the rowdy atmosphere a distraction: sobbing models bawled out by impatient Russians; Italians singing loudly to their guitars; Jews arguing about a specially Jewish style of art; the sculptor Zadkine noisily cutting stone in the studio below his—all against the disturbing noise of animals being slaughtered in the nearby abattoir. And then there were the constant interruptions from the always hungry, always filthy Soutine, bursting in in his typically Neanderthal manner, scavenging for food and bringing his evil unwashed smell with him.[38]

Chagall and Soutine were both ruthless with work that dissatisfied them: they threw out paintings at an alarming rate—dumping them into the dustbin or even hurling them straight out the window. Soutine, who was notoriously secretive about showing his work, frequently slashed it violently to shreds first.[39] Chagall might be in Paris, but his head and heart were still in the shtetl. Night after night, he stayed up painting dreamlike, supernatural visions of the old Russia he had known as a child—peasant huts, domed churches, synagogues, beggar violinists. Soutine, who had had poverty ground into him in the shtetl near Minsk, had no such nostalgia and seemed doomed to abject self-abasement and degradation. He repelled people not just with his rank appearance but with his work too, some of which was disturbingly fixated on the blood and gore of the abattoir. He painted sides of beef on meat hooks and other food—skinned rabbits, chickens, pheasants—and plates of stinking fish obsessively. Perhaps it was his perverse way of staving off the gnawing hunger he had to endure; he found his artistic food standing for hours in the Louvre admiring his favorite old masters, especially Rembrandt: "This is so beautiful," he told sculptor friend Chana Orloff, "that I am going crazy."[40]

Chagall was luckier than the vast majority of his fellow artists; he received a regular stipend from his patron and was careful with his money: "I was the millionaire of La Ruche with my hundred and twenty-five francs," he later joked. Inevitably, his perpetually broke fellow artists constantly cadged loans from him. When they did manage to scrape a few sous, they paid off their models, visited the nearest bordello, and drank their melancholy away in one of the cafés of Montparnasse, such as the Rotonde, where they sometimes met up with Modigliani and the Spanish painter Picasso or writers such as fellow Russian Ehrenburg or the French poets Apollinaire, Blaise Cendrars, and Alexis Léger. They went to exhibitions, museums, and galleries together and shared in artistic discussions, though Zadkine was one of the few of the artists' group who mastered French sufficiently well to argue about poetry with Raymond Radiguet.[41]

Ehrenburg recalled the highs and lows of new ideas that often ran on a short fuse: "Every month the poets and painters issued various artistic manifestos overthrowing everything and everyone, but everything and everyone remained as before." What did it matter? Life in Paris, with all its vicissitudes, expanded their world, as Ehrenburg captured so eloquently: "Paris taught me, enriched me, beggared me, put me on my feet and knocked me down."[42]

To the "tidy and conservative French," this chaotic Russian artistic incursion during the years before World War I—of Jews and Christians, rich and poor, from the stage of the Châtelet to the smoky cafés of Montparnasse—was unfailingly entertaining, if at times incoherent: "the Russians were so splendid, so Scythian, so untrammeled! They galloped like wild Tatars right across the tidy geometric gardens. There was nothing Latin about them, either in their liturgy . . . or their logic."[43] No surprise, therefore, that the straitlaced Lenin had, by June 1912, had enough of Paris and its distractions. "Why the hell did we go to Paris," he later complained to his wife, Nadya; as far as he was concerned, the city was "a foul hole."[44] Political infighting and an endless stream of visitors had worn him down and frayed his nerves. He was frustrated at being so far from Russia, where a network of his underground activists were propagandizing and agitating with ever more violence for the overturn of the tsarist system. He wanted to be nearer the seat of the action should revolution come. So he and Nadya packed up their few possessions at the rue Marie-Rose and, with little more than a few clothes, books, a chess set, and their toothbrushes, headed east to yet another bolt-hole, this time in Galicia—then part of the Russian empire's Polish borderlands.

The turbulent world of émigré art and politics of Montparnasse, in all its dynamism, its creativity—and its suffering—could not have been further removed from the tinkling Belle Époque salons of Boulogne-sur-Seine. Here Grand Duke Paul and Countess von Hohenfelsen had continued to lavish millions of francs on their opulent home and the sedate fine dining that went with it. The dinners they hosted were always exquisite: *"filets de soles Parc-des-Princes"* or *"mousselines d'éperlans Walewska"* or *"boeuf braisé Parisienne,"* followed by tempting selections of *"truffes, soufflés, gaufrettes"*—all served on the finest Sèvres porcelain.[45] The Romanov grand duke and his wife remained oblivious to the lives of their less privileged compatriots on the other side of the city; nevertheless, they were anxious to return to Russia. The problem, as always, was Olga's irregular position as a morganatic wife and the continuing ban on her presence there, although Nicholas II had made a concession for the wedding of Paul's daughter Maria Pavlovna in May 1908. But it had not been a comfortable return for Olga; the tsaritsa, still rigid with disapproval, had cold-shouldered her and had received her only in private. Paul's fury at the persistent marginalization of his wife ate away at him and affected his already poor health. Then finally, in November of 1908, Olga was allowed to return for the burial of Grand Duke Alexis in St. Petersburg and thereafter was given permission to remain officially.

Nicholas had his reasons for conceding his favorite uncle's return to favor; since the 1905 revolution he had become increasingly politically isolated and needed the ever-loyal Paul's support. Paul had useful connections in Paris too, as one of the important cogs in the Franco-Russian alliance. Although Olga sensed the dangers of a return after the safety of Boulogne, given the increasingly unstable situation in Russia, she began looking for a suitably grand mansion. Disliking Paul's town house in St. Petersburg, she set her heart on finding somewhere at Tsarskoe Selo near the tsar's residence, the Alexander Palace. But no existing house suited the couple's exacting requirements. A new palace with Louis XVI-style interiors was therefore built at speed to their precise specification, employing fifty workers and craftsmen sent specially from Paris. Olga with her usual imperiousness took command of an enterprise that would eventually cost over 1 million francs (around $4.5 million today).[46] She spent hours making a long inventory of the furniture and artworks at the house in Boulogne that was to be carefully packed up and transported by rail at enormous cost to Tsarskoe Selo. But she didn't stop there, and made new acquisitions in the Paris art and antiques houses even as the couple prepared to leave, promising their Paris friends that they would retain the house in Boulogne and return every autumn.

Paul and Olga's return in grace to Russia came in 1913, in time for the Romanov tercentenary celebrations, but it was not till May 1914 that they were able to move into their magnificent new mansion, complete with a staff of one hundred servants and a wine cellar stuffed with ten thousand bottles.[47] The same atmosphere of grace and sophistication prevailed there as in their Paris home. Paul quickly resumed his influential place at court and finally saw his long campaign for Olga's official recognition rewarded when Nicholas II granted her a new Russian title—Princess Paley (using the name of a Ukrainian clan—Paly—who were early ancestors of Olga's Karnovich birth family). This title, and with it the right to transmit it to her son and two daughters by Paul, spared Olga the embarrassment of the Germanic-sounding Hohenfelsen name, now that war with Germany had broken out. Missing his lifelong connection with the military, Paul was eager to return to his old regiment of the guards, but he would have to wait some time for a new commission.

Passing through Paris in the summer of 1913 prior to returning to St. Petersburg, Russian diplomat Anatoly Neklyudov was taken aback by how many Russians were in the city. "The best St. Petersburg society was well represented," he noted; never before had Paris struck him so much as "the town of pleasure and thoughtless luxury":

> *It was the time of the appearance of the famous tango, of "Persian balls" etc. There were "tango suppers" at Ciro's, and "tango teas" all over the place, at which in the afternoons, evenings and nights, professionals, amateurs, cocottes, women of the world, Grand-Duchesses even swayed gracefully or fluttered comically about in new American dances.*[48]

Russians, he noted, "filled the small theaters, the smart restaurants, and the new dressmakers' showroom," all spending money with reckless abandon.

> *It was as if some one was urging on all these people by whispering in their ear: "Hurry up. Hurry up, and enjoy yourselves; these are the last months of your thoughtless, brilliant, and luxurious existence.*[49]

One of the generation of Russian young blades dancing the night away that year was Grand Duke Paul's son Dmitri Pavlovich, who made regular visits to his father in Paris, where he could indulge himself to the hilt on his lavish private income. The American ballroom dancer Irene Castle recalled being pursued by Dmitri when she was appearing with her husband and dance partner, Vernon, at the famous supper club the Café de Paris. Dmitri had been so taken by their performance that he threw a hundred-franc note on a plate and passed it around the tables, collecting more than five hundred francs, which he "gracefully presented to the lovely Irene."[50] The young grand duke was so suave, he could pass for an Englishman—"blond, smooth-shaven, tall, slight," and—like his uncle, Tsar Nicholas—he was "possessed of a definite Oxford accent."[51] It was clear that he had "grown up with the best of everything." He had "the charm befitting his rank," recalled Irene, "and about as much restraint as a pin wheel in a strong wind." Dmitri would confidently swoop her round the dance floor at the Café de Paris; and with equal panache drove the Castles at breakneck speed, blasting his horn as he went, through the city streets "in a car twice as long as we had ever seen before, at what appeared to be eighty miles an hour." Dmitri wined and dined the Castles at l'Abbaye on the Left Bank; he begged them for the lyrics to American ragtime songs, which he said his father Paul was "crazy about"; and took them on the Grand Dukes' Tour round the dives of Paris. When Vernon was absent for a couple of days, Dmitri showered Irene with orchids, cartons of Russian cigarettes, and "a set of the most beautiful diamond and onyx buttons from Cartier," making it clear he was "mad for her." Nothing deterred this louche, self-confident Russian grand duke: the world, and its women, was at his feet, and in 1913 the money to enjoy it was limitless.[52]

Grand Duke Dmitri's hedonistic lifestyle marked the high point of the Russian enjoyment of the Belle Époque. The outbreak of war in Europe in August the following year brought inevitable and dramatic changes to the émigré community in Paris. The aristocracy, like Paul and Olga before them, headed back to their grand mansions in St. Petersburg. The literary couple Dmitri Merezhkovsky and Zinaida Gippius, along with other Russians in their circle, set off back to Russia, under the same impression—that they would soon be back. For how could Zinaida resist "those wonderful Paris springs" that she loved so dearly? "Those who did not know Paris before the war in 1914," she later reminisced,

> *had never seen the real Paris—lively, merry—above all merry—every young street boy whistling the same tune (at that time "the cake walk")—the soft tinkling of little bells on the fiacres, the nightingales singing in the thickets of the Parc Muette; even the pleasures of the absurd Trocadéro with its waterfall and stone animals; the simple little hookers on the Boule-Miche and the Rat Mort;* the wonderful street smells and the iridescent light.*

Everything about Paris in the spring brought her such joy. She and Dmitri were infinitely sad to have to leave "*la douce France.*"[53]

Over at La Ruche, Marc Chagall packed up and left Paris in 1914 to go back to the shtetl for a visit. He had shut up his studio, tying the door handle with wire, as the key would not lock, and leaving a whole stack of paintings inside. Other rolled-up canvases that he took with him were left behind en route, in a gallery in Berlin. He never saw any of them again. Back in the shtetl at Vitebsk he turned out an enormous new body of vivid canvases and married his sweetheart, Bella; war would keep him in Russia for the time being.[54]

When war was declared in Paris in August 1914, many of Chagall's fellow Russians enthusiastically volunteered at mass recruitment rallies held at the Esplanade des Invalides. In all, some forty thousand foreign nationals residing in Paris came forward to enlist, including over six thousand Russians—about one fifth of the Russian population of Paris.[55] Among them were several of Ehrenburg's old

---

* Boule-Miche—colloquial French shorthand for the boulevard Saint Michel; Rat Mort—a café in Place Pigalle, Montmartre, that was a notorious haunt of prostitutes.

café companions from the Rotonde and from the émigré library on rue Gobelins. Many of the volunteers were poor Jewish workers from immigrant families who had settled years earlier in the 4th arrondissement or political exiles who did not want to risk arrest back in Russia. However, according to the newspaper *Le Temps*, by August 24, 57 percent of the Russian volunteers had already been turned down on health grounds—among them Ehrenburg.[56] He assumed it was because he was "too weedy" ("One cannot with impunity prefer poetry to beef for a period of three or four years," he argued).[57] Soutine enlisted in a work brigade but was soon dismissed for poor health, suffering from stomach ulcers and anemia. Eventually, ten thousand Russian Jews in Paris left for Spain or the United States, having been given the ultimatum: enlist or leave the country.[58] Others returned home to serve in the Imperial Russian Army. After his rejection, Ehrenburg chose to stay, despite suffering numerous interrogations by the French police about his German-sounding name. He worked night shifts at the Montparnasse goods station unloading shells and wrote articles on the French war effort for the Russian press, spending time at the front with other journalists.

Unfortunately, the Russian volunteers did not fare well in the French army. They were not taken into the main French fighting force but sent to outposts of the Foreign Legion, despite insisting that they wanted to join regular French units.[59] The experience was a dreadful one for many of the 3,393 Russians enrolled in the legion by December 10, 1914. They were insulted and ill treated, and their requests for a transfer refused. The following year twenty-seven legion recruits rebelled and were court-martialed; seven were executed.[60]

During the First World War, the Ballets Russes seasons had continued at the Châtelet, although in order to stay afloat financially the company was also now touring and appearing regularly in Monte Carlo. The most notable production staged during the war years was that in May 1917 of a new ballet entitled *Parade*. Depicting a Paris street fair of conjurors and acrobats, with choreography by Léonide Massine, it was based on a one-act scenario by the French writer Jean Cocteau. The music by the avant-garde French composer Eric Satie was guaranteed to offend, including as it did the sound effects of typewriters and a car horn, and the arresting cubist city-scape and costumes designed by the blazing new talent on the Paris scene — Pablo Picasso — were equally provocative.

Ehrenburg remembered *Parade* as the only happy event in Paris during the war. *Le Tout-Paris* duly turned out and hated everything: the modernist music, the choreography, and especially Picasso's costumes and sets. *Parade*'s reception, though noisy, was not as bad as that for *The Rite of Spring*: "People sitting in the stalls rushed toward the stage, shouting 'Curtain!' in a real frenzy," Ehrenburg recalled with amusement. Audience members were so incensed when the dancers retaliated by making fun of their protests, that they "lost their heads entirely," howling "Death to the Russians!" and "Picasso is a boche!" The following day, the French press suggested that rather than offend Paris audiences, the Russians would do better launching an offensive against the Germans "somewhere in Galicia."[61]

Diaghilev had hoped for a scandal with *Parade* to rival that of *The Rite of Spring* four years earlier and boost ticket sales. He was disappointed; the ballet was performed only four more times that season, and thereafter slipped down the repertoire. Within a year, such had become his financial difficulties that in 1918 he transferred the Ballets Russes company to Madrid and then to London. The premiere of *Parade* had, however, succeeded in ensuring that Paris was the place where "the avant-garde elbowed its way into mainstream European elite culture."[62] It also launched the career of Pablo Picasso, who married Olga Khokhlova, one of the ballerinas in the Diaghilev company, the following year at the Russian Orthodox Cathedral on rue Daru. Thereafter she would be his principal life model.

Then came 1917, and suddenly the Russian community had far more serious preoccupations than art. In early March, after a week of protest marches, strikes, and riots, the long awaited revolution had broken out in Petrograd (as St. Petersburg had been renamed on the outbreak of war). On March 16 Nicholas II abdicated the throne of Russia and his brother Mikhail declined to take it in his stead. On hearing the news, Lenin, who had moved to Switzerland in September 1914, left his safe house in Zurich and, with his Bolshevik entourage, hastily made his way back to Petrograd, eager to capitalize on the struggle that the Provisional Government was having in imposing order.

Ilya Ehrenburg recalled how the Russian émigrés in Paris had been very excited by the news of revolution and had celebrated noisily, drinking and singing in the bars and cafés of Montparnasse. A large group of them solicited the Russian ambassador Alexander Iswolsky at the embassy on rue de Grenelle for help in getting home. A plan was devised to send the political exiles, now eager to enjoy the freedoms of a Russia liberated from the tsars, back in batches—"the first to go would be émigrés belonging to the more important political parties."[63] But there was also by now another reason for them to want to leave Paris—a growing anti-Russian campaign in the French press led by *Le Matin*. Ever since the revolutionary disturbances of 1905, the French police had become increasingly alarmed at the growing numbers of Russian émigrés flooding into the city. Paris had become the "grand headquarters of Russian revolutionaries" and around twenty-five thousand of them had congregated in the capital. Their loyalties to France and its alliance with Russia were being increasingly called into question.[64]

By April 1917 the French press was publishing hostile articles insinuating that the Russians had "always adored the Prussians, that they were irresponsible and inclined to betray their friends."[65] There had been growing antipathy too between French and Russian troops based together in France. Ehrenburg was anxious to get home, but having come to France without any official papers in 1908, he had to trail around various embassies and consulates in order to get the passport and visa he needed to leave. Shortly before he did so, he met up with old drinking partners at the Rotonde, including the Mexican artist Diego Rivera. Rivera was happy for him; Ehrenburg was going to "see the Revolution, the real Revolution!" Rivera had witnessed the one still going on in Mexico and it had been "the gayest thing imaginable," he told him. He hoped, in parting, that he would see Ehrenburg again. But "perhaps not": he might be thrown into prison, or be shot; such was the way of revolutions.[66]

Having secured the right papers, Ehrenburg prepared for the train home. That last evening in Paris, he walked along the banks of the river Seine, "looking about me yet seeing nothing. I was no longer in Paris and not yet in Moscow. . . . I was happy and unhappy. My life in Paris had been dreadful, and yet I loved Paris."[67] He eventually arrived in Moscow in July 1917; four months later he witnessed the Bolshevik seizure of power. But it was not the end of his Paris story, nor that of other Russians whom Ehrenburg had befriended in the city. Many of them would soon find themselves oppressed and hounded by the new socialist order back in their Russian homeland, in ways far worse than they had experienced under the tsars. The Romanov grand dukes would see their fine palaces taken from them and their family condemned as enemies of the new state. In a very short space of time, many Russians would be fleeing back to Paris again.

—⟫•⟪—

CHAPTER 4

"We Had Outlived Our Epoch and Were Doomed"

When they took possession of their lovely palace at Tsarskoe Selo just before war broke out in 1914, Grand Duke Paul and Princess Paley knew, in their hearts, that their generation was living on the brink of disaster and that a return to Russia was risky for them. But after twelve years of exile in Paris, the enforced inactivity of his life there had weighed heavily upon Paul; as a lifelong military man, he wanted to serve again in the army.[1] He returned, however, with a deep sense of fatalism: in August 1915, he and Olga confided over dinner with the French ambassador to Petrograd, Maurice Paléologue, that the tsar and their kind were already "marked down."[2]

Although, given the outbreak of war, Paul's request to return to the army had been granted when Nicholas II gave him the command of the First Corps of the Imperial Guard, persistent ill health prevented him from taking up his appointment at army headquarters at Mogilev until May 1916. Paul and Olga's twenty-year-old son, Prince Vladimir Paley, a gentle, sensitive soul and budding poet, had meanwhile been serving in the Hussars since 1915 and now became his father's orderly officer. Unfortunately, Paul's long years out of the army had left him ill-equipped to cope with the demands of a wartime command and, after leading the guards in a disastrous attack on July 27, 1916, during the Brusilov offensive, he was relieved of his command and sent back to Tsarskoe Selo.[3]

Paul and Olga were fifteen miles out of the city, at Tsarskoe Selo, when revolution broke in Petrograd in 1917. Maurice Paléologue dined with them one last time, in April. Paul, he recalled, was still wearing his general's uniform and seemed calm; there was about him an air of "unaffected dignity," but "lines of woe [were] deeply etched upon his haggard face." His wife was "simply trembling with grief and exasperation." Indeed, Olga had already told a friend how she lay awake at night imagining their home in flames, "and all our beautiful collections pillaged and sacked."[4] As they passed through the elegant rooms on their way to lunch, the same thought struck all three of them, remembered Paléologue:

> *We feasted our eyes on all this splendor, the pictures, the tapestries, the profusion of furniture and treasures of art. What was the good of all that now? What would become of all these marvels and glories? With tears in her eyes, the poor Princess said to me:*
>
> *"Perhaps this house will be taken from us quite soon—and I've put so much of myself into it."*[5]

Paul's eldest daughter, Maria Pavlovna,* had recently arrived on a visit and noticed how distraught her father was that his attempts to persuade the tsaritsa, in Nicholas's absence, to make political concessions at the eleventh hour had failed. When the tsar abdicated

---

* Maria had divorced her Swedish husband Prince Wilhelm in March 1914 and returned to Russia. On September 19, 1917, she remarried—to Prince Sergey Poutiatine.

at Pskov on 16 March, no one in the Romanov family had had the courage to face Alexandra, and so it had fallen to Paul to go and give her the bad news. The revolution had "cut him to the heart," but he did not blame the revolutionaries, Maria wrote: "It was all, he said, the result of the terrible blindness of the past regime."[6]

By the summer of 1917, the Russian aristocracy was witnessing the end of days: "There is no country called Russia anymore," Paul told Maria Pavlovna, "only a country called Revolution, which must be protected at any price."[7] On March 20, 1917, the Provisional Government had issued a decree making the palaces of the imperial court—the Winter Palace and those at Tsarskoe Selo, Peterhof, and Oranienbaum state property. All monies belonging to the imperial family were transferred to the Ministry of Finance, and crown lands—the income from which provided the lavish appanages enjoyed by the grand dukes—were confiscated by the state. For now, the Romanovs were left with only their privately owned homes in Petrograd and their personal possessions.

After the Bolsheviks seized power in the second revolution in November, things became much worse for the aristocracy. Lenin revoked all private ownership of land, and by February of 1918 had confiscated three quarters of all estates in Russia.[8] Anyone deemed "bourgeois" faced the brunt of the Bolsheviks' wrath. In the Russian sense of the word, *bourgeois* meant anyone considered to be privileged, not just financially but also culturally. The intelligentsia of old prerevolutionary Russia, along with the aristocracy, was thus collectively deemed to be "enemies of the revolution."[9] The number one target in Lenin's sight lines for attack, expropriation, and eventual "liquidation"—a word that would become all too chillingly familiar over the next few years—was the Romanov family. Back in 1901 Lenin had declared that in Russia "it was necessary to cut off the heads of at least a hundred Romanovs" to achieve the socialist state, and throughout the winter of 1917–18 vehement class hatred against the old imperial elite mounted.[10] "Death to the aristocrats" was the cry everywhere, recalled Maria Pavlovna: "We were entirely in their power and nothing but chance could help us."[11]

Expropriations and house searches became daily occurrences, with intimidating gangs of revolutionaries wreaking destruction on the homes of the wealthy and heading always, as a priority, for their wine cellars. The aristocracy were forced to share their living space with numerous worker families and given only the most basic food rations. Reduced rapidly to penury, they began selling their few remaining possessions in order to survive, while every possible way was found to humiliate them and strip them of their dignity. By the winter of 1918, the new Bolshevik government had made it obligatory for all the bourgeoisie to work—at jobs as abject as possible, such as sweeping the streets, cleaning toilets, and digging graves.[12]

Just before the revolution had broken in Petrograd in March 1917, Grand Duchess Vladimir had fortuitously left the city for Kislovodsk, a fashionable spa located in the Caucasus between the Black and Caspian seas, to be near her son Grand Duke Andrey, who was undergoing treatment there.[13] She rented a pleasant villa, albeit modest by her standards, and was not expecting to be gone for long. She had therefore left behind at the Vladimir Palace in Petrograd "all her lavish court robes, her trains of velvet and brocade, most of her wonderful collection of furs, [and] the greater part of her priceless jewelry."[14] Before long, however, revolutionaries arrived in Kislovodsk, and she was placed under house arrest for two months; for the first time in her life, Grand Duchess Vladimir had to learn to go without things.

Her eldest son, Kirill, had meanwhile been the first Romanov to get out of Russia—by rail to Finland with his pregnant wife Victoria and two daughters in June of 1917. He settled on an estate at Haikko for three years, from where he could keep an eye on the situation at home. He lived in hopes of the restoration of the monarchy to which he laid claim as next in line and turned down offers of refuge from the governments of Sweden and France. In 1920 the Germanophile Kirill and his wife opted to settle in Coburg at the Villa Edinburg. Throughout that summer of 1917, meanwhile, other members of the Romanov family with residences in Crimea had headed south. The dowager empress Maria Feodorovna had traveled from Kiev to her daughter Xenia and son-in-law Sandro's villa at Ai-Todor, to be joined there later by her other daughter, Olga, and her husband, Nikolay Kulikovsky. On arrival, Olga had had the good sense to divide her mother's jewels among several cocoa tins and hide them around the house. The Bolsheviks often turned up to make searches of the property, prompting a regular scramble to hide the tins in crevices along the nearby cliff edge.[15]

Elsewhere in Crimea, the tsar's uncle, Grand Duke Nikolay Nikolaevich, was staying on his brother Peter's estate at Dulber; Prince Felix Yusupov and his wife, Irina, were living at their palace at Koreiz. Felix had managed to smuggle out some of his most prized valuables from his palace on the Moika in Petrograd with the help of a rather shadowy Englishman named Bertie Stopford—a sometime art and antiques dealer and possibly unofficial spy based in St. Petersburg.* Stopford came to the rescue again in saving Grand Duchess Vladimir's fabulous jewel collection of Fabergé and Cartier pieces—much of the latter acquired on her many trips to Paris. In Petrograd that July, he had managed, with the help of Grand Duchess Vladimir's son Boris, to get into the Vladimir Palace via a secret passageway and locate her jewels still in the safe in her dressing

---

* Stopford had helped Cartier extend his client base to St. Petersburg and open a branch there, thanks to his connections at the Russian court. It seems likely that this enabled Stopford to pass on gossip and intelligence gleaned there to the British embassy.

room. He folded them carefully in newspapers—in all 244 items, including 25 tiaras—and in September 1917 smuggled them out in two Gladstone bags to the safety of London.[16] The dowager empress Maria Feodorovna was less fortunate; the authorities confiscated the remainder of her fabulous collection of imperial jewels from the Anichkov Palace, her home in Petrograd.

Throughout the summer and autumn of 1917, those of the aristocracy who were able—particularly members of the court who lived out at Tsarskoe Selo—as well as officials of the tsarist civil service and provincial nobility, were leaving Russia in ever greater numbers. For many with second homes there or family connections in Paris or the Riviera, getting to France was the major objective. They had two options: by rail from Petrograd, north across Karelia into Finland, and from there up to the Swedish border to get a ship to Europe. There was also the possibility of traveling south through mostly hostile Bolshevik-controlled territory to the Black Sea. The only other route was almost impossible, but some who left early managed to escape on the Trans-Siberian Railway to Harbin in Manchuria, or to travel right across to Vladivostok and take a boat to Japan or California. But this option evaporated once civil war gathered in Siberia and the strategic railway line became a focus of the fighting.

After the end of World War I in November 1918, German troops who had been occupying Ukraine and Crimea—and thus providing a modicum of protection for the Romanovs there—withdrew, and the situation became ever more dangerous. Local political factions were now subjecting those members of the imperial family holed up in Crimea to frequent house searches and arrest. Trotsky's newly formed Red Army, composed mainly of conscripts, was rapidly approaching Crimea in its pushback against the White Volunteer Army of counterrevolutionaries in southern Russia, and by the end of 1918 it was imperative that the Romanovs were evacuated to somewhere safer—by sea via Malta to France or England.

Shortly after the Bolshevik coup in November, Grand Duke Paul had been arrested at his palace at Tsarskoe Selo, suspected of involvement in a monarchist plot. The Bolsheviks held him for three days at the Smolny—the former school for daughters of the nobility that was now the headquarters of Lenin's government. Some of the hard-liners wanted to remove Paul immediately to the Peter and Paul Fortress on the River Neva; others, to the notorious naval stronghold at Kronstadt. Meanwhile, Paul's Bolshevik guards seemed rather embarrassed with their prisoner, even addressing him as "Comrade Highness." They found him a rickety armchair and sat him down and "begged him to read the newspaper to them and explain it," they being illiterate. "It must have been strange," wrote French diplomat Louis de Robien, "to see this Romanov in general's uniform and wearing the order of St. George,* with his majestic look and superb presence, reading *Pravda* to a group of four disheveled sailors."[17]

While Paul dealt with his situation with amazing composure, if not serenity—as several observed—his wife, Olga, was busy behind the scenes. She had rushed at once to the Petrograd Soviet, where "with the energy and persistence inherent in her, she did not desist until the decision was revoked," remembered her stepdaughter Maria Pavlovna.[18] Olga succeeded in enlisting the help of a doctor, who confirmed Paul's fragile state of health—he had an ulcer and a weak chest—and he was released on condition he did not leave Petrograd without official authorization.[19] He returned to his home at Tsarskoe

* The highest military decoration of the Russian Empire.

Selo only to witness most of his vast and very valuable wine collection smashed to pieces by Bolshevik officials.[20]

In point of fact, in August 1917 Paul had already asked permission to go to Sweden—the nearest neutral country offering refuge, only twenty hours by steamship from Petrograd—perhaps as a stepping-stone back to his home in Paris.[21] With the war still raging, he could not travel by rail due west directly to Europe. To economize, he and Olga had moved out of their palace,* which they could no longer afford to heat, into a smaller dacha in the grounds of Grand Duke Boris's English-style villa.[22] Soon all three of the automobiles that they had brought back from Paris were confiscated.[23] Nevertheless, he and Olga seemed grateful still to be together; the stiff and formal Paul had always seemed "the last man in the world one would have expected to make so romantic a marriage," but the couple clearly adored each other.[24] When Louis de Robien visited them at Tsarskoe Selo in February 1918, almost all their original sixty-four domestic staff had been let go. They shared their meager rations of brown bread, with one of their last good bottles of Mouton-Rothschild. They had no money, they told Robien, and were now obliged to sell their art treasures and paintings, but Paul, he noted, "seems to bear it all with a rare greatness of spirit. He has not lost his optimism and still has hope; he says that good may come out of this excess of evil, some day."[25]

Paul's hopes must have evaporated in March 1918, when Lenin's government issued a decree commanding all members of the imperial family to report for registration to the All-Russian Extraordinary Commission for Combating Counter-Revolution and Sabotage—known as the Cheka—in Petrograd. The Bolsheviks were now preparing to send all the Romanovs into internal exile—variously, at

---

* The Bolsheviks soon expropriated the palace and turned it into a museum. Olga was allowed to keep only the icons and family photograph albums.

Vologda, Vyatka, and Perm—until they had decided what to do with them.[26] When he arrived to register, Paul and Olga's son, Prince Paley, was offered the chance to repudiate his father, but Vladimir had refused and was sent into exile in Vyatka, despite his mother's protests that he was a Paley, not a Romanov. But she did at least manage to save Paul from being sent away, having once again brandished a doctor's certificate attesting to Paul's ill health at Cheka headquarters.[27] But Paul knew even then that he was living on borrowed time. He intimated as much to his daughters, Irina and Nataliya, when walking with them in the garden: "He spoke to us at length about all that he owed to our mother," recalled Irina, "all that she had brought to him which he had never known in his life before, and about all that she had been to him."[28] Not long afterward, an offer came to help get Paul out of Russia, which he refused.

That same month, the tsar's brother Grand Duke Mikhail (Alexandrovich), who had declined to take the throne after Nicholas's abdication, was arrested and sent into internal exile at Perm.* For three months, he had been allowed a degree of freedom there. Then suddenly and without warning on the night of June 12–13, he and his secretary, Nicholas Johnson, were taken into the forest outside the city and murdered. Barely a month later, Mikhail's brother Tsar Nicholas; his wife, Alexandra; and their five children, Olga, Tatiana, Maria, Anastasia, and Alexey, were all brutally murdered, along with their servants and doctor, at Ekaterinburg in the Urals. The following day, Alexandra's sister Ella, who was being held at a schoolhouse not far away at Alapayevsk, was taken out to a nearby mineshaft, thrown in, and left to die, along with her companion, Sister Barbara; Grand Duke Sergey Mikhailovich; Princes Ioann, Konstantin, and

---

* Mikhail insisted that he would only take the throne if he were endorsed as tsar by a proper, democratically elected constituent assembly.

Igor—all sons of Grand Duke Konstantin Konstantinovich—and Prince Paley, who had been imprisoned there with them.

Not long after so many of her closest relatives had been brutally murdered in the Urals, Paul's eldest daughter, Maria Pavlovna, and her husband, Sergey, decided they must make their escape out of Russia. The grand duchess's jewels were sent ahead to Sweden; she sold some remaining pieces to raise money for their journey and sewed a few other items into her clothing.[29] Prior to leaving, she had gone to visit her father and stepmother at Tsarskoe Selo. It had been such a beautiful summer day: "on the lawns, in the high grass, daisies lifted their white heads; grasshoppers whirred lustily, and yellow butterflies fluttered here and there." It was August 1918, but none of them yet knew that Vladimir, Prince Paley, had already been killed and they could not bear to talk about "any hope of reunion, even in a distant future." As a sad-faced Paul saw them off, Maria knew that it was for the last time.[30]

Maria and Sergey headed south to Orsha (in modern-day Belarus) by train, hoping to get beyond into German-occupied Ukraine. But as luck would have it, the train was grindingly slow and full of soldiers, and they had no passports, no permits to leave, no Ukrainian visas, and were likely to be apprehended at any time by Bolshevik patrols. At the checkpoint at Orsha all they could do was plead to be allowed to pass through. Exhausted, thirsty, and hungry, they spent long hours in agony waiting for a decision; finally using what little money they had to bribe the officials, they got on a train to Kiev on August 4.[31] The city by that time was filling up with refugees from northern Russia, all arriving "in rags, hungry, often without money," telling tales of the endless cruelties of the Bolsheviks. Everyone, it seemed, was desperate to travel the three hundred miles south from there to Odessa and get a boat to safety.[32] Maria and Sergey had by now gratefully accepted the offer of a refuge from her cousin, Marie, queen of Romania; both of them were sick with the Spanish flu, but an escort of young White officers saw them safely to the border with Bessarabia. In the dark of the railway carriage lit by a single candle, Maria could just make out their faces: "These strangers, people I had never seen before, were closer to me now than my own kin; they were a part of my own being; they contained all that I was leaving."[33] But just as she was about to abandon Russia forever, Maria Pavlovna received the news she had been dreading: her father was in prison.

By late summer of 1918, Grand Duke Paul had been the last senior Romanov still living at Tsarskoe Selo; but on August 12, the Bolsheviks finally came for him. Once again Olga wore herself ragged trying to protect her husband, producing medical certificates about his illness, but to no avail. Paul was taken first to Cheka headquarters and then to join three other grand dukes under arrest at the Shpalernaya Prison in Petrograd: the brothers Georgiy and Nikolay Mikhailovich and their cousin, Dmitri Konstantinovich—all members of Nicholas II's wider Romanov family. These three had already been held in Vologda since the beginning of July and had been transferred to the Shpalernaya on July 21. All the grand dukes were in their fifties; they were but four among seven hundred prisoners in Bolshevik hands—admirals, ex-ministers, ex-senators, hundreds of army officers, and several priests.[34] Each of the Romanovs had a cell seven feet long by three feet wide with an iron bed; their prison food amounted to bad black bread and "dirty hot water with a few fish bones floating in it," which made them ill. But their families were at least allowed to bring them clean linen, cigarettes, and some food at regular intervals, and they were let out into the exercise yard once a day. Grand Duke Georgiy even succeeded in smuggling letters out to his wife.[35]

Olga was allowed to visit Paul twice a week. Leaving her daughters at Tsarskoe Selo, day after day she traipsed to the Shpalernaya Prison carrying heavy baskets of food, but it exhausted her; her determination to keep going was superhuman, considering that she too was now very ill—suffering from breast cancer.[36] Yet all she concerned herself with was Paul's health, which by now was in serious decline. So much so that on December 6 he was transferred to the prison hospital at Goloday Island, located near a bleak burial ground used for criminals at the far end of Vasilievsky Island. It was a long trek for Olga in intense cold to get there with her heavy baskets of supplies.[37] Messages, meanwhile, had arrived secretly, offering Paul an escape to Finland, which would have been possible given the lax security at the hospital. "A mad desire for liberty took hold of me," he told Olga, but he would not agree, fearful that if he escaped, his three cousins in the Shpalernaya Prison would be shot in revenge.[38] There were those, however, who were desperately trying to help behind the scenes: the Danish ambassador, Harald Scavenius, had made repeated efforts to secure the release of the four imprisoned grand dukes. But his appeals had all come to nothing, even though King Christian had offered to take the grand dukes in and pay a ransom of $70,000.[39]

By the end of 1918, there should, in fact, have been five Romanovs languishing at the Shpalernaya Prison. But by a miracle, the thirty-year-old Prince Gavriil Konstantinovich—a nephew of Grand Dukes Nikolay and Georgiy—had been released, once more thanks to the efforts of an indomitable wife. Prince Gavriil was, like Paul, seriously ill. Suffering from TB, he had managed to fend off arrest until August 15. However, after Grand Duke Paul's arrest, it was inevitable that Gavriil would be taken, and he was also incarcerated at the Shpalernaya. His wife, Antonina*—a purposeful woman, much like Olga Paley—persuaded Gavriil's physician, the TB specialist

---

* Antonina Nesterovskaya was another morganatic Romanov wife. She had been a member of the corps de ballet at the Mariinsky and danced with the Ballets Russes in Paris from 1909 to 1911. It was another ballerina, Mathilde Kschessinska—who also landed herself a Romanov husband, Grand Duke Andrey—who introduced Antonina to Prince Gavriil in 1911. As with Paul and Olga, the tsar banned their marriage, as did Gavriil's mother, but after Nicholas's abdication they married secretly in April 1917.

Dr. Ivan Manukhin, to make representations to the influential critic and writer Maxim Gorky, whom he had also been treating for TB, begging him to appeal directly to Lenin.[40] Gorky may have been a Bolshevik sympathizer, but he was deeply opposed to the brutal wave of killing that the Bolshevik seizure of power had sparked and had already warned Grand Duke Mikhail's widow, Countess Brasova, to get out of Russia while she could.[41] He now wrote to Lenin on Antonina's behalf:

> *Dear Vladimir Ilyich! Make a small yet noble favor: let ex-Grand Prince Gabriel out of prison. First, he is a very good man. Second, he is temporarily ill. Why should we make martyrs out of people?*[42]

Antonina's maid took the letter by train to Gorky's son in Moscow for hand delivery to Lenin.[43] The situation, meanwhile, took a serious turn on September 12, 1918, when Moisey Uritsky, head of the Cheka, was assassinated. The whole city was gripped with fear as the Bolsheviks instituted summary arrests, executions, and house searches — "there was literally not a single family where people were not arrested," recalled Antonina — and worse, the government declared that all Romanov prisoners were now hostages and would be shot, should any more government commissars be killed.[44]

After several days of agonizing wait, a message finally came back from Lenin, agreeing to Gavriil's release — but only into the care of the Gerzoni Clinic on Ligovskoy Prospekt for treatment.[45] Gorky was horrified, claiming the clinic would kill Gavriil if he went there, and insisted on taking him under his own protection. "They won't dare touch him in my apartment," he said. And so the couple was given a large room at Gorky's comfortably appointed home on Kronversky Prospekt. Here they shared meals with a curious company of friends and hangers-on, including Lunacharsky, Chaliapin, and various

Bolshevik celebrities. With Gorky's assistance, Antonina applied for a permit for them to leave Russia. It took yet more agonizing delays and the worsening of Gavriil's health before they were finally allowed to do so.[46] At 5 A.M. on November 11, 1918, a frail Prince Gavriil and his wife, a maid, and their precious bulldog boarded the train for Beloostrov and the border with Finland, where they made their way to a sanatorium in Helsingfors (Helsinki).[47]

Hoping for a similar outcome, Olga Paley—who, with Antonina, had often shared joint visits with their husbands at the prison—also beat a path to Gorky's door, pleading for his help, but he was in bed, sick with bronchitis, at the time. On November 27 the letters that Grand Duke Georgiy had been managing to smuggle out to his wife informing her of the prisoners' desperate situation stopped; Olga last saw Paul on Christmas Day 1918. Day after day, the four men had heard the sound of cell doors being opened as people were taken away to be shot; rumors that they would soon be released evaporated. Paul told Olga that he was waiting to hear his own death warrant at any time.[48]

In mid-January, Gorky, who had now recovered from illness, was able to take the train to Moscow to see Lenin, as he had promised Olga, to try and intercede on behalf of the four imprisoned Romanovs.[49] Lenin had resisted his pleas for a long time but finally had agreed that there was no sense in holding the grand dukes any longer and that they could be allowed to go abroad. Having secured Lenin's agreement, Gorky prepared to return to Petrograd—taking on trust Lenin's piece of paper ordering their release. However, as he did so, instructions were wired, on Lenin's authority, to Grigory Zinoviev, head of the Petrograd Soviet, to go ahead and execute them.[50]

On the evening of Tuesday, January 28, Grand Duke Paul was brought from the prison hospital to the Shpalernaya and then at 10 P.M. the following day to the forbidding Peter and Paul Fortress. His three Romanov relatives had already been transferred to cells there, in the notorious Trubetskoy Bastion. It was almost twenty degrees below zero in the cold dawn of January 30, 1919* when, having been told to remove their shirts and warm coats, Grand Dukes Nikolay, Georgiy, and Dimitri were led out from the Trubetskoy Bastion, each held by the arm on either side by guards; Paul, too weak to walk, was carried out on a stretcher. Somehow, Nikolay had been allowed to carry the pet cat he had adopted in prison. As the three grand dukes passed the Peter and Paul Cathedral, where all the Russian tsars lay interred in splendid sarcophagi, they instinctively took off their caps and crossed themselves. Such gestures of faith weren't going to help them, jeered one of the soldiers: "We are going to shoot you, and we are not going to bury you under slabs of marble, but under slabs of wood."[51]

The three men conducted themselves with considerable calm and dignity as they were lined up in front of a shallow ditch in front of the mint that already contained the bodies of thirteen prisoners. As the execution squad prepared, Nikolay asked one of the guards to take care of his cat "in memory of me." Grand Duke Paul, who was too sick to stand, was placed on his stretcher beside them. Grand Duke Dmitri, who was devoutly Orthodox, was still praying out loud "for the salvation of the souls of his executioners" when Commandant Galkin and two henchmen shot them with their revolvers.[52] Galkin rewarded his men afterward with a book and half a loaf of bread; one of them helped himself to Grand Duke Georgiy's boots and ran round the streets bragging about it.[53]

In Moscow, Maxim Gorky was just about to board the train back to Petrograd thinking he had saved the grand dukes when he saw the

---

* English-language sources till now all give January 28 as the date of the executions, but most recent Russian sources state it was the 30th. The execution was announced the following day in *Petrogradskaya Pravda*, without giving the date, time, or reason for the execution. The Bolsheviks claimed it was in retribution for the murder of German communist leaders Karl Liebknecht and Rosa Luxemburg in Berlin on January 15.

news in *Petrogradskaya Pravda* that they had been shot. Such irony, wrote Georgiy's widow later, "to be buried two steps from the place they had a right to be buried."* The Cheka refused to release the men's bodies to their families, but it is said that one of Dmitri's adjutants managed to rescue his body from the trench a few days later and buried him in the garden of a private house.[54]

Maria Pavlovna heard the news of her father's execution—which had come via King George in London—at the Cotroceni Palace in Romania, where she had taken refuge with Queen Marie. It was the final confirmation that her "Russian life was over." She and her kind had, she sadly admitted, "outlived our epoch and were doomed." "Everything disappears into the past, everything which is good everything which is bright and the only thing that's left is the terrible reality."[55] But at least Paul's widow, Olga, had by then been able to get their two young daughters, Irina and Nataliya, out of Russia—to the care of sympathizers at a sanatorium in Finland. Olga sold some of her jewels to arrange her own escape, by sledge across the Gulf of Finland, evading the searchlights of the forts at Kronstadt, to the safety of Terioki. She was reunited with Irina and Nataliya in Rauha on March 25, 1919, where she received a letter confirming that her beloved son, Vladimir, of whom she had had no news for almost a year, had been murdered at Alapayevsk.[56]

Princess Paley's home for the next year would be Sweden, where she dreamed of a return to Paris to take possession once more of the home she had created with Paul at Boulogne-sur-Seine. Perhaps that desire was more profound than it might have been; for she had now been operated on for the breast cancer, which perhaps she had neglected too long while fighting for her husband's life.[57] "In spiritual

---

* There have been numerous searches for the bodies of the other grand dukes in the grounds of the Peter and Paul Fortress, and although in 2009 remains were found of more than a hundred victims during excavations of a mass grave by archaeologists, there is yet to be any formal identification of them.

terms, I am a dead being," she wrote to a friend. "However, I have to live for the two young girls." Returning to Boulogne would be a "real ordeal," for all her best past memories were there "and the image of this beautiful past stands before me in all its implacable cruelty."[58]

When the execution of the four grand dukes was announced in *Pravda*, the British government, having failed to help the Romanovs murdered in the Urals the previous July, became increasingly worried. In England, the dowager empress's sister Queen Alexandra was constantly urging the government to rescue the remaining fifteen members of the imperial house still languishing in Crimea. Extremists in the Yalta Soviet had been agitating to execute them all, and they could and should have left sooner, but rescue had been delayed by the dowager empress's extreme reluctance to leave Russia.[59] She still adamantly refused to accept that her son Nicholas and his family had all been killed, and there had been no word about the fate of her other son, Grand Duke Mikhail, either. By December 1918, her son-in-law Sandro had become deeply frustrated and decided to wait no longer at Ai-Todor. When a contingent of British navy ships arrived in Yalta, he left on one of them—HMS *Forsythe*. In so doing, he had to admit to experiencing a "horrible sense of acute humiliation caused by the fact that a grandson of Emperor Nicholas I [who had fought the British in the Crimean War] had to be rescued from Russians by Britishers."[60]

As they said goodbye at the port of Taranto in southern Italy, the commander of the *Forsythe* had laughingly apologized to Sandro: "Sorry not to be able to sail you straight into the palm-garden of the Ritz in Paris."[61] But really, what other option was there? Here he was "a man of fifty-three, without money, occupation, country, home or even address, brooding over the past, dreading the thought of falling asleep lest [he] should dream of those who were gone."[62] And so from Taranto Sandro caught an express train to Paris. But things were quite different this time: he was now an exile, and he arrived "unheralded and unexpected. No bemonocled representatives of the Russian Imperial Embassy awaited me on the platform of the Gare de Lyon and no gold-braided delegates of the Presidency of the French Republic rushed forth to escort me through the 'special exit.'"[63] Penniless or not, he installed himself at the Ritz, that favorite Romanov watering hole. Already he found himself bitterly regretting having failed to take the advice of friends in London and New York before the war to keep "at least a quarter of my fortune somewhere outside of Russia, preferably outside of Europe." An American industrialist friend had offered to invest a few hundred thousand dollars in the United States for him, but Sandro had foolishly turned him down. "I stand and fall with Russia," he had declared dramatically. But all three of his brothers—Grand Dukes Nikolay, Sergey, and Georgiy—had been murdered by the Bolsheviks; and now Russia too had fallen and he didn't even have the money to pay for his room.[64] But thank God he was in Paris. The city still smelled the same—still that unmistakable aroma of fresh baked baguettes. For a man who had escaped near-certain death in Russia, "no expensive perfume could have smelled better."[65]

It was not until April 11, 1919, that the British dreadnought HMS *Marlborough* brought out the remaining colony of Romanovs, who had been corralled together at Dulber, in Crimea. Maria Feodorovna; Grand Duchess Xenia and five of her six sons (the eldest, Andrey, had left with Sandro earlier); Grand Duke Nikolay Nikolaevich and his wife, Anastasia, and his brother Grand Duke Peter and his wife, Militsa; the Yusupovs; Prince Sergey Dolgorukiy, his daughter Olga and niece Sofka; Prince Nikolay Orlov; as well as various children, staff, and governesses. But at the very last moment, Maria Feodorovna had refused to leave until the British brought in several more Allied warships to take on board the thousands of refugees who had fled the advance of the Bolsheviks in northern Crimea and were now besieging Yalta begging to be evacuated also. "A state of chaos reigned among this throng of terrified and distraught people," recalled Sir Francis Pridham, first lieutenant of the *Marlborough*: "Children became separated from their parents and husbands from their wives and it is doubtful whether some of these unfortunate creatures ever met again. Many arrived on the pier with no other possessions than the clothes they wore."[66]

Elsewhere on the Black Sea, Grand Duchess Vladimir had been stranded for some time. In October 1918, with the Reds threatening to take the city from White forces, she had had to endure a long and arduous 373-mile trek west from Kislovodsk with her sons Boris and Andrey to the Black Sea fortress town of Anapa. She deemed Anapa an "awful hole," but when she was offered evacuation on a British warship she nevertheless felt, on the strength of recent White successes in the region, that it was her duty to stay in Russia in hopes of a recovery of the counterrevolutionary cause.[67] When White fortunes yet again changed for the worse in May 1919, Grand Duchess Vladimir was forced to go back to Kislovodsk, with Andrey and his mistress, the ballerina Mathilde Kschessinska.* The situation was getting extremely dangerous: the family were enduring regular raids and searches, which every time left them with fewer and fewer possessions, as their cupboards and closets were broken open and robbed. Grand Duchess Vladimir wrote to a friend, Alexander Ouchakoff, in Paris complaining about how difficult her life had become: "At my age it's hard to sleep in a bad bed, not to have enough linen, clothes, no baths, no dresses or furs for the winter and to eat badly." She asked Ouchakoff to raise money for her by selling a car she had bought in Paris in 1913; he even managed to get the still-creditworthy grand

---

* The couple were not able to marry until after his mother's death in 1920, for Grand Duchess Vladimir had opposed a morganatic marriage. They married in Cannes, January 30, 1921.

duchess various items from Paris shops to send to her in Kislovodsk.[68] Thankfully, Bertie Stopford had at least reassured her that her Cartier jewels were safe and sound in a London bank vault.

Finally, at the end of 1919, the grand duchess made her way out of Russia, by train to the port of Novorossisk, where she arrived tired and disheveled but still manifesting her indomitable grand-ducal style. She then had to spend six weeks stranded in her railway compartment waiting for a ship to Italy but finally sailed on February 13, 1920, on the *Semiranisa* with Andrey, Mathilde, and their son Vova—the last Romanovs to escape the Bolshevik terror. Their feelings at the time "defied description," Kschessinska later wrote, for they understood only too well the significance of their departure: "We were leaving part of ourselves in Russia, part of our lives, our hearts. . . . Of all the trials we had endured or had to endure, this was without doubt the bitterest and most painful."[69]

Arriving in Venice on March 10, Grand Duchess Vladimir was met by the ever-loyal Bertie Stopford. He saw her safely onto a train for Cannes, where in her inimitable style she took up residence at the Grand Hotel.[70] Stopford, meanwhile, had taken her precious jewels to Cartier in Paris to be valued. The grand duchess was planning to meet him there to discuss their disposal when she was taken seriously ill with an abscess on her kidney. She took herself off to the northeastern French spa town of Contrexéville, but her health rapidly declined and she died there, at the Hotel La Souveraine, of heart and kidney failure on September 6, 1920, without being reunited with her much-loved jewels. In the event, Kirill had the pearls, Boris the emeralds, Andrey the rubies, and their sister Elena the diamonds. But many of these would soon be sold off piecemeal* to support an uncertain new life in exile.[71]

---

* These included the grand duchess's favorite tiara of diamond loops with pearl drops, made for her by the imperial court jeweler Carl Edvard Bolin in 1874. It was purchased by Queen Mary in 1921 for £28,000 and is frequently worn by Queen Elizabeth II with emerald drops.

Grand Duchess Vladimir was the last Romanov to leave Russia and the first to die in exile. She and her relatives who got out were, of course, the lucky few. They still had enough supporters and even assets abroad, and ready cash or jewels to fund their exit. Yet for some Russian aristocrats, their pride made it hard for them to admit defeat and flee: "I'm not going anywhere," insisted Princess Ekaterina Meshcherskaya. "I'm not going to sit in the doorway of some foreign embassy, like a beggar, to ask for protection against my own motherland."[72] With the Whites now facing imminent defeat, many thousands of her compatriots—desperate, ordinary, poverty-stricken Russians—thought differently and had fled the fierce fighting and were heading south in search of a boat to Europe.

By the end of 1919, the port of Odessa was flooded with Russians fighting for places on a ship. Soon their exodus would create a refugee problem of a kind never before seen in Europe. And many of these thousands of destitute Russian refugees would be heading for Paris.

CHAPTER 5

"I Never Thought I Would Have to Drag Out My Life as an Émigré"

astille Day, July 14, 1919, was a great day for Paris; the streets thronged with people celebrating the victory parade as they watched the massed troops of the French and their wartime allies march past. It was a special moment for those first émigré Russians who had fled the revolution and had already managed to get to this, their chosen city of refuge. Here they were out in force on the streets of the city that they hoped they would be able to call home. Standing among them, Sandro—husband of Xenia, the murdered Tsar Nicholas's sister—contemplated the current exodus of his fellow countrymen to France:

> They stood in little groups in the Champs Elysees, on the Grands Boulevards and in the shady streets of Passy, and they talked as only Russians can. Not listening to each other, repeating the self-same argument over and over again, excelling in pantomime and reaching the uppermost heights of drama. . . . There must have been not less than one hundred thousand of

them in Paris on that day, and this was only the advance guard,
only a small fraction of the approaching hosts of refugees.[1]

Sandro's estimate of the number of Russians may have been on
the rather generous side, but he counted himself blessed to have escaped being murdered like his three unfortunate brothers. It would
take some getting used to, he admitted to friends, this business of
"How It Feels to Be Poor."[2] He could not lay hands on any cash in
Paris; he owed money to his tailor, his haberdasher, and his shoe-
maker, and after a couple of months his credit at the Ritz had totally run out. There was nothing left but to sell his one remaining
and much-treasured asset—his numismatic collection. But all those
carefully acquired coins minted in prehistory by Goths and Byzantine Greeks, Phoenicians, and Macedonians together raised only
about five percent of their prewar price.[3]

All this made it very difficult for Sandro, from a position of now
greatly reduced prestige and influence, to make representations to
delegates on the interests of a free Russia at the Versailles Peace
Conference and open their eyes to the dangers of Bolshevism. It
was equally difficult for the former Russian ambassador to Paris,
Alexander Iswolsky, to do so. He was now a "refugee from the
Reds" and living in an attic room at the Meurice Hotel—the kind of
accommodation to which "one of the class to which the valets of important visitors were generally assigned," as U.S. journalist Stephen
Bonsal noted when he visited. Iswolsky, who had been summarily
relieved of his position in May 1917, was sick, dejected, and recovering from the Spanish flu: "I am a man without a country," he told
Bonsal in despair. "Today Russia is a vacuum."[4]*

Consider the sad fate of another eminent Russian exile whom

---

* Three months later he died in Biarritz, a broken man.

Bonsal noted struggling to cross the street and who was now almost blind and quite lame:

> *Today, for perhaps the hundredth time in this catastrophic year, I witnessed an incident which reminded me of how quickly the pomp of power passes, how near to the highest place in the capitol yawns the abyss by the Tarpeian Rock. I saw Count Cassini, so long ambassador extraordinary of Holy Russia, running through the sleet and rain on the Place de la Madeleine to catch a bus to take him to the modest suburban retreat, or refuge, with which the French government has provided him.*

"I grant you that thousands of other people were doing the very same thing at this crowded hour, but the difference is that they have done it every day of their lives; they are inured to it," Bonsal added. But when he had first seen the count back in 1896, he had been "lording it over all China." At the time, he had been "practically Viceroy of the Far East":

> *When he moved through the streets of Peking, sotnias* of Cossacks dashed ahead and cleared the way for the little man with the monocle who for four years, with the dreaded power of Russia behind him, dominated four hundred million Chinese and made them do his bidding.*[5]

In a miniature of what was now a mass exodus from Russia, France had seen its own displacement of people during 1791–93, when, after the fall of the Bastille, several thousand French aristocrats had fled Paris. Prior to that Louis XIV had, with the revocation of the Edict of Nantes of 1685, driven up to half a million Protestant

---

* A Cossack military unit of about 100 to 150 men.

Huguenot refugees out of France to Britain, the Netherlands, and elsewhere. But the thousands of refugees who left Russia between October 1917 and March 1921 and headed for Paris came from a much wider cross-section of society, with loyalties to a whole range of political parties, social classes, and religions.[6] They were often loosely referred to as "White Russians," the assumption often mistakenly made by this that they were monarchists. A more accurate attribution is "anti-Bolshevik," for not all Whites were monarchists by any means, and plenty of ordinary, nonaffiliated Russians saw themselves as Whites in the emotional and spiritual sense of a shared hatred for communism. All had rejected the political aspirations of the Bolsheviks—even some socialists, who abhorred the brutality of Lenin's methods. But in general, the very first to flee Russia were those closely tied to the old aristocracy and tsarist system and most likely to bear the brunt of Lenin's demands for revenge.[7]

Soon whole swathes of the Russian population were on the move—civilians uprooted by the civil war that developed over the winter of 1917–18. As the émigré writer Zinaida Shakhovskaya observed, "All of Russia had become nomadic: millions of people walked, rode, raced across its wide expanses in search of either their loved ones, or food, or the army with which they wanted to fight."[8]

In the early days of the civil war, there were at least chances for those fleeing to make it through thinly controlled Bolshevik areas by rail and road, using a combination of stealth and bribery of officials. Escape south had been much easier all the time the Germans controlled Ukraine, but now the escape route via Crimea was becoming extremely precarious.

The White military resistance to the Bolsheviks unfortunately never really gained momentum. It was always hamstrung by having no overall leader and no unifying political objectives, consisting as it did of several regional armies made up of ex-tsarist military and volunteers. Their fractured campaign never had much hope of overcoming the onslaught of the newly established, and growing, Red Army. The first setback came in the northwest, when General Nikolay Yudenich's seventeen thousand White troops were defeated outside Petrograd in October 1919. This triggered an early wave of White Russian refugees, who fled north into Finland and the Baltic countries, and from there west into Germany and Czechoslovakia.[9] Those anti-Bolshevik army officers—many of them Cossacks—who got away, went southeast to their homelands on the river Don or along the Volga, where they could regroup and launch a counterattack. In Siberia, meanwhile, an anticommunist mix of socialist revolutionaries, liberals, right-wing social democrats, and many Cossacks had gathered around Admiral Alexander Kolchak, based at his headquarters at Omsk.[10] Kolchak became something of a folk hero and was considered the de facto supreme leader of the Whites; but he was a navy man with no experience of combat on land. Although he had some initial successes in Siberia, when the Red Army counterattacked he rapidly lost ground, and by October 1919 had had to evacuate from his base at Omsk. His White forces were finally defeated in Siberia in February 1920; not long after, Kolchak was captured and summarily executed. Many refugees from this collapse headed east along the Trans-Siberian Railway to Manchuria and China, and a considerable colony of White Russians grew up in Harbin. But it was the crushing defeat of the leader of the anti-Bolshevik forces, General Anton Denikin, that turned the tide. His Volunteer Army was cornered in the Don Cossack country of southeastern Russia in March 1920, finally ending hopes of a counterrevolution. This triggered an unprecedented mass stampede of White troops, many with their families following, from Novorossisk and other Black Sea ports, especially Odessa and Batumi. There followed scenes of utter chaos as some of the Whites, unable to get away from the Red Army, "simply crossed themselves and jumped into the sea."[11] A desperate appeal was sent out to the British, who had backed Denikin's government and had evacuated the Romanov family the previous April from Yalta. They now rallied to help transport thousands of White Russian military and civilians to Constantinople, which for the last year had been a transit point for Russian refugees heading for Europe.[12]

One of the first of the Russian intellectual elite to escape to Paris was the popular satirist and writer Nadezhda Lokhvitskaya, who wrote under the pen name of Teffi. Hugely popular in prerevolutionary Russia and a favorite author of Nicholas II, she had been on a reading tour of Ukraine when, in the spring of 1919, the advance of the Red Army had forced her to flee south to Odessa. In the late summer she was able to secure a passage on the *Grand Duke Alexander Mikhailovich* (named after Sandro) from Crimea to Constantinople. Her sense of sorrow was profound as the ship "slid down the map, down the huge green map across which, slantwise, was written *The Russian Empire.*" Everyone was frightened, looking back over their shoulder as the land faded from sight. Behind her a woman wailed aloud as she grieved her loss—"long, obstinate wails, interspersed with words of lament." Its sound was chilling, recalled Teffi, "a terrible, black, tearless wail. A last wail. Over all of Russia, the whole of Russia." Against her better instincts, she had turned and taken one last look back:

> And like Lot's wife, I am frozen. I have turned into a pillar of salt forever, and I shall forever go on looking, seeing my own land slip softly, slowly away from me.[13]

Such feelings were common to many of the evacuees. The writer Aminodav Shpolyansky—later known in Paris as Don-Aminado, vividly recalled the day the French ship *Dumont d'Urville* raised anchor and sailed from Odessa to Constantinople—it was the twentieth of

January 1920. It was a date he would remember forever. He and his traveling companions (including the writer Alexey Remizov, who also settled in Paris) were silent as they left port, each thinking their own thoughts, although the bitter significance of this departure was one they all shared.[14] When will we return to Russia? In a couple of years, they thought; but then as the journey went on, "subsequent predictions of the amount of time got longer and longer, depending on temperament and optimistic outlook," and their mood became ever more hopeless.[15] Aminado and his companions traveled on by steamer to Marseilles—and then by train to Paris via Arles, Tarascon, Lyons, Dijon, "without plans, without a program, and in 4th class," "overcoming everything, sleep, fatigue, thoughts and feelings, confusion, spiritual restlessness . . ."[16]

The distinguished historian and novelist Henri Troyat, born Lev Aslanovich Tarassov in Moscow of an Armenian family, remembered the terror as an eight-year-old enduring the sea journey by steamer from Yalta to Novorossisk—the family's passage obtained with great difficulty by his father—in a raging sea storm with most of the passengers rolling and bumping against each other, groaning and passing round bowls in which to vomit. And from there, shortly afterward, another boat, this time to Constantinople. It was February 1920 and perishing cold; their boat was covered in snow and looked unreal, like a "construction of crystal and sugar, with stalactites of ice hanging from every protrusion." As it probed its way out into the frozen sea

> *an emerald channel opened between the blocks of ice. Huge white masses, disturbed by the movement of the ship, pivoted and moved slowly apart. It was very cold. The coast of Russia faded in the mist. My parents looked miserable, impoverished, lost. Around them people were crying.*[17]

Zinaida Shakhovskaya, along with her sister and mother, also left Novorossisk in February 1920—on a German hospital ship, the *Hannover*, that had been captured by the British. She recalled that cathartic moment of departure, and how an elderly priest began reciting prayers as they sailed. "The sun played on his pectoral cross. Women, old people, and children began to kneel. Many began weeping, without shame, in the face of the sea in the face of the earth. . . . We sailed on, and the sun was setting over our misfortune."[18] From Constantinople they took passage on the *Cherkessenko,* which was already crowded with Armenian refugees and where they trembled with the cold under a canvas canopy on deck. "Around everything is gray, dirty, hopeless. Rain seems to flood both the past and the future," she noted in her diary at the time. "Paris seems so far away, and it's hard for us to imagine that one day we will be there."[19]

Undoubtedly the most preeminent of the Russian writers to leave during what became known as the first wave of the White Russian emigration was the writer and poet Ivan Bunin, who was revered as a leading voice of the Russian intelligentsia and a master of the short story in the tradition of Anton Chekhov. He had been at the height of his success when war and then revolution broke, which triggered bouts of despair that his best days as a writer were over. With his partner, Vera Muromtseva, he had moved south from Moscow to Odessa as the civil war spread. Bunin dreaded the thought of having to abandon his homeland, his world, his inspiration; "from the bottom of his soul," observed fellow writer Valentin Kataev, Bunin sensed completely "the collapse, the death of old Russia, and the end of all former ties."[20] And so he had hung on in Odessa, along with several other leading figures—writers, doctors, lawyers, academics—in hopes the Bolshevik regime would collapse. But he had written very little in these final thirteen months in Odessa, and at times had felt suicidal.[21] All his worst premonitions about Russia had come true; Kataev could see that "he did not want to become an émigré, cut off from his country," which is why Bunin had remained in Odessa even when it was occupied by the Red Army in August 1919. Nor did he disguise his counterrevolutionary views, while one by one his similarly minded but more fearful friends were packing and leaving, including fellow writer Alexey Tolstoy, who was also heading for Paris.[22]

On December 20, Vera recorded their decision finally to leave in her diary: "The Bolsheviks are coming, like Atilla, like clouds of locusts. They are destroying everything in their path." She and Bunin had visas for Constantinople; but beyond that? They inquired about refuge in Serbia but were told it was already crowded with Russians. Bunin wanted to go to Paris, but Vera objected at first: "Paris is cold, starving, and most likely we will be treated arrogantly." Soon, however, she was persuaded that the Balkans was not a good option; either way, they could only do what so many other refugees were doing: they would carry Russia away with them "and try to preserve it abroad until we return."[23] Finally, they received word of third-class tickets available for the *Dmitry* leaving Odessa on February 8, 1920. "My heart is very heavy," Vera wrote on the second:

> Soon we will be émigrés. And for how many years? All our hopes have been dashed, even our hopes to see our loved ones. How everything has gone to pieces. . . . I never thought I would have to drag out my life as an émigré.

They could hear the shelling overhead when, on February 6, Bunin and Vera decided to set off for the ship. They loaded their belongings onto a small cart "driven by a very old and tipsy man" and made their way to turbulent scenes at the wharf, of frightened people, many with no baggage, some even without tickets, running and jumping on board the *Dmitry*.[24] They were then stuck on board for four days before finally, on February 9, the ship headed out to sea, but the choice between staying or leaving had been an invidious one, as Vera noted: "Before us darkness and terror. Behind us—horror and hopelessness."[25]

Among the many Allied vessels involved in the evacuations from Odessa in February 1920 was HMS transport ship *Rio Negro*, captained by Evan Cameron. The scenes at the waterside in Odessa horrified him when he arrived. "The noise and pandemonium were terrible . . . on the wharf was a swarming mass of humanity, obviously haunted with fear of the approaching Bolshevist." Many of the refugees were verminous and had been living in a state of destitution in Odessa all winter waiting for evacuation. The sight was "pitiable in the extreme." Cameron and his crew spent all night taking people on board, in the bitter cold and under the constant noise of gunfire. Don Cossack cadets—young boys for the most part—were the only line of defense between the ship and the approaching Red Army. When a mass of the remnants of the White Army struggled to board the Russian transport ship *Vladimir* close by, so fierce was the struggle that Russian soldiers on the ship opened fire on their own countrymen to keep them back.[26] With the Bolsheviks now entering the docks, the *Rio Negro* was forced to lower the gangway and sail on February 7, leaving hundreds of desperate people behind on the wharf, "many of whom were kneeling in the snow, imploring us to take them on board." As the ship drew away, Cameron could see "every conceivable sort of conveyance . . . small handcarts, carriages, and beautiful cars litter[ing] the wharf, together with tons of luggage, all deserted." For the most part, he noted, "the people we saved were mostly women of the upper classes, charming and refined" and all now huddled together on our rough troop decks. "Again and again they said, 'Thank God we are on a British ship!'"[27]

As the *Rio Negro* steamed out of the harbor with 1,400 refugees on board (it had only been fitted to carry 750 troops), Captain Cameron heard the rattle of machine guns, the whistle of bullets through the air, and the ever-approaching boom of field guns. Out at sea, he soon discovered that many of the passengers were very sick with typhus; the solitary Canadian doctor on board had no nursing staff and very few supplies. Out in the open waters of the Black Sea "a gale of wind, a heavy sea, and blinding, lashing, biting snow greeted us."[28] Due to the overcrowded, fetid conditions below, some of the passengers lay down on deck, covered in deep snow, preferring the cold there than the terrible fug below. Their ship passed a tug in distress, but Cameron, having radioed the fleet for help, had had to make the agonizing decision not to take another twenty passengers on board his already seriously overloaded vessel. The *Rio Negro* eventually entered the Bosporus in a blizzard and sailed on to Salonica, where the Serbs agreed to take his passengers, sending special trains to collect them.[29]

The final crushing defeat of the White counterrevolution against the Bolsheviks came with the rout of General Wrangel's forces in the autumn of 1920. Wrangel had taken charge of the remnants of Denikin's army after its defeat at Novorossisk, but admitted his action was merely "galvanizing the corpse" of an army that was already in retreat and heading for defeat. He was, nevertheless, determined to save the honor of the White cause in Russia, to "show the world" that it was "dying but not surrendering."[30] By mid-October 1920 the situation had become hopeless. Forced into the bottleneck of the Crimean peninsula—a position that many strategists had considered to be militarily impregnable—Wrangel's forces were unable to hold back the onslaught of the Red Army. There was only one way of escape and that was by sea. Wrangel therefore ordered all warships of the Black Sea fleet loyal to the Whites and all merchant vessels to come together in a huge armada, which would evacuate refugees from the ports of Sebastopol, Feodosiya, and Kerch. Wrangel was reluctant to leave until the last people had been taken on board and personally supervised the loading of the ships before finally departing Crimea on an old cruiser. This evacuation was effected under the official supervision of the French government, which had backed Wrangel's anti-Bolshevik campaign and had sent troops to Odessa in support.

During November 14–15, 1920, this veritable armada of 126 heavily overloaded vessels, with men, women, and children crammed into every available space, made their escape from Crimea. There is no certain figure of how many exactly sailed: at the least 136,000—of whom 70,000 were military—as estimated by Wrangel in 1923, but later Soviet intelligence suggested 146,000 evacuees, of whom 29,000 were civilians.[31] The nearest twentieth-century equivalent to such a mass evacuation would be that of 4,500 Jewish refugees from France to Palestine in 1947. In 1920 biblical analogies were certainly drawn, with one evacuee talking of the Wrangel evacuation fleet as "the Holy Ark that was destined to save the remnants of Great Russia."[32]

During the evacuation, Wrangel had wished to prioritize his troops, as he had had no means with which to provide for so many civilians; but he had been completely overwhelmed by refugees from every strata of Russian society.

Boris Alexandrovsky, a doctor from a Red Army field unit captured by the Whites who accompanied the evacuation of wounded White officers and men, witnessed the extraordinary mix of evacuees crammed into an uneasy interaction on board the *Kherson*. How ironic it was, he wrote, that

> *I, a representative of the younger generation of pre-revolutionary*
> *Moscow intelligentsia, the son of a doctor and a doctor myself,*
> *was standing there, tightly crammed in with a crowd of former*
> *tsarist and White officers, that is, the caste that I and all my*

peers and comrades in every stage of my life, my origins, edu-
cation and upbringing, had so deeply despised.[33]

Yet here they all were sailing away from Russia together, and they
would take that heady mix of competing personalities and causes
with them to their various places of exile. But was there any common bond that united them? Yes, confirmed Alexandrovsky; they
all shared one unassailable hope:

a shared confidence that the Soviet government was a tempo-
rary phenomenon and that in a few months or at most a year
it would be replaced by something else. What exactly, none
of them knew. But it united the whole heterogeneous mass of
people filling the ships of the Wrangel fleet, sailing through the
waters of the Black Sea into the coming unknown.[34]

Right now, however, it was all about survival, for as Alexandrovsky soon observed, some of the ships were completely unsea-
worthy. Natalia Melenevsky confirmed this; she was on board the
Gregor, a wretched "wreck of a ship, an empty barrel without bal-
last, without a rudder, without sidelights, without an engine," and,
worse, without lifeboats.[35] It had to be towed through the fog by
a British ship, and everybody on deck was hurled back and forth
along with their meager belongings as they sailed into the full force
of a Black Sea storm—the bora. On all the ships, the refugees were
crammed in together like herrings in a barrel; there wasn't enough
room on board for them to lie down and sleep properly. In addition,
the weather had turned cold and thousands had to travel on the open
decks in a piercing rain. Nobody had been allowed to bring heavy
luggage. Although families brought some provisions, food supplies
ran out within a day; there wasn't enough water to go round, and
very rapidly hunger and thirst became a serious problem. Nor were

they able to wash for days, and their clothes became infested with lice; typhus began to take hold. And then, under cover of darkness, there were the rats—huge rats, which crawled out and started running around the passengers as they huddled together trying to sleep.[36] The journey across the Black Sea was made worse for all evacuees by the appalling unsanitary conditions on the ill-equipped, overcrowded vessels on which they traveled. On the *Trini*, for example, there were only two lavatories for six hundred people. As Alexandrovsky later recalled, babies were born during the journey and some people died; their bodies, after a perfunctory service, were lowered over the side. One boat, the destroyer *Zhivoy*, being towed by a torpedo ship broke its rope and sank with 257 on board.[37]

The overloaded fleet of ships, with raised yellow sanitary flags warning of infections on board, moved at a snail's pace across to Constantinople, many of them listing badly from overload. They took on average five days (though some inadequate vessels took up to nine) to get there. En route, the dirty, exhausted, and hungry passengers continued to argue noisily and passionately, as Alexandrovsky recalled, about the collapse of the White army, its political consequences for Russia, and who was to blame. Even as they caught sight of the first glimmer of the Bosporus, the Russian refugees were still arguing, and failed to take in its "panorama of one thousand and one nights" sparkling in the Golden Horn, the unforgettable sight of sugar-white palaces, the thin needles of minarets and mosques of the magical Constantinople skyline, with its focal point the domes of the ancient Hagia Sophia.[38] For most, now was not a time for enjoying the view. As musician and singer Alexander Vertinsky later recalled, all he could think of as his ship docked was the unwanted exile to come:

All the palm trees, all the sunrises, all the sunsets of the world,
all the exoticism of distant lands, everything that I saw, all that

I admired, I would give for a single, cloudy, rainy, tearful day in my homeland.[39]

But now at least the half-starved Russians could eat: Turkish and Greek merchants plied their oars on every kind of fishing vessel and boat as fast as they could out to the fleet and swarmed round offering dates, Turkish delight, figs, lemons, oranges, fish, fried lamb. Having no Turkish money, all the refugees could offer as payment were "rings, brooches, amulets, bracelets, silk scarves," while the military men traded their weapons. "For one fried fish and a couple of oranges"—a gold wedding ring was exchanged; for "three doughnuts fried in mutton fat and half a pound of halva"—somebody's precious turquoise earrings were lowered down in buckets on ropes. Priceless family heirlooms were gladly given in return for fresh drinking water or a precious loaf of white bread; the eager traders came away with the last vestiges of the Russian refugees' remaining assets, lowered down to them below.[40]

Not all the ships were allowed to land, but once those that were had safely moored, there was no method or order in the way in which this desperate crush of humanity was disembarked. People crowded and shoved and pushed on deck—anything to get ashore, at any cost, out of the hellhole of the cabins and holds below, thus making it impossible for any effective measures to be set up for quarantining and disinfection or separating the already infectious from the sick and wounded.[41] A rabble of clamoring refugees, many of them ragged and emaciated, began to scatter across the city: "former governors, prosecutors, excise officials, nobility, general staffers, hussars, ulans, dragoons, Cossacks, gunners, cadets, newspaper editors, reporters, photographers, singers, artists, musicians, doctors, engineers, agronomists, schoolteachers, maids of honor from court, officers' wives"—a kaleidoscope of the prerevolutionary Russian bourgeoisie, nobility, and intelligentsia, as Alexandrovsky later recalled.[42] And this is not to mention those from the various anti-Bolshevik political groups, including the Cadets, socialist revolutionaries, and Mensheviks. Most of these indigent refugees, brutalized by the hardships they had endured, were well educated, but where would they stay while waiting for safe passage to Europe and how would they earn their living? American relief workers of the Near East Mission in Constantinople despaired at the "pathetic appeal of the refined-looking men and women who stood hopelessly on the street corners of Constantinople with the newspapers offered mutely for sale." One of the aid workers was stopped one day on the street by a Russian baron:

> *He was in full uniform of the Russian Royal Brigade, minus his sword, which he had sold to buy his dinner the previous night. He asked for work, but what could a Russian baron do, who knew nothing but how to fight and command a regiment?*[43]

Other White officers maintained their dignity as the last bastion against the despair of their defeat: "parading the Grande Rue de Pera in the exotic finery of Cossack kit complete with diagonally placed breast cartridge pockets, top boots, long black coats and elaborately decorated silver daggers."[44] Those professionals who could doctor, or drill teeth, teach, translate, or write a legal document set themselves up in backstreet rooms up the crooked, cobbled lanes of Galata—in the European part of the city across the Golden Horn on the west bank—and managed to survive. Some of the more canny and unscrupulous ones preyed on their less fortunate compatriots, snapping up for a song their gold cigarette cases—gifts from the tsar with diamond-studded imperial eagles—ornate snuffboxes, heavy gold fob watches, and family diamonds, selling them in the city's flea markets; precious family icons were always the last to go.

Constantinople was one great big bazaar, full of the hum of traffic, the snarling of street dogs, the shouts of street sellers and beggars. But for the mass of bewildered and exhausted refugees camping out in the most rudimentary vermin-infested accommodation, life that winter of 1920–21 was desperate. There were many displaced children too, who in the exodus had become separated from their parents and had ended up sleeping in huddles in the streets, reduced to begging. Some Russian women, desperate to feed their children, were forced to sell most of their clothes, leaving themselves with nothing to wear on the street outside.[45] Everywhere you looked in the city, you saw the rawness and suffering of Russian lives reduced to nothing: former generals working in laundries or kitchens; countesses, princesses, and their kind scrubbing floors and washing dishes or standing on street corners or on the Galata Bridge to Pera, trying to sell a blouse, a uniform, a handful of medals, bunches of violets, a pair of boots, or an old fur coat. Crimean currency was valueless, and when they had sold off all their valuables, all that was left for female refugees as a last resort was prostitution and the seedy nightlife of the city's cabarets, dance halls, and drug dens.[46] Seeing the proud Russian aristocratic class being "degraded into the parasites and pleasure-givers of a Levantine city was cruel," wrote Captain Evan Cameron.[47]

Many distraught people continued to search fruitlessly for relatives from whom they had become separated during the evacuation. Day after day they came and searched the waterfront. A newspaper for the refugees was started up, full of pitiful messages:

I'm looking for Pyotr Ivanovich Dobrokhotov, staff captain of the 114th Novotorzh Infantry Regiment. There is no information about him since the first Odessa evacuation. Please write to . . .

Those who know anything about the fate of Shura and Katya Petrova, 17 and 19 years old, from Novocherkassk are urgently asked to inform their mother at . . .

Companions on the second Novorossisk evacuation and on the upper deck of the steamer Rion *please urgently inform your address at . . .*

Shurik, please respond! Mum and I got a visa to Argentina. Write to this address . . .[48]

Alexander Vertinsky was able to get work singing in a chic cabaret restaurant and managed to raise enough money to buy himself a Greek passport and a ticket to Constanta in Romania, but obtaining a visa or passport to travel on to a new home was a major hurdle for many of the refugees. After arrival in Constantinople, thousands languished for weeks or months, waiting while the Allied governments argued over who would take them and while arrangements were made for them to travel to destinations in Europe. As the wait grew ever more protracted, a rapid process of Russification took place across the city. Russian was heard everywhere; on the rue de Pera, especially, signs went up for Russian restaurants, cabarets, shops, offices, doctors, lawyers, pharmacies, and even schools. Smirnov vodka and Russian caviar became available for those with money.[49]

During that waiting period, some of the male ex-military refugees were lured into joining the French Foreign Legion—thereby signing away five years of their lives for the deserts of North Africa, the jungles of Indochina, or death by sunstroke or tropical disease in some backwater of the French colonial empire. For the most part, though, Wrangel's defeated army was transported to Gallipoli and settled in a military camp there; fifteen thousand Don Cossack soldiers and civilians were taken to the Greek island of Lemnos and other islands in the Sea of Marmara, where they endured far worse conditions in the hot, barren landscape, living in tents with little food and water.[50] Another six thousand refugees who were not disembarked in Constantinople, or the alternatives of Beirut or Alexandria, were stranded for some time at the town of Bizerta in the French protectorate of Tunisia. A considerable contingent of White officers and their families opted to sail across the Adriatic and settle in Serbia, then part of the newly created kingdom of Yugoslavia, or other Balkan states such as Bulgaria and Romania. But as the League of Nations, the French government, the American Red Cross, and various relief agencies combined to try and assist the refugees in finding a place of settlement, some governments prevaricated over the extent to which they were willing to offer a refuge and in particular how much they were willing to contribute financially. Eventually, the French government let it be known that it was prepared to take the majority of the Russians under its protection.[51] There was every good reason for this: after four years of devastating war and the loss of many thousands of men, France urgently needed workers to rebuild its industry and work in the mines and factories of northeastern France, as well as the agricultural sector.

Over the last century numerous attempts have been made to quantify the exact scale of the Russian emigration. Huge confusion prevailed over the precise numbers at the time, because no official registration of refugees was carried out in Constantinople and other stopover points, and estimates of numbers conflict considerably. But the closest approximation appears to be that one million Russians fled Bolshevik Russia, many of them heading for the big European cities of Berlin and Paris.[52] Over the next five years, Constantinople* would

---

* In 1924 it reverted to the name Istanbul.

be a transit point for around 250,000 of those Russian refugees. In 1922 there were about 35,000 living in the city but their numbers had dwindled to around three thousand by 1930.[53]

Some time after returning home to England, Captain Cameron of the *Rio Negro* received a letter from Vera Evdokimova, one of the Russian refugees he had taken on board his ship. From Constantinople she had eventually obtained passage on a steamer to Marseilles with her husband — "eight days without warm food and everyone was ill because of the terrible weather." But then:

> *At last Marseilles and Paris. . . . All my life I shall not forget our arrival in the evening at Paris. We arrived at the Gare du Nord with only 50 francs between us. We did not know anyone, we were both tired and hungry, all alone in immense Paris and destitute.*

It had been difficult starting life over again with nothing, but she had managed to get a job at a *maison de couture*. "Can we dream of returning to Russia?" Vera asked. "I do not think so. Therefore we try to be courageous, and in spite of all, try to live!" As Captain Cameron read these words, he wondered what had happened to all those other people he had brought to safety. "Where have they gone? What are they doing?"[54]

What became of the thousands of other members of "Russia's refugee army" who arrived in Paris penniless and traumatized but grateful to have escaped the civil war in Russia?[55] Hunger and deprivation might well dominate over their lives in the first difficult years of readjustment in France, but Paris offered hope of something better. As writer Mark Vishniak recalled of his own arrival with his wife on the train from Marseilles on May 23, 1919, with everything they possessed in two wicker baskets, it seemed that here was "a new Mecca, a new Babylon." But which way would the dice of fate fall for them in Paris? Anything right now was better than life back in "Sovdepia," as the émigré Russians were now referring to the alien new order imposed on their beloved homeland by the Bolsheviks.[56]

CHAPTER 6

"Paris Is Full of Russians"

I n December 1921, an ambitious young American writer eager to make his mark arrived in Paris with a commission as European correspondent for the *Toronto Star*. His name was Ernest Hemingway. His wife, Hadley, had money from an inheritance that had enabled them to rent an apartment on rue Cardinal Lemoine on the Left Bank. From here Hemingway threw himself into the vibrant and stimulating life of a city embracing the artistic avant-garde and American Jazz Age culture. "Paris was where the twentieth century was," declared Gertrude Stein, a long-standing American resident and friend.[1] But it wasn't just the Americans who were flocking there. "Paris is full of Russians," Hemingway told the readers of the *Toronto Star* on February 25, 1922:

> *They are drifting along in Paris in a childish sort of hopefulness that things will somehow be all right, which is quite charming when you first encounter it and rather maddening after a few months. No one knows just how they live except by selling off jewels and gold ornaments and family heirlooms that they brought with them to France....*

"Just what the Russian colony in Paris will do when all the jewels are sold and all the valuables pawned is somewhat of a question," added Hemingway. He observed the Russians daily, gathering in the cafés on the boulevard Montparnasse, waiting for "something wonderful to happen" but increasingly having to face up to the inevitability of finding work. "It seems a pity," he concluded: "they are such a charming lot."[2] Russian charm had certainly helped some of the exiled Russian aristocracy in the early days of flight into Europe, when they were able to call in favors and exploit old family connections to cadge for loans. But the money was rapidly running out for most of them, and charm and hope alone were not enough to survive on. In those first difficult days of exile, it was the Russian women who proved to be the most enterprising.

One of the first members of the Russian imperial family to settle in Paris was Grand Duchess Maria Pavlovna, for her links to the city through her late father, Grand Duke Paul, were strong. After receiving the news in February 1919 that he had been shot, she and her husband, Sergey Poutiatine, had managed to get visas for Paris. Maria longed more than ever to see her brother Dmitri, to whom she was very close. The siblings had been separated since the end of 1916, when Tsar Nicholas had banished Dmitri to the Imperial Army on the Persian front after his involvement, with Felix Yusupov, in the murder of Rasputin. It probably saved his life, for after the revolution Dmitri did not return to Russia but accepted a commission in the British Army in Tehran and spent the remainder of the war in obscurity there. When he arrived in Paris in November 1918, he stayed at the Ritz, where he met up with Sandro, who found it very odd "to see a Russian Grand Duke wearing the uniform of an alien nation." But, as he added, "the rescued ones cannot be choosers."[3]

Dmitri had moved on to London by the time Maria Pavlovna arrived in Paris from Bucharest the following April. Her return as a refugee rather than an entitled Romanov had been difficult and humiliating. She and Sergey had not had the money for a hotel and had gratefully accepted the offer of staying with Russian friends in Passy. But being back in the city rekindled many painful memories of her father, Paul, and the lovely mansion at Boulogne-sur-Seine that Maria had visited in happier times, and she felt a great longing to see it again.[4] When she drove up to the house for the first time in five years, it all looked exactly the same. "The paths were swept, the bushes clipped, only there were no flowers in the beds." But old Gustave, the concierge, and his wife, Josephine, were still there, and together they sat down and wept the loss of Grand Duke Paul.[5] Maria felt herself "immediately plunged into the old atmosphere. It seemed as though the door on to the stone terrace might open and my father, wearing his old tweed cape, would come down into the garden followed by the two little girls."

Inside, the house was eerily bare and silent: "all my father's collections and every object of value had been transported to Russia a few months before the war . . . the glass cases were empty, there were hardly any pictures on the walls, and the furniture stood huddled together, under sheets." And now, of course, the splendid palace at Tsarskoe and everything so carefully transported there from Paris was gone—confiscated by the Bolsheviks.[6] With the spring sunshine pouring through the tall windows of the dining room, Maria stood there reminiscing, as many familiar scenes flooded back to her. She remembered her father's always punctual arrival at table for lunch at 12:30 and how her stepmother was never, ever ready on time; how Olga often arrived late, "laden with neatly tied parcels and cardboard boxes" from her latest shopping expedition.[7] Maria and Dmitri had seen very little of Paul between 1902 and 1908, but she vividly remembered her father showing her excited brother the Paris attractions and their stepbrother, Vladimir Paley, writing plays for their little sisters, Nataliya and Irina, to perform. The memories she relived at Boulogne that day—part sad, part happy—"were mine to carry through life," Maria wrote—"sometimes as an inspiration, sometimes as a warning."[8]

Maria and Dmitri were finally reunited in London a few weeks later. But bad luck seemed to dog her, for it was here that she and Sergey received news from Queen Marie that their little son Roman, whom they had left in the care of Sergey's parents, had died of bowel disease. Broken and racked with guilt at her admitted indifference toward her child, Maria kept Roman's death to herself, hiding the news even from her friends.* For a while Maria, Sergey, and Dmitri shared a rented house in Kensington, but in May 1920 the Poutiatines decided to move to Paris. The months of disruption and rootlessness since fleeing Russia all compounded Maria's feelings of loneliness and insecurity; she arrived in Paris with little or no sense of how she would make her way and earn a living. But she knew that in order to survive, people of her class who were now settling here in their thousands, without means, would have to endure the humiliation of finding a job for the first time in their till now privileged lives. They would have to take off their "fantastic costumes," and with them their pride, and don everyday clothes. More important, they would need to change their outmoded, entitled attitudes.[9]

Shortly after her return, Maria had an extremely painful reunion with her stepmother, when Olga Paley came to Paris from Finland to settle Grand Duke Paul's estate. Maria was taken aback when they met. Gone was the "magnificent self-assurance" that once had commanded attention wherever she went:

Her face was deathly pale and transparent, terribly aged and lined. She had grown smaller, she seemed to have shriveled up, smothered as she was in her black widow's clothes heavily

* By her own admission Maria had never had strong maternal instincts. She had left her older son, Lennart, behind in Sweden after her divorce from her first husband, Prince Wilhelm, and was estranged from him for many years.

trimmed with crape.... Her grief had completely changed
her; she was a broken miserable creature who could hardly
speak, hardly think.[10]

By the end of the summer, Dmitri had followed Maria to Paris,
and in autumn 1921 Olga Paley came back to live there permanently
with Nataliya and Irina.[11] But not at the grand house at Boulogne;
this had to be sold to pay off debts. She bought a small house nearby
in the rue de la Faisanderie, where she retreated, surrounded by her
memories. In her final years, and suffering a profound grief over
Paul's murder that never left her, Olga threw herself into work for
underprivileged Russian émigrés, organizing fund-raising lotter-
ies and charity balls in Paris, including a particularly sought-after
annual ball in Biarritz. Patronized by American millionaires and
the cream of European officialdom and the aristocracy, each year
it raised enough money to fund Olga's numerous good causes until the next one. "My grandmother could not sit and watch these
wretched people," her grandson wrote later; "the poverty was over-
whelming."[12] With this in mind, Olga founded a committee to work
with Russian refugees, which assisted many in dealing with the authorities over their residency in France and wrote to ministers on
their behalf.

Through it all, she remained kind and gracious but was tormented
to discover many of the precious items from her home at Tsarskoe
Selo being sold off by the Bolsheviks in the Paris and London auc-
tion houses. In London, at the King's Bench Division in November
1928, she brought an action vigorously opposing the sale of various
objets d'art and furniture from Tsarskoe, including her beloved piano,
by a syndicate of dealers and merchants. Olga rightly claimed that
the Soviet state had stolen them, but the dealers countered that they
had been sold to them by the Leningrad Gostorg (the Soviet import–
export agency) as "part of the nationalised property of Russia."[13] To

save them was, for Olga, a matter not of their value, but of what they represented of her old and happy life with Paul.[14] The stress reduced her to a pitiful figure. Maria Pavlovna recalled her stepmother's decline with considerable sorrow: "She had grown stout and in the morning padded around the house in worn-out slippers and an old dressing-gown, her hair hanging in strands about a still beautiful but tired face."[15] But still Olga persevered with her letter writing, sitting at her desk for long hours, telephone in hand, trying to help others until the cancer returned. She died on November 2, 1929, at the age of sixty-two, and was buried at the Colombes Gabriel Péri Cemetery in France. "I see her again, as I saw her in June last at Christie's," wrote the correspondent of the *Daily Mirror* in a brief obituary, "a pathetic figure watching the sales of her pictures, furniture, and objects of art from her palace at Tsarskoe Selo." The sale, he noted, had included two portraits of Alexander II and a Canaletto.[16]

In her memoirs, published in 1932, Maria admitted that she had moved to Paris "in the illusion that immediately upon my arrival a new life would open up before me." But like most of her class, she had no idea about money: the Russian aristocracy had never carried cash or written checks; they had left that to their minions to deal with. Not long after getting to London, she had already, reluctantly, begun selling off the jewels that she had retrieved from safekeeping in Sweden. They might once have had considerable value, but in the early 1920s the market was being flooded not just with Russian jewels but with those of other European aristocrats dispossessed by the war, and Maria's realized only low prices. Sandro had noted the widespread fleecing of his compatriots desperately "peddling" their valuables in London and Paris, and how the middlemen dealers conspired to keep the prices down, thus ensuring that the Russian émigrés got so much less back than they had paid. They had all left Russia anticipating that their salvaged valuables "would surely take us right into the 1930s." But they were mistaken. Sandro's wife Xenia's stunning Romanov pearls had lasted "just three years, to a minute."[17]

Sandro had had great difficulty finding work in London, as too had Maria Pavlovna during her brief time there. It wasn't just a matter of earning a living, which was pressing, but also she had needed to find something to occupy her now empty time. There was, fortunately, one skill she shared with many other refined, well-brought-up Russian women of her class: needlework. Maria later told an interviewer that she had "always like[d] to fiddle with a needle" and that back in St. Petersburg she and Empress Alexandra "used to amuse ourselves by making dresses for the little Grand Duchesses"—the Romanov sisters Olga, Tatiana, Maria, and Anastasia.[18] In London she took up these skills again, as well as knitting American-style sweaters to commission—knitted goods being in demand due to the postwar shortage of good quality fabric. The work was very labor-intensive, and no matter how hard she tried she could not manage to earn more than six pounds a week from her endeavors. So she also started copying designer dresses and making fine lingerie for Russian friends—by hand, for she had no sewing machine.[19] Once installed in Paris—the center of the fashion world—Maria knew she could do much better. She set herself up with a Singer sewing machine, bought on credit, and a cutting table. She took a short course in machine embroidery in order to use her sewing machine more efficiently, while she sought a Parisian clientele. She went out little and stuck to her own narrow class of aristocratic exiles. Many of them had suffered far greater trials than Maria had—materially and emotionally—but they never discussed the trauma they had endured. "All our conversations still turned around one subject," remembered Maria—the past:

This past was like a dusty diamond, which we held to the light in the hope of seeing the sun rays play through it. We spoke of the past, we looked back to it. And speaking of the past we sought for no lessons but tirelessly and aimlessly went over old ground seeking whom to blame for what had befallen us. Our future as a whole we could not imagine, while our return to Russia, of which we were then so certain, we pictured only under very definite auspices. We lived side by side with life but were afraid of meeting it.[20]

This vein of nostalgia, of a deep, fatalistic yearning for the world that they had lost, was something that dogged so many of Maria's generation of exiles in Paris and made it impossible for many of them to adjust to their new environment. One such was Maria's brother Grand Duke Dmitri Pavlovich, "a Romanov Hamlet" who seemed perpetually tormented by his past, blighted by the early loss of his mother, a lonely childhood, and the murder of so many of his relatives during the revolution.[21] Once the possessor of the fourth largest fortune in Russia, Dmitri had arrived in Paris in November 1918 "with less than a hundred francs [eight dollars] in his Grand Ducal pockets, and 'only one extra shirt.'"[22]

Of all the Romanov family members in exile, Dmitri seemed the most aimless, moving between the London and Paris social sets and staying at the Ritz in both capitals, even when it was beyond his means, unable to manage what little money he had. Underneath the effortless charm and suavity, he had always been lonely, and vulnerable. His state of "feverish idleness" as a down-on-his-luck playboy might have continued had not Dmitri's increasingly penurious situation forced him to look for work.[23] In London in the spring of 1919, he took some lessons in economics from Hugh Dalton at the London School of Economics in an attempt to better manage what money he had left. But in essence Dmitri had only one asset that he could exploit: he was a handsome, seductive ladies' man, and women fell for him with predictable regularity. He was always on the lookout for well-heeled connections who might steer him toward better prospects; he knew that his best option would be to find himself a wealthy wife. With this in mind, he had briefly pursued the wealthy American divorcée Consuelo Vanderbilt after being introduced to her in London by Lord and Lady Curzon. Like many of the women who were courted by him, Consuelo found Dmitri "an exceptionally handsome man, fair and sleek with long blue eyes in a narrow face."[24] He had, she conceded, a kind of stealthy grace, but she wisely thought better of marrying him.

Dmitri continued to be dogged by bad luck in love as well as in his personal fortunes. For a while he pursued an American dancer, Teddie [Theodora] Gerard, who had been appearing in "a criminal-adventure farce" — *The Eclipse* — at London's Garrick Theatre.[25] Teddie later sold her story to the U.S. press, relating how the "unhappy prince" had poured out stories of the terrible murder of his family, in between playing "low wailing" Russian folk music to her on his guitar at a Christmas party in Mayfair in 1920. Pale and mournful, Dmitri seemed the classic "ghost at a feast."[26] A few months later, he was back in Paris and staying at the Hotel du Rhin, frittering his time and money away in clubs and restaurants, but once more forced by his money troubles to move in with his sister Maria and brother-in-law Sergey, this time at their apartment on rue Miromesnil.

Some suggested that with his brooding, matinée-idol good looks Dmitri should try Hollywood, but by spring 1921 the twenty-nine-year-old had new preoccupations; he was once more chasing an older woman of means.[27] This time, it was the French fashion designer Gabrielle "Coco" Chanel, who currently was dominating the postwar fashion world. They had in fact first met on a visit Dmitri made to Paris in 1911, when Chanel was working as a milliner on rue Cambon, and crossed paths again at a dinner party at the Ritz on

January 22, 1921, introduced by Dmitri's then lover, the French actress Marthe Davelli. At the end of the evening, Chanel drove Dmitri back to his apartment; she stayed till dawn, for they had, he noted
in his diary, "suddenly found [them]selves on an amazingly friendly
footing."[28] Davelli seemed quite happy to pass Dmitri on to Chanel;
he was, she had found, "a little expensive for me."[29] The jealous Paris
gossips were soon busy discussing how the "little shop girl" Chanel
(who had worked her way to success from very humble origins) had
set her cap at a handsome Russian grand duke. Chanel had in fact
only recently been engaged in a brief, covert affair with Stravinsky,
who had returned to Paris from Switzerland to work on a production of a new ballet, *Pulcinella,* for Diaghilev. Chanel's introduction
to Diaghilev by Stravinsky came at a time when the Ballets Russes
were in dire financial difficulty, and she had become an important
new financial backer.* Stravinsky, his wife, and their children were
at the time without a Paris base, and in September 1920 Chanel had
invited them to stay at her art nouveau villa at Garches in the Paris
suburbs. Stravinsky might have been short and rather unattractive,
but his dandified vanity more than exceeded his stature.[30] The brief
liaison Chanel enjoyed with the tempestuous composer—and which
may well have overlapped with that with Dmitri Pavlovich—appears
to have been conducted not under his wife's nose at Garches but at
Chanel's suite at the Ritz. She had, however, found Stravinsky too
intense and impetuous; the charmingly relaxed Grand Duke Dmitri
was far less taxing company, and he was always so effortlessly decorative. For now, as friends cynically remarked, Chanel was into
Russian men—it was her "Slavic period."[31]

Chanel later remarked that "Princes have always filled me with
immense pity"; the poetic-looking Grand Duke Dmitri, who was

---

* Having attended the premiere in 1913, Chanel provided the funds for *The Rite of Spring*
to be revived in Paris in 1920, though with new choreography by Massine, for no one could
remember Nijinsky's original. The costumes were made at her sewing workshops.

eight years younger than her, certainly fascinated her. His tragic Romanov history and cultured top-drawer aristocratic connections were the door to elevation of her own social status and a distancing from the humble peasant roots to which her rivals loved to draw attention.[32] Dmitri Pavlovich was the perfect escort; but he was not a wealthy one. Gone were the days of that charmed life when he could take a lover to breakfast at Maxim's and shower her in orchids and jewels from Cartier, as he had done with the dancer Irene Castle in Paris in 1913.[33] By 1921 he was fast running through the proceeds of the sale of his palace on St. Petersburg's Nevsky Prospekt.[34]

A persistent myth attaches to Dmitri's involvement in the creation of Chanel's legendary No. 5 perfume, launched in May 1921. It has been suggested that in 1920, when she was looking to create her own brand of perfume, he had introduced Chanel to the Russian-French *parfumier* Ernest Beaux. But since the couple did not meet till January the following year, it seems more likely that Chanel had already sought Beaux's help of her own accord. It may perhaps be true that the idea for the iconic glass-stoppered square bottle in which No. 5 was marketed came from Dmitri. For apparently Chanel, who was fascinated by Russian design, had asked him to describe the Russian military uniform, and in so doing he had sketched an image of the vodka flask issued to officers of the Imperial Guard.[35] Either way, in a very short space of time Chanel No. 5 became a worldwide best-seller and made Chanel's fortune.[36]

A few weeks into their relationship, she and Dmitri took off for Monte Carlo "to bask . . . in the sun" in her shiny new motorcar—a blue Rolls-Royce convertible Silver Cloud that Dmitri had helped her choose. They each chipped in fifteen thousand francs for the trip; it may not have been much for Chanel, but Dmitri was perilously close to running out of money. The hotel manager felt uncomfortable presenting his bill; to do so was extremely *infra dig* with Romanovs. But Chanel insisted.[37] During their holiday, Dmitri idly amused himself playing golf; he and Chanel dined at Ciro's exclusive restaurant and spent their evenings gambling at the casino, where Dmitri showed he had not shaken off the inveterate gambling habits of the Romanovs. Thereafter Chanel discreetly paid him an allowance, in hopes perhaps of marriage and the title Grand Duchess; they frequently traveled together in Europe, and she seemed happy to indulge him.[38]

Dmitri wasn't in love with Chanel; he considered her a valued friend, but as a proud Romanov he felt humiliated that she was the one with the money and he was perceived as a kept man. Worse, she was a commoner, which he felt might damage his standing in the émigré monarchist circles in Paris in which he moved. "I have had enough of gallivanting around France in a morganatic situation," he confided to his diary, remembering the profound damage that such a marriage had done to his father. He and Chanel tried to keep their relationship secret; to avoid scrutiny, she installed him at the house in Garches, now vacated by the Stravinskys, where she "guarded him like a beautiful pet animal." In 1922 they spent another sybaritic summer together, this time at Biarritz.[39] But by the end of 1923 the relationship had petered out, Chanel by then embarking on a long affair with Hugh Grosvenor, 2nd Duke of Westminster. She and Dmitri remained lifelong friends, however, she preserving a tender pity for his rootless life; for as Chanel so sharply observed, he shared that same quality of all the dispossessed Russian grand dukes: they were "diminished, almost emasculated by their poverty in exile." True, "they looked marvelous, but there was nothing behind. Green eyes, fine hands and shoulders, peace-loving, timorous. They drank so as not to be afraid. They were tall and handsome and splendid, but behind it all—nothing: just vodka and the void."[40] Separation from Chanel pushed Dmitri toward honest employment once more, and by 1924 he had become "an Imperial super-salesman" (Sandro's witty words) for the Grand Société de Vin de Champagne, based in

Rheims, eventually becoming a member of its board of directors. "The cursed stuff cost me so much money before," Dmitri quipped, "that surely it ought to support me now. With all due modesty, I do maintain that I know more about the vintages of champagne than even the Widow Cliquot herself."[41]

Dmitri Pavlovich can, however, take credit for giving his sister Maria an important leg up in the couture business when, in the autumn of 1921, he introduced her to Chanel. Having already succumbed to the Slavic style of Diaghilev and the Ballets Russes, Chanel was captivated by Maria's Russian-style embroidery.[42] There were also shared personal sympathies: both had lost their mothers when young and both had been taught to sew by nuns.[43] Maria proved to be far more capable and organized than Dmitri, and she did not allow her Romanov pride to get in the way of earning a living. In December 1921 she spent a week at Chanel's workroom improving on her embroidery skills. She had tried to keep a low profile and "be one of them," but the other girls could tell she was a Russian refugee; it took some time for them to warm to her and share their skills. But no sooner had Maria "astonished them by her talent and aptitude, not only in actual sewing but in designing also," than the girls "grew cold toward her, believing that she was the precursor of other Russians who would eventually 'get their jobs.'"[44] Such hostility in the workplace would be encountered time and again by the Russian émigrés in Paris.

Aware of the indigent position most of Maria's compatriots then found themselves in, Chanel seized the opportunity to undercut her French rivals by hiring Maria's services, for she offered extremely competitive prices. She placed her under an exclusive contract to produce embroidered sweaters and Russian-style embroidery for blouses and tunics for her 1922 collection. Privately, a fashion expert from Fifth Avenue told Maria that her designs would have "a worldwide influence on this year's styles," but it was Chanel, of course, who would garner the accolades rather than the self-effacing Maria Pavlovna. But she was glad, she told American journalist Basil Woon, that the work she and other former Russian nobles were doing would "add to the funds of the hospitals and schools we have founded in Paris." Not just that, but, she added, "we are determined that, if we can't rule Russia, we are at least going to have a good try at leading the world of women's wear." Woon was struck by Maria's "nervous energy driven by an indomitable will," and the fact that she worked twelve to fourteen hours a day.[45]

Chanel, for her part, also helped other former Russian aristocrats, such as Count Kutuzov, ex-governor of Crimea, employing him as head receptionist at her atelier on rue Cambon, as well as hiring numerous Russian women as salesgirls, seamstresses, and models. She also volunteered advice on Maria's rather unfashionable hairstyle and took the scissors to it. She suggested she should go on a diet too, in order to liven up her dowdy, downtrodden appearance, for the plain, square-jawed Maria looked well over her true age of thirty-one. It was, Chanel advised, "a great mistake to go round looking like a refugee. . . . If you wish to do business, the first thing is to look prosperous."[46]

In March 1920 another Romanov refugee, Prince Gavriil Konstantinovich, who had narrowly escaped execution by the Bolsheviks, had arrived in Paris with his wife, Antonina Nesterovskaya. Finding themselves, like their Romanov relatives, short of money, Antonina, like Maria Pavlovna, proved to be extremely enterprising as a breadwinner. A petite powerhouse of energy, she established her own fashion business: the House of Bery, on rue Vital, in September 1921, having abandoned the idea of setting up a dancing school in Paris. Soon her business was attracting rich American patrons, an added attraction being the presence of tall and languid Prince Gavriil, who made a habit of offering unsolicited Romanov charm by sitting in the salon, regaling customers with photographs and stories

of his life in imperial Russia.[47] Gavriil became friends with the émigré Polish painter Tamara Lempicka, doyenne of the new fashionable art deco style, who famously painted him in military tunic, in
all his Romanov self-confidence.

Soon even Grand Duke Dmitri's former associate Prince Felix
Yusupov and his wife, Irina, would be testing the water of the world
of couture. One might not have imagined they would need to seek
gainful employment in Paris, for when the Yusupovs fled Russia,
Felix had been able to bring some of his family's prodigious wealth
with him. Indeed, Sandro had considered his son-in-law the "nabob
of the lot"—Felix having been the only royal able to smuggle a substantial fortune—in the shape of two Rembrandt portraits that he
had spirited away from the Yusupov Palace in Petrograd—as well
as his prized collection of snuffboxes, a famous black pearl necklace
that had supposedly come down from Catherine the Great, and a
pair of diamond earrings that had belonged to Marie Antoinette.[48]
Such valuables were small potatoes to Felix, whose income before
the revolution had been in the millions. As Sandro sardonically remarked, his prodigious spending had been "sufficient in itself to explain the short duration of the Rembrandt proceeds."[49]

After spending a year traveling between Paris, Rome, and London, Felix and Irina had bought a house at 27 rue Gutenberg, in
Boulogne-Billancourt. Once installed, Felix was delighted to receive
a phone call informing him that a small pouch of diamonds that had
been left with the jeweler Chaumet some time previously, when
Chaumet had been remodeling some of Irina's parures, was awaiting collection.[50] They had forgotten all about them; their limousine,
mothballed for the last five years in Paris, was also recovered. For
the next few months the Yusupovs spent an aimless time commuting
between Paris, Biarritz, and an apartment they owned in Knights-
bridge while trying to decide where to settle permanently. Having
chosen Paris, Felix was horrified to discover that his and Irina's in-

surance policy—the pouch of Chaumet diamonds—had been stolen from his desk.[51] As his money supply ran out, Felix sought ways of replacing it. In 1924, he and Irina established a fashion house named "Irfé" at rue Duphot—the name made up of the first two letters of their names. The ethereal-looking Irina, a granddaughter of Tsar Alexander II, with the natural svelte figure of a mannequin, was the face of their brand in Irfé's publicity photographs. Thanks to the Yusupovs' impeccable Paris connections, the first collection was launched at the Ritz on place Vendôme.

Such was the interest of the British and American press in the fortunes of the dispossessed European royals, especially the Russians, that in 1921 an American journalist, Frederick Collins of the *Woman's Home Companion,* tracked some of them down in Paris for an article entitled "What's Happened to Royalty?" "All these pampered pets of fortune have dropped out of our knowledge," the headline noted. "But where were they now, what do people think of them and what do they think of themselves?" The article featured a photograph of Maria Pavlovna in the sitting room of the modest two-room apartment where she lived, not far from her workshop, and drew the reader's attention to the fact that although she had once been "heiress to the most magnificent private collection of jewels in the world, the beads she wears in this picture are glass."[52]

In the early days of her fashion business, Maria, Sergey, and his parents, Prince and Princess Poutiatine, together worked hard at their first modest premises, with occasional, largely ineffectual, input from Dmitri, who, according to journalist Basil Woon, who visited the atelier, "drew some designs."[53] It was Maria who invested all the energy in the business, with advice from Chanel behind the scenes. Indeed, Dmitri seemed incapable of raising the energy for any kind of useful employment. He seemed crippled by a lack of will to turn his life around. Nevertheless, his past involvement in the Rasputin murder made him an object of perennial fascination with the European press, although he never cashed in on it; that for him was a point of honor. It was the elusive Grand Duke Dmitri Pavlovich whom Frederick Collins had been particularly intent on interviewing in Paris. He was still the very "epitome of a Russian grand duke"—"slender, well-groomed . . . and concave at the waist line," but of course, unlike the grand dukes of old, his wealth was gone. He dined out on his charm and his good looks, relying on others to foot the bill. Collins followed Dmitri round Paris for days and repeatedly tried to engage him in conversation, but Dmitri "would not go beyond the ordinary civilities." Eventually he cornered his prey at a club called the Acacias, drinking with a group of wealthy celebrities that included the Princess Murat, American impresario Florenz Ziegfeld, bestselling novelist Elinor Glyn, the Infante Don Luis of Spain, and the Dolly sisters—famous vaudeville artists from New York. Strange company, but right now, as Dmitri confided, "This is not Paris. It isn't anything." And yet—just now, for a dispossessed Russian *"it is the world."* And it was one in which Collins felt it was "safe to say anything, even to a Grand Duke"—except perhaps to ask him "how it feels to be 'broke.'"[54]

At last Dmitri warmed to him, and Collins managed to get a photograph—the first publicity shot of Dmitri since 1912, so Collins claimed. How did the Grand Duke live, he asked, curious about what he was doing for money. Dmitri was somewhat surprised: "How did all my class live? We knew nothing, that is, how to do nothing." But he had friends, and he had taken out a loan—and another loan—and intended to pay them back—"and live." He was in the process of floating a company, he said; it was either that or end up like many of his former army colleagues, who were now in Paris working as chauffeurs and taxi drivers.[55] The company in question was, of course, his sister Maria's embroidery workshop, which had been set up "in the servants'" hall of a modest house in what Collins termed "the Harlem of Paris"—at 48 rue François Premier. Dmitri's "grand plan," Collins revealed, was for this enterprise to "give employment to émigrés of noble birth." In another interview for the American press, he talked vaguely of working on various designs as an inventor and that he had "started an office where ex-Russian officers can work at solving mechanical problems"—a venture of which nothing more was heard.[56]

Having found Maria Pavlovna's workshop at the end of a dark, low passage and up a narrow flight of stairs, Frederick Collins could not but be moved by the sight of its occupants. "A slender, bent old lady in a black cotton dress and a scrupulously clean gingham apron had come in with an armful of blouses, dress patterns, scarfs and suit, embroidered in marvelous designs." They were, Collins told his readers "unlike anything I had seen in the windows of the Rue de la Paix." He was impressed; even more so when the lady with the "fine face and the deeply tired eyes" turned out to be the dowager Princess Poutiatine, Maria Pavlovna's sixty-five-year-old mother-in-law, who worked at the embroidery workshop along with several Russian émigrés.[57] The garments in her arms, she proudly told him, had all been made by her daughter-in-law. The princess seemed so tired, and thin, and "silently sad, except when her eyes lighted up over some beauty in her daughter-in-law's handiwork." Collins found her husband up some rickety back stairs, "dressed as a retired banker might be dressed of a late afternoon at his home on Chicago's North Side, in a clean starched collar, a light silk tie, and a well-cut buff-colored summer suit." The prince told him that he designed and made items in the workshop, where he and his wife also lived. His noble face reminded Collins of King Edward VII. He felt intensely sorry for "this courtly old gentleman," now "bent over an ironing board like a tailor's apprentice." He was "the picture of a race declassed!"[58]

In another room upstairs, Collins was shown "a dozen members of the nobility" hunched over embroidery machines—"*working for a wage of two francs an hour!*" He was horrified: a franc then was worth about eight cents; two francs were "a tip for the boy who carried your bag." A day's work in Maria Pavlovna's atelier paid a dollar and a half—but it was "enough to keep the Countess Apracsine [Apraksina]—once a great St. Petersburg beauty—from starvation" and support other former ladies of the Imperial household who worked there. "It was a living, nothing more, for beautiful, sapphire-eyed Princess Massalski [Massalskaya]," who claimed to be a cousin of the tsar and admitted how hard it had been at first—"for you see, I had always had everything." At the end of his visit, Collins could only conclude that in the poignant setting of this émigré Russian workshop "there lies, so close to the surface that a jewel may scratch it, the tragedy of the human heart."[59]

By now Maria Pavlovna had created her own brand name, Kitmir,* with her stepmother, Princess Paley, providing financial support in the venture. In August 1923, Maria moved to much bigger premises at 7 rue Montaigne, with MAISON KITMIR now displayed in gold letters above its courtyard entrance. Here she had a team of Russian women producing embroidery and beautifully beaded handbags, belts, and shawls—all exclusive to Chanel.[60] Her mother-in-law too found a degree of success with a hat-making enterprise—Chapka, at rue Saint Honoré—producing beautifully embroidered cloche hats, modeled for Paris *Vogue* by the émigré Princess Trubetskaya. By 1926 Maria Pavlovna had ended her exclusive deal with Chanel and was supplying her embroideries to two hundred businesses, having supplemented her workforce with fifty French machine embroiderers,

---

* The name was that of a legendary dog from Persian mythology; it was considered lucky by Russians, and had been given to one of three dogs of a great friend of Maria's—the former Russian ambassador to Washington, Boris Bakhmetiev.

keeping her Russian compatriots, whom she considered "incomparable," for the beautifully crafted hand embroidery.[61]

In part 2 of his series on the Russian émigrés in Paris—"The City of Exiles"—Frederick L. Collins visited the salon of Madame Yteb on the rue Royale. The owner in question was Baroness Elizaveta Hoyningen-Huene—Yteb being a reversion of her pet name, Betty. She was in fact the daughter of an American—Anne van Ness Lothrop—who in turn was a daughter of the former American ambassador to the court of Alexander III. Anne had married into the Russian aristocratic Hoyningen-Huene family and produced three children: Betty, Helena, and George. The family had lost everything in the revolution and, in 1918, had landed in London, where Betty and Helena, like other decorous young ladies of the Russian aristocracy, had turned to needlework.[62] Betty had been first briefly married to Baron Wrangel—brother of the White general—and was still trading on the kudos of that name and its romantic connections, despite being recently remarried to a British army officer, Lieutenant Colonel Charles Buzzard. With Charles's financial support, she decided to open a fashion house in Paris, starting extremely modestly in a small flat on the Left Bank, where she gave work to some of the first Russian refugees to arrive. By 1922 she had moved to the more prestigious establishment at rue Royale. She employed her artistic brother George to illustrate Yteb's advertisements for the fashion magazines and also to help in designing the actual clothes, which, like the fashions at Kitmir, exploited the popular Slavic style.[63]

The Yteb salon was managed by another aristocrat, Princess Koughoucheff (Kugucheva), whom Frederick Collins was told had "sold her last jewel to buy the material for a few cakes which she sold on the streets of Constantinople in order to keep alive her mother, her old governess, and her two young children and who had tirelessly worked distributing clothes and food to the refugees there before coming to Paris." One of the salon's best fitters was Countess

Gourno, and two of their mannequins were Russian women of the nobility. All worked to the strict rule that they must be able to retain their positions on their merits alone.[64]

With sewing, millinery, and knitting thus proving to be the quickest, easiest, and most immediate route out of poverty, twenty-seven fashion houses were established in Paris by Russian émigrés between 1922 and 1935. Everyone in the Russian colony—from the highest to the lowest born—knew someone who worked in the fashion trade, and casual work could easily be found by reading the small ads posted on the noticeboard at the Russian Orthodox church on rue Daru. By the mid-1920s this industry employed well over three thousand Russian women.[65] Among them were Princess Lobanova-Rostovskaya at Maison Paul Caret on rue de Rivoli; Princess Ourousoff (Urusova), who ran a *maison de couture* at 108 boulevard Haussmann producing hats and embroidery for Worth; Maison Tao on l'avénue de l'Opéra, run by three Russian princesses, its name the initials of the surnames of Mariya Trubetskaya, Mariya Annenkova, and Lyubov Obolenskaya; exquisite lace-trimmed lingerie by the House of Hitrovo; the workrooms of Countess Orlova-Davydova's premises, "where fifteen titled women do exquisite knitting for the dressmaking trade" under the label Mod; the sewing shops of Countess Bobrinskaya in the boulevard Flaudrin; right down to Princess Shakhovskaya and her two daughters, living in a single room in Versailles and embroidering linen—"but not too well."[66] But this, of course, is not to include the innumerable unrecorded women earning a pittance doing piecework at home. English journalist George Orwell in his classic work *Down and Out in Paris and London* was particularly struck by one Russian émigré mother who lived in a "small arid room" at his pokey Hôtel des Trois Moineaux—a "rickety warren of five stories, cut up by wooden partitions into forty rooms"—who "worked sixteen hours a day, darning socks at twenty-five centimes a sock, while the son, decently dressed, loafed in the Montparnasse cafés."[67] The French writer Anaïs Nin recalled one "authentic White Russian" who sewed for her. She was "quiet, well-bred" and, much to Nin's dismay, now earned her living as a seamstress. "When she came to get work from me," Nin recalled, "she asked if instead of taking it home she might stay and sew in my home just to breathe again some beauty and grace she had once known in her own home."[68]

The list of young Russian noblewomen now working as mannequins was equally impressive. The couture houses favored them because they were well educated, elegant, had perfect manners, and, most important, spoke very good French.

Some of their parents, however, resisted such employment, which they perceived as a debasement of their daughters' status. But the fact was, the couture houses loved the willowy, fine-boned Russian women. The work was far less taxing than factory work, and a model could earn considerably more than a waitress or a shopgirl. The names of Russian ladies from the *Almanch de St. Petersburg* now parading decorously in the Paris couture houses were endless: Baroness Tiesenhausen, two Baronesses Meden, the *demoiselle* Nossovitch, two Obolensky princesses, one of General Lokhvitsky's daughters, one of the Eristova princesses, Princess Tumanova, Countess Golenicheva-Kutuzova, the *demoiselle* Bazhenova, countess Grabbe, the *demoiselle* Bobrikova—and eventually even one of Olga Paley's daughters, Nataliya, who would become one of the most successful of them all.[69]*

Tales of émigré Russian nobility struggling with adversity seemed to strike a chord with the European and American press. There were so many little tragedies of hardship: "Countess L," once at the heart of Russian court society, now providing for "her blind mother and

---

* She found fame as a fashion model as Natalie Paley and, after a brief marriage to couturier Lucien Lelong, tried a brief career in films. Her second marriage to theatrical impresario John C. Wilson took her to New York in 1937 and provided an entrée into elite American society.

invalid husband giving manicures and selling silk stockings." Or "Countess O," once enormously wealthy, "now support[ing] her family by decorating porcelain for several big Paris stores and painting flower panels to order." A countess friend of Felix Yusupov's worked as a washroom attendant, while her husband looked after the customers' coats.[70] The *Tatler* found it all rather quaintly endearing: "how plucky, how brave" these aristocratic Russian ladies were; women such as a "certain beautiful princess" who lived in a cheap hotel, where she "paints landscapes on velvet hats for which the milliners clamor"; such reduced circumstances did not, however, prevent her from remaining "a grande dame, who receives a circle of Russian friends, who, with quiet dignity, sip their tea (without cakes) while the mistress of the room continues her work. The new poor of Paris, you will see, are not idle."[71]

At the end of his series of investigative articles on the plight of the displaced Russian aristocracy, Frederick Collins admitted that he had set out with no concept of the scale of the Russian migration—or "hegira," as he called it—or of its consequences:

It is as if the President of the United States, the governors of all the states, most of the doctors and teachers and judges and preachers and bankers and manufacturers and merchants of Kansas City and Chicago and Seattle and New York and every other American city, most of the big men of the small towns— with their wives and grown children and little babies—were to be suddenly expunged from our American life, and dumped without warning or resources into foreign lands and foreign conditions. It is as if you and I and all the people we know were pauperized and exiled!

Collins could not but be impressed with the courage and humility of the many former aristocrats he had met, most of whom seemed undaunted, with "heads up and eyes front, exiled but unafraid!"[72] But survival in Paris in the early 1920s was hard; the help wanted ads of the French press were full of menial jobs that required none of the skills that the cream of the former intelligentsia had to offer. So many square pegs were forced into round holes, perhaps none more so than the legions of ex-army Russians with little or no skills other than an ability to drive, for nothing more truly represented the economic plight of those first émigrés in Paris than the aphorism then doing the rounds: "The men drive taxis and the women sew for a living."[73]

—⟶••⟵—

CHAPTER 7

"How Ruined Russians Earn a Living"

O ne day in April 1922 a visitor to Paris driving a mud-spattered touring car, who had been on the road for three days from the Riviera, pulled into a large garage on the avenue des Ternes. It was past midnight, and the only person on duty was "a white-haired man of erect carriage and patriarchal mustache, who wore overalls and carried a hose."

"I want my car washed and made ready for tomorrow morning," said the tourist, who was also a magazine writer of some repute. "Here," and he tendered a ten-franc note.

As the old man took the proffered note, there was something about him that rang a bell in the American journalist's memory; "pardon me, but haven't I met you somewhere before?" he asked. The old man smiled in response: "You have. You were my guest at Smolensk in 1915." It turned out that the dignified old car washer was a former general of division, Krasnilov, who had scored a remarkable victory at the Pripet Marshes during the Russian advance on Galicia in World War I—a success "that had made his name adored in Russia."* Not long after this encounter, the old general obtained slightly better employment for a few francs more a week, this time opening the doors of limousines delivering wealthy Americans to "a famous jewelers on Rue de la Paix" (Cartier perhaps?)—but as such this was the best, most congenial employment he could hope to find in his new home.[1]

Other senior military figures had fared little better in Paris. Frederick L. Collins had found "the monumental figure of Admiral Possokhow [Posokhov]"—"massive head and noble features, built on the Michel Angelo plan"—in his cheap furnished rooms, located in abject obscurity down a "smelly side street, through a low doorway, across a cobbled courtyard, up three flights of shadowy stairs."[2] In his heyday, Admiral Sergey Posokhov had been commander in chief of the imperial naval forces at the White Sea port of Archangel and had been the proud owner of four Rolls-Royces in Petrograd. Now aged seventy-six, he had been rejected as being too old to work as a chauffeur, which he would have preferred, and was reduced to peddling lengths of woolen material for men's coats and suits. But he did have some silver that he had left in the safekeeping of the British consul at Archangel and "when I do not earn enough I sell a piece." With his cheerful courage, the old admiral "painted the Russian picture for what it is: 'Exile.'" Posokhov told how his old friend, "General Wadinow [Vadinov]"† was reduced to upholstering chairs in a little shop near the Gare de Lyon but, Posokhov assured Collins, the general and his wife seemed to have adapted and had "forgotten the splendors of their great house in Sebastopol."[3]

---

* General Krasnilov is hard to trace in World War I but during the civil war is known to have commanded Don Cossack troops in an attempt to take Tsaritsyn and cut off the Volga. This army was defeated by the Reds in March 1919, and its remnants joined Denikin's Volunteer Army.

† Possibly the intended name is Alexander Vadin, 1866–1946, a former major general who emigrated to Paris. Sergey Posokhov died in Paris in 1935.

Grand Duchess Maria Pavlovna remembered a whole company of former Cossacks—some eighty from the same regiment—who worked as porters and freight handlers at the Gare de l'Est. Apparently several of the officers among them had refused offers of better work "rather than break up the unit." Their loyalty to each other was undimmed even in exile; they shared the same wooden barracks in the rail yard, which they proudly decorated with photographs, arms, uniforms, and a regimental flag that they had managed to bring out of Russia during the evacuation.[4] Perhaps the most extreme example of former officers reduced to the bottom of the employment pile were the White Russian dustmen of Cannes, who were notable for being "very elegant and glamorous in their military tunics." There were also many Cossack ex-officers who kept chicken farms in and around this luxury resort.[5]

By 1926 around 35,000 émigré Russians had chosen to live in Paris; by 1930 their numbers had swelled to over 43,000—though some sources claim that it was as high as 50,000.[6] Out of these, only a very small proportion of doctors, dentists, lawyers, university lecturers were able to find work in their chosen profession in Paris, because of French employment regulations and the requirement of French nationality. Some got around the rules by working exclusively for the Russian émigré colony—such as former Russian ambassador to Paris, Vasily Maklakov, who ran the Russian Emigration Office and provided a legal service for émigrés. A few Russians sat for the relevant French exams and even opted for French citizenship in order to be able to work in their professions. Inevitably, however, in those first years of the emigration a great deal of valuable Russian talent and expertise failed to find an outlet; the émigrés were largely "dumped on a glutted world market at the bottom of a postwar economic depression." While they might be welcomed and worked like donkeys in rebuilding the devastated northeastern regions of France recovering from the Great War, in Paris they frequently found themselves viewed as unwanted competitors in the job market.[7] In order not to inflame resentment, the émigrés were advised to keep their heads down and stick to their own. Although a few notable French journalists—Jean Delage, Charles Ledré, and André Beucler—supported the émigrés' struggle to live and work and wrote sympathetically about them in the French press, British and American newspapers were largely fixated on tales of the downfall and impoverishment of the aristocracy.

The first port of call for those Russians who lacked friends or contacts in the city, who spoke no French, and who were seeking employment or training in practical work was the welfare committee known as the Zemgor, located on rue du Dôme. A contraction of the Russian for "The United Committee for the Union of Zemstvos and the Union of Towns," it had originally been founded in Russia in 1915, and was reconstituted in Paris in 1921 by Prince Georgiy Lvov, former prime minister of Russia, specifically to assist Russian emigrants. At this same time, the League of Nations also stepped in, appointing Norwegian Arctic explorer Fridtjof Nansen high commissioner for refugees, with a brief to assist the many displaced Russians and persons of other nationalities in settling and finding jobs. This led in 1922 to the creation of the Nansen passport, and with it the painful official definition of the Russians in France as *apatrides*—stateless. True, the new passport provided official identification for those who had lost their passports, visas, or ID papers in their flight from Russia, but it also took away their sense of self, first and foremost, as Russians.

Another important early source of help and welfare was the Russian Red Cross—patronized by aristocrats such as Grand Duchess Maria Pavlovna—which also established a branch in Paris. The situation for the émigrés had become more pressing in 1921, when the new Soviet government issued a decree depriving anticommunist Russians living abroad of their citizenship; many Russians in Paris now feared that French recognition of the Soviet government would result in their deportation. While the Zemgor helped find jobs for four thousand of the new arrivals, sheer economic necessity meant that many émigrés—particularly from the former aristocracy—succumbed to a "drastic proletarianization" in the kind of work they were forced to accept.[8] Those for whom the Zemgor could not find work in Paris were sent into the French countryside to work in agriculture; others, to the industrial works of Normandy, or the huge Schneider & Cie steelworks at Le Creusot in eastern France, or the mines and factories of Decazeville in the south. A few were sent even farther afield to Corsica, where there had been a desperate shortage of manpower since the war.[9] The press reported with a degree of surprise and pity in articles such as "How Ruined Russians Earn a Living," fascinated in particular by the "Princess as a Cow Keeper," a reference to Count Paul Ignatieff, now running a dairy farm at Garches, with his wife, the former Princess Meshcherskaya, who rose at dawn to milk the cows.[10] A Prince Gudachev was also keeping cows at La Gironde, and other Russians were learning animal husbandry and pig breeding.[11] "Making money growing mushrooms" was the chosen pursuit of an unnamed count, and "Colonel Skouratoff" and his wife, like several other Russians, was making a go of market gardening, "growing salad greens in a small garden out at St. Germain."[12]

In Paris, itself, some of the French-speaking, well-educated former Russian aristocracy and White Russian officers managed to get jobs in banks or offices, as clerks or bookkeepers. Vladimir Troekurov, an ex-captain of the Imperial Guards and bodyguard of the former tsar, was working as a clerk in a Paris bank. Having good English was also an advantage to those seeking work as reception staff and doormen in hotels and department stores because of the large numbers of American and English tourists in the city. But for the majority of male refugees, the only recourse was to take

fairly low-grade and drab jobs such as washing dishes, waiting tables, cleaning windows, working in factories, or being a driver. The
Russian People's University, founded in Paris in 1921, tried to help
them by offering technical courses on a shoestring budget; by far the
most popular was auto mechanics for aspiring taxi drivers. At a time
when few people owned a car, taxis were in huge demand, especially
during the busy holiday seasons and when big events were running
in Paris, such as an international exposition.

Taxi driving was therefore the first choice of many Russians and
greatly to be preferred for the autonomy and independence it allowed.[13] For this reason, the Russian taxi drivers were top of the
heap—the "aristocrats of the émigré work force."[14] It also meant
they had to work in the city, which provided them with more contact with their own colony and friends.

The first Russians who took up driving cabs in Paris were former
members of the Russian Expeditionary Force sent to fight in France
in 1916 and who, because of the revolution, had never returned
home.[15] Entry rules were strict: a work and residence permit was required, plus a permit to drive, which in itself served as an important
identity paper. Most of those in the new wave of emigrants opted to
study for the "knowledge" exam at night school and learn the layout
of the Paris streets in their spare time, while holding down make-do
jobs during the day; but it was demanding for those with little or no
French. They were finally able to drive professionally when they
completed their certificate—renewable every two years—paid their
65 francs, and also passed a medical examination.[16] The Paris auto-
school course cost the considerable sum of 120 francs ($120 then;
around $1,800 in today's money)—a large amount for émigrés
to find, but various veterans' organizations in the émigré community helped organize and run training courses for Russian drivers
and also translated car manuals for them. Once they had their permits, taxi driving promised an income of $50–$80 a month (roughly

$750–1,250 today).[17] For a lucky few, taxi driving provided sufficient income for them to save and eventually move on to something better.

But first there was the matter of being taken on by one of the taxi garages. The vast majority of Russians drove for one of the big three: G7 and its red Renaults, G3 and its new blue Renaults, and the Citroën garage, which between them owned six thousand vehicles; each taxi was shared on a rotation with two other colleagues. The remainder worked for smaller companies owning between ten and two hundred taxis, or a company called Spakt with its yellow Peugeot taxis.[18] The big garages liked the Russians, who tended to be better educated, more polite, more honest, and—because they needed to hang on to their jobs—less likely to upset the clients. They didn't make aggressive demands for tips either (according to émigré writer Andrey Sedykh, elderly Englishwomen and provincial French curates were the meanest tippers). Rich women especially preferred the Russians for ferrying them around on shopping trips or to restaurants or the theater. Aware of this preference, some Russian taxi drivers even advertised their nationality by painting the Russian bear emblem on the doors of their cabs.[19] The Russian drivers quickly became noted as "ambassadors" for some of the better-known Russian cabarets and restaurants, rather like maîtres d'hôtel, by being regularly on call outside for customers.[20]

Drivers of the red Renault taxis from the G7 garage based on avenue Wagram, which had a virtual monopoly, had to pay a daily rental for the use of their taxi and buy their own petrol. On average it would take a long, tiring twelve to fourteeen hours of work each day, preferably of numerous short-duration hires, for which they could earn a better turnover of tips, to make a profit. In one of the first studies of the Russian emigration, W. Chapin Huntington related a typical story—that of General A, a former commander of the Siberian corps of the Russian army. Even though he was over seventy, the general studied for the taxi driver examination but was only able to clear 80 cents a day because his poor health prevented him from doing long hours. His wife found factory work—but for a pitiful 48 cents a day. It was their son's wage at the Renault car factory at $1.50 a day that was crucial to the family's survival. The son too had taken the taxi driver exam but was so weakened by overwork and a poor diet that he had collapsed at the wheel and had had to be hospitalized.[21]

A few drivers managed to earn enough to obtain their own vehicles and work independently of the control of the big garages. This was usually achieved by working in pairs; the men shared the same cheap hotel room, and even the same bed, on a rotation: one drove the taxi by day while the other slept and vice versa.[22] During the decade 1920–30 there were 3,000–5,000 Russians registered as taxi drivers in Paris, but no two sources agree on the precise figure.[23] So ubiquitous became the Russian cab drivers that by 1926 they had two unions (as well as several other smaller groupings based on political allegiances). The General Union of Russian Drivers (L'Union Générale des Chauffeurs Russes), created in March 1926, was the first and became by far the largest. It had probably the most highly qualified board of former imperial officials enjoyed by any trade union: a judge for president, a barrister for vice president, an examining magistrate as general secretary, a captain of the guard as assistant secretary, and a former notary and colonel as treasurers.[24] At its headquarters on rue Letellier in the 15th arrondissement, the union provided a library, canteen, hairdresser, gym, and a pharmacy selling discounted medicines; it also offered free medical and legal consultation and had a rest home fifty miles outside Paris. Within two years it had branches at Nice and Lyon and some nine hundred members.[25] The Association of Drivers and Automobile Industry Workers (L'Association des Chauffeurs et Ouvriers de l'Industrie Automobile) had about seven hundred members by 1929. Both unions established mutual-assistance funds and supported military invalids and children's charities. They also established summer vacation facilities for members. By 1928 the union even had their own newspaper, *Russkii shofer* (Russian Driver).

It did not take long for the Russian taxi driver to enter into the folklore of 1920s Paris. It became a well-known joke that the man driving your taxi might well be a Russian count, a prince, a former general—or some other once-distinguished personage; soon the taxi driver was appearing in novels, plays, and the cinema, most notably Joseph Kessel's 1927 novel *Nuits de princes,* which featured a Russian doctor, Maxim Shuvalov, who worked as a cabbie, and which was made into a film in 1930. As Anaïs Nin recalled:

> *Paris was full of White Russians who had once lived luxurious lives. It became a cliché, like the hard-luck stories of prostitutes. One knew that every taxi driver was in the past a Russian prince, who had lived in a palace and had chauffeurs of his own. They ran all the night clubs, they wore their sumptuous uniforms while performing doormen's duties. They wept and told stories so frequently that one ceased to believe in them.*[26]

But not all taxi drivers were men—one aristocratic exception to the rule was Princess Sofya Dolgorukaya, a trained physician whose medical qualifications were not recognized in France. She had had to support her family in Paris by driving taxis at night. At least she had a passion for cars, but she complained that the hours were very long and that often when waiting at the cabstand "a client would pass her by in favor of a man-driven cab."[27]

Pavel Bryunelli—a Russian despite the Italian-sounding name— very much typified the case of the well-educated émigré forced to settle for manual labor. An admirer of Pushkin, he had arrived in Paris dreaming of becoming a poet, but had been forced instead to take a succession of jobs, first in a language school and then a chicken farm at Versailles. When this enterprise failed, he headed for the automobile industry, and then for a series of factory jobs but found it hard to knuckle down under the strict hierarchical factory system and the humiliating bullying by foremen. All this while his wife worked as a secretary, his daughter sewed shirts, and his father-in-law, formerly a Russian state councillor, was reduced to "carving wooden boxes that no one would buy." Bryunelli persisted in his dream of achieving the independence of taxi driving. Finally, after being blighted by family tragedy, he gained his permit.[28]

Russian writer Gaito Gazdanov, who had fought with Wrangel's army, had a long career as a Paris taxi driver. He arrived in Paris in 1923 and had been driven by hunger to take work unloading barges at St. Denis alongside a collection of refugees and criminals recently released from jail; then he moved on to washing locomotives at the Chemins de Fer du Nord depot. It was, he recalled, "easy but unpleasant work; it was done out in the open; in the winter the water was icy cold, and after only the first hour I was usually soaked from head to foot, as if I had been caught in a heavy shower of rain."[29] Later he worked in a factory and then an office; he taught French and Russian for a while, and it was only "after the total inadequacy of these occupations" became clear to him that he took the exam testing him on his knowledge of the streets of Paris. He thereafter spent the best part of twenty-four years driving a taxi at night and writing novels and short stories during the day.

During that time, Gazdanov became acquainted with the dismal and "piercingly depressing" nighttime suburbs of Paris and their pervading stale smell of dirt and decay. Everywhere he drove during his long, lonely shifts he witnessed the most abject of the city's lowlife, the sight of whom filled him "with pity and revulsion."[30] He picked several of them up for fares regularly, including elderly gentlemen still wishing to do the Tournée des Grands Ducs around the brothels and dives of the city. Many of his late-night clients were prostitutes "all drenched in strong cheap perfume."[31] Occasionally he took pity on them, befriending in particular one lost syphilitic, alcoholic soul—a once beautiful prostitute named Jeanne Raldy—and witnessing her pitiful descent toward a lonely drug-addled death.[32]

Gazdanov's view of his Parisian home was a deeply melancholy one: he found the émigré world particularly difficult and joyless as he watched his fellow countrymen "drag around an identical and irremediable sadness everywhere"; for those driving taxis, every evening's work brought so much "human vileness."[33] One of his fellow Russian taxi drivers, a highly educated linguist who had worked in the foreign ministry before fleeing to Paris, remained, as did so many, totally alienated from the work yet seemed to have no aspirations for something better. They met at night on the taxi stand at Passy and discussed their lives, their politics, their hopes for Russia, Europe—humankind—but agreed that "the world in which we live continues to exist only in our imagination. Our individual lives are over."[34] Gazdanov became attached in particular to two such middle-aged taxi driver philosophers: Ivan Petrovich and Ivan Nikolaevich. Together the three Russians would sit in cheap bistros over a dinner costing eight francs "and argue over a state of which they were not citizens, about money they did not have, about rights they did not possess and about barricades that they would not be building." Gazdanov remained cynical about the aspirations of his two companions. They talked of a world that was "dreamy and absurd and about as far as one could get from reality." Against the odds they still nursed dreams of "an imaginary future Russia"; they "sobbed about their lives and turned more and more to drink." Paris for them was not benign; it was malevolent, the place where dreams were dashed.[35] The "dull drone of nighttime voices" at the late-night cafés that Gazdanov visited resonated with the Slavic sorrow of his

compatriots, men unable to come to terms with the "lost possibili-
ties of happiness." The answer for many was to deaden their despair
with alcohol; as one of Gazdanov's drinking companions said: "You
have to drink otherwise you can't stand it."[36]

Writer and critic Roman Gul remembered the same morose camaraderie among Russian taxi drivers and the grim conditions in
which they had to live when he first arrived in Paris. Jobless and
without means, he had been taken in by an aspiring poet friend,
Georgiy Leontiev, who had invited him to share his room in the
inappropriately named "Golden Lily Hotel." It proved to be little
more than a rooming house for Algerian street traders and Russian
taxi drivers. "The stench of the lavatories, of unmade beds, of on-
ions and garlic" hit him as soon as Gul opened the front door. Up a
narrow spiral staircase like a corkscrew, he entered a room furnished
with little more than two iron bedsteads and a mirror between them;
but it was better than being homeless.[37] While Georgiy drove his
taxi by day, Gul walked the streets of Paris or sat in the Luxembourg
Gardens, a lonely stranger, a refugee—but at least a free one. He
joined his friend in a grubby bistro for a late-night meal at the end
of his shifts. Georgiy drank a lot, and so did his taxi driver friends; in
fact, they all drank far more than they ate. Of course, not all Russian
cabbies drank themselves to death, Gul averred: "Many had a family
life, many got out of driving and became a part of French life; many
saved money and bought their own cabs. Many managed to get on
their feet." Nevertheless, Georgiy and his drinking companions—all
of them former White Russian staff officers—showed Gul the dark
side of the Russian emigration—"the world of the Russian driver
who drank himself to the bottom without ever wanting to get out
again," with no future other than taxi driving.[38]

Eventually, so many Russians coming to Paris were taking work
as taxi drivers that their French counterparts complained about the
unfair competition. In 1926 the French labor minister, Antoine Du-

rafour, banned foreigners from taking the qualifying exam, leaving in the lurch seven hundred Russian candidates who were in the middle of preparing to take it. An intervention was made requesting Russian refugees be exempted.[39] The request was granted, but this sounded the first of many warnings of the difficulties Russian émigrés would increasingly face in the French labor market in the 1930s.

In Paris of the 1920s the Russian émigrés settled in several distinct areas. Those with money such as the Yusupovs lived in upmarket Boulogne-sur-Seine, or Passy out at the 16th arrondissement. Poorer Russians opted for cheap rented accommodation in the 15th arrondissement of Vaugirard. But by the end of that decade, a very clearly demarcated Russian enclave had grown up in an industrial neighborhood at Billancourt, the southernmost tip of land just beyond the posh Bois de Boulogne, facing the river Seine.* Located only three miles from the imposing mansions of the Bois—such as that of Grand Duke Paul and Princess Paley on avenue Victor Hugo—Billancourt was grubby and run-down and very much the other side of the tracks in social terms, with none of the bucolic pleasures of the Bois. From the early 1900s it had become home to the French aviation and automobile industries and the French film industry, which set up studios there in 1922.

Working as an extra on films provided a means of income eagerly embraced by White Russians living in the area. One producer commented on being besieged by "Russian aristocrats reduced to abject poverty" and desperate for work. "I have four statuesque Russians available whenever I want them. They are all titled. One was a general and another a colonel in the Czar's Imperial Guard.

* Billancourt was annexed to Boulogne in the 1860s and from 1924 was known as Boulogne-Billancourt.

Now they are all kitchen hands in a Paris hotel." No wonder the
Russians persisted in trying to get into films: there was always the
hope that it might transform their lives. "If he turned out to be *photogénique*," mused one of the characters in Nina Berberova's *Billancourt Tales*, "his whole life would start over. He would have plenty
of money. . . . One fine day he might decide to have something tasty
to eat or buy himself new trousers."[40] Several Russian actors tried to
establish themselves in the Paris industry, but the one who proved
the most *"photogénique,"* and for a while the most successful, was
Ivan Mozzhukhin. Known to French audiences as Mosjoukine and
extremely striking, with his large, expressive, pale eyes, Mozzhukhin
had already established himself in Russian films before fleeing Yalta
in 1920, bringing with him only a few prints of the seventy films
he had already made. At Films Albatross, established by Russian
exile Iossif Ermolieff in Montreuil, in Paris's eastern suburbs, he
worked on several popular silent films in the 1920s, such as *Le Lion
des Mongols*, *La Maison du mystère*, and the biopics *Kean* and *Ca-
sanova*. Unfortunately, he made the fatal mistake in 1926 of trying
to make it in Hollywood. It was a disaster; his thick Russian accent
killed his career stone dead when talkies came in, and Mozzhukhin
returned to Paris, reduced to working as a dancer in cabaret, and
died in poverty of TB in 1939.

For those émigrés who had not been lucky enough to break into
the most sought-after work of taxi driving, a range of harsh factory
work was the only option—and the best place to find it was in the
industrial outlets at Billancourt, notably the Renault car factory. In
fact, Billancourt became so dominated by the Russian community
that they referred to it in Russian as *Biyankursk*—punning on the
name of the Russian industrial city of Kursk; and they called their
employer to whom they were indebted *Musyu Reno* or *dyadya Lui*

(Monsieur Renault, Uncle Louis). "Mr. Renault loves us," the Russian workers would say, "he understands the misfortunes visited on us Russians; he has even given money to the Russian Red Cross."[41]

Concentrated around the place Nationale and surrounding streets such as rue de Solférina, rue de Saint-Cloud, avenue Édouard-Vaillant, the Russians of Billancourt lived mainly in cheap third-rate hotels and pokey furnished rooms in what was effectively a whole miniature Russia of its own. Such was the "Russianness" of the community that many of the first émigrés in Billancourt never bothered to learn French. The population of this little town—or *gorodok*—as portrayed in a famous short story by Teffi, stubbornly refused to integrate and came to consider the central place Nationale as their own Russian national square. Here they fiercely preserved the Russian way of life: there were Russian shops—complete with their own signs in Cyrillic—three Russian clinics, three dentists, two bakers, two butchers, twenty-three Russian restaurants, as well as a host of cafés, drapers, and hairdressers. At Pyshman's grocery store you could get new Soviet Russian canned goods as well as "Moskva" toffees, *pirozhki* brought in from Filippov's famous bakery, and traditional Russian icons and painted wooden spoons.[42] Public lectures were held on Russian-interest subjects, and in 1928 Billancourt set up its own branch of the Russian People's University; a Russian secondary school was built on rue d'Auteuil the following year. Billancourt had a very active Russian cultural life and even a cabaret on rue Traversière with its own Caucasian dancers and gypsy singers, where you could see "some wild Circassian squatting dance at two in the morning" and a "double-chinned singer with a splendid bosom, in a homemade spangled dress," who sang nostalgic Russian songs such as "I Won't Talk of My Hidden Sufferings."[43] Here you could drink vodka and munch on pickled cucumber and herring or freshly made blini; for all its limitations, Billancourt was the best place in Paris to feel like being back home in Mother Russia. In 1927 the community finally got its own purpose-built Russian Orthodox church, Saint Nicolas-le-Thaumaturge on rue Point-du-Jour; before that, the priest had been obliged to hold services in a makeshift church in an abandoned garage or the back room of a restaurant, to the constant noise of popping corks, the clutter of crockery, and raucous laughter.[44]

Every day's end, you could see hundreds of Russians pouring out of the Renault factory gates at quai Point-du-Jour. You could spot one by the fact he was generally cleaner and better dressed and even wore a tie; many, as émigré writer Nina Berberova noted, still had a military bearing about them. Old habits and discipline died hard. Renault had hired considerable numbers of immigrant workers in the post–World War I years, peaking in 1924. Indeed, Renault had been sufficiently perspicacious to recruit many of his ex-military workforce while they were still stranded in refugee camps in the Dardanelles and especially at Bizerta in Tunisia; others were hired in Bulgaria and Serbia. Recruitment literature was specially printed in Russian to assist this. The French government had also found Russian workers for French farms by this same means.[45] Sometimes whole companies of former Whites were recruited as a group, and they stuck together in Billancourt; one group of Kuban Cossacks established themselves there in 1926. Loyalty to the flag and to the regiment was paramount always. An inbred sense of organization and military discipline also meant the ex-military workers were renowned for being punctual and reliable.[46] French reporter Georges Suarez, sent to Billancourt to do a story on the Russian émigrés for *Le Petit Journal*, noted also that the Russians were distinguished by "having the correct attitude." For this reason, the crime rate among them was exceptionally low. A trained eye could recognize them "by the clean cut of their face, by their energetic and loyal gaze, by their athletic shoulders." They struck Suarez as proud but courteous, reluctant to talk about their former lives. "In misery and in work they remained refined." They resisted being drawn into strikes for this same reason; the experience of oppression and dispossession in Russia, followed by flight and exile, had defused any desire to confront their employers, although their left-wing French coworkers frequently branded them as blacklegs and strikebreakers.[47] In 1923 the Renault factory was employing around six hundred Russians; by the end of 1926, at its height, the Russian workforce numbered around five thousand, of whom 30 percent lived in Billancourt. In all, about 20 percent of Russian émigrés worked for Renault and the nearby automobile plants at Citröen, Peugeot, and also the luxury automobile maker, Delage.[48] The French automotive industry became such a mainstay of the Russian emigrant community that, by the late 1920s, 34 percent of registered Russians in France were employed by it. Yet although the White Russian assembly line workers were considered hardworking and reliable, they were paid only about two dollars a day in the late 1920s, at a time when Ford workers in the United States were getting a statutory five dollars.[49] For this reason, many Russian car workers saw the assembly line at Renault as only a stopgap on the way to something better—in most cases, taxi driving.

Everywhere you went in Billancourt, there was no escaping the perpetual, distant hum of machinery; the long wail of the factory siren punctuating the stages in the working day, the "smell of machine oil wafting through the streets," along with the dust and pollution.[50] The denizens of Billancourt, ignored almost entirely in literature and in contemporary memoirs, provided fertile ground for the short stories of Russian émigré writer Nina Berberova, who herself lived at Billancourt on rue des Quatre Cheminées from 1924 until 1932. In her *Billancourt Tales,* first published in the émigré newspaper *Poslednie novosti* (Latest News) in 1928 and 1930, she remembered the overcrowded tenements, the dusty streets, the claustrophobic heat and lack of air in high summer, the sense of so many "irreparable lives" stunted by poverty, hunger, and hard work, and the pride of a shared common tragedy.

> *Many of us have breathed, sighed, and gasped here. . . . In the summer, dust swirls against the pediments of the Renault factory and the children cough; in the spring the men who are out of work go to the riverbank and there they lie for a long time, eyes closed.*

> *. . . This was life. Billancourt did not believe in tears. For a proper existence, for a place of their own in the world, people repaid the world with their labor, which smelled of sweat, garlic, and alcohol.*[51]

Berberova's vision of life at Billancourt seems a particularly negative and jaundiced one, focusing on its shabbiness and poverty, and the wretched loneliness and insularity of many of the émigrés. It is the most despairing of all portraits of émigré Russians in Paris, depicting them as "the destitute stupid, stinking, despicable, unhappy, base, deprived, harassed, hungry Russian emigration (to which I belong)."[52] Here the predominantly male Russian population of Billancourt—("A woman doesn't live in Billancourt," wrote Berberova, "she flees to Paris")—buried what talents they might have brought out of Russia with them. All that was available was grueling manual labor.[53] "I saw them at work," she recalled,

> *pouring steel into open-hearth furnaces, next to Arabs, half naked, deafened by the noise of the air hammer they handled, screwing bolts into a moving conveyor belt to the whistles of transmissions, when all around trembled and rocked and the high ceiling of the gigantic shop was not visible at all, so one*

had the illusion that everything trembled beneath the open sky, black and threatening, in the dead of night.[54]

Car workers out at Billancourt struggled to earn half of what their compatriot taxi drivers made; a few made it out and into more successful careers, such as the naval engineer Vladimir Yurkevich. Like many of the refugees, he had fought with Wrangel in Crimea; in Billancourt he worked at a lowly job as a turner at Renault, then as a draftsman at a shipyard, eventually becoming a leading designer of ocean liners in New York. But for most there was little chance of an escape from the tediously repetitive part work of the Renault assembly line, modeled on those of Henry Ford's automobile factories in the United States. Sergey Rubakhin was one of so many unremembered Russians who ended up in Billancourt. He had joined Wrangel's army at the age of eighteen and, evacuated from Crimea in 1921, had arrived in the Dardanelles with only "my rags and my lice." After some time in Bulgaria, he moved to France and worked in a locomotive factory, then as a miner, a dishwasher in a restaurant, and a docker before finding work at the Renault factory. He recalled how his job consisted of placing a single pin in a transmission cog and fixing it in place with pliers; then repeat . . . and repeat:

And there you were. That was it. I became the pin champion. Pins in the morning; pins in the afternoon; pins in the evening. I saw those pins everywhere. At times my eyes glazed over, my pace slowed; but the conveyor belt kept on moving, pitilessly. The bosses yelled at me and fined me. After six months I couldn't take any more; I gave up on the pins.[55]

Rubakhin took a job on the railway but had an accident and was laid off for six weeks. The Russian Red Cross in Paris helped him get back on his feet. They suggested he should try taxi driving. It seemed like the ideal job: no bosses, no orders, no assembly line—just him, the driver, as "sole master before God." No more orders from tyrannical gang masters and no more of the interminable political squabbles with his Russian coworkers that punctuated émigré life. A friend who ran a restaurant lent him 4,000 francs to buy a vehicle, and he was able to pay him back after a year.[56] When interviewed later in life, Rubakhin noted how his children had become thoroughly assimilated, and their children too; for them "Russia was something as distant as Gaul was to a Frenchman." But he still kept the Russian festivals and an icon burning in the corner, and his French wife had learned to bake traditional Russian *kulich* at Easter.

One of the first writers to arrive in Paris and tune into the sense of abandonment and despair shared by so many newly arrived Russians was Teffi. It came in a short, poignant story published by *Poslednie novosti* in April 1920, and was entitled in Russian "Ke Fer?"—a transliteration of the French expression *que faire?*, meaning "What to do?" The title was also an echo of a famous 1902 political pamphlet by Lenin—"Chto Delat?" and the repeated refrain of decades of debate over the accursed question plaguing Russian politics: "What is to be done?" The story told of a newly arrived former Russian general who found himself on the place de la Concorde, pondering his bleak prospects in Paris. In exile the Russians continued to ask this question, persistently and to exhaustion. Teffi was one of the first to write of her dismay at how the emigration had divided rather than united people, how hardship and uncertainty about their status had eaten away at them like a malady and eroded the grandeur of spirit once admired in them:

> We—les Russes, *as they call us*—*live the strangest of lives here, nothing like other people's. We stick together, for example, not*

*like planets, by mutual attraction, but by a force quite contrary
to the law of physics—mutual repulsion. Every* lesrusse *[sic]
hates all the others—hates them just as fervently as the others
hate him.*[57]

Que faire? became proverbial among the émigré community in
Paris, because it encapsulated their sense of hopelessness and the
Russian fatalistic attitude toward life. Teffi's first impressions of her
fellow émigrés in Paris, like those of Nina Berberova, seemed particularly depressing. She struggled like Berberova with an overwhelm-
ing negativity: "We don't believe in anything, don't expect anything,
don't want anything," she wrote in her story "Nostalgia." "We have
died. We feared a Bolshevik death—and have met our death here."[58]
She left Paris for a while, but in August 1923, after having spent
an unhappy couple of years in Berlin, she returned and found a
degree of adjustment and philosophical acceptance in the Russian
colony: "what formerly tormented, humiliated, disturbed them [the
émigrés], what seemed like a mockery of fate, they now accept as
necessary—it's a good thing, they say, that we have that at least."[59]
Teffi was in fact one of many émigrés from the cultural sphere
who arrived in Paris from Berlin in and just after 1923. Hers had
been only a brief and unsuccessful sojourn in the German capital,
but in the first years of the emigration Berlin had been the primary
objective of many, the quickest and easiest European capital to get
to, located at the crossroads of major exit routes via Finland, Poland,
and the Baltic states. As a result, it had rapidly attracted the cream
of the Russian intelligentsia and initially had assumed the mantle of
cultural capital of the Russian emigration. But all that soon changed:
for a while it had been much cheaper for émigrés to live in Berlin
than Paris, but the collapse of the German mark in 1923, followed
by stringent currency reforms and the subsequent stabilization of
the mark, had pushed up prices in Berlin, which the struggling

Russian community could not afford. Their savings vanished; many lost their jobs, and the higher cost of living forced many writers, poets, and artists to move to Paris.[60] All of this new intake flocking to Paris shared a passionate desire to protect and preserve their culture and their sense of Russianness—and the inspiration in art, music, and literature that sprang from it. This new injection of talent revitalized the émigré community of Paris, bolstering it with a sense of mission to preserve their beleaguered heritage at all costs. It would prompt French journalist Jean Delage to declare that "real Russia, civilized Russia, friend of order and liberty . . . is scattered all over the globe but all her heads, all the control levers, are in Paris."[61]

---&>··&>---

CHAPTER 8

"We Are Not in Exile, We Are on a Mission"

W hen Ivan Bunin and his partner, Vera, arrived in Paris at the end of March 1920, via Bulgaria and the Black Sea crossing from Crimea, they were bemused to find so many fellow nationals in the city. "I like Paris . . . but I've hardly seen anything here except other Russians," Vera wrote in her diary on April 4. "Only our [French] servant reminds us that we're not in Russia." Since Bunin had been a literary celebrity and still popular back home, he and Vera were invited to the Russian embassy for dinner during the Orthodox Easter celebrations.* "There were a lot of people there, all from Tolstoy's world: counts, countesses, princes—people from another life who still have not lost their place in 'society.'"[1]

Bunin at least had a literary reputation that preceded him, but he now needed to find a French publisher for his work. He also

---

*Despite the Bolshevik takeover in Russia, the old Russian embassy in Paris continued to serve as a meeting place for émigrés, with Russian ambassador (until 1924) Vasily Maklakov acting as intermediary between French bureaucrats and Russian refugees until France's formal recognition of the newly established Soviet Union in 1924.

had strong feelings about encouraging the continuing survival of non-Soviet Russian literature—the kind of writing that had been stifled since 1917. Those writers who had not departed then were now being driven out by the first manifestations of a new kind of Soviet censorship. Paris seemed to be an obvious choice as a cultural and political beacon—a city where writers could exercise their creative freedom. "People are saying that our literature now occupies a more esteemed place than ever before," noted Vera. Its survival was essential: it was "a repository for Russia." But leaving their audience behind in Russia created a new problem for the literary émigrés: they were faced with building a new but much smaller one in exile than the one they had enjoyed at home. Getting published in Paris was going to be difficult, even for someone as eminent as Bunin, who already admitted to being in a "most regrettable" situation both "materially and spiritually." The current émigré Russian press in Paris was tiny, much of it short-lived, and it paid a pittance; one émigré newspaper had already asked Bunin to write for it—but on credit. This was not at all what Bunin—a writer who had been ranked alongside Tolstoy—was used to. Here in Paris there were *so many* Russian writers, all in one place, all struggling to survive.[2]

Bunin was already longing to be able to return to Russia. Novelist Alexey Tolstoy (a distant relative of *the* Tolstoy) held similar hopes; in Paris in early 1921, he was already confidently predicting that "bolshevism will be finished by March." Like Bunin, he had been forced to flee at a time when his literary reputation was growing, and he had found the privations of émigré life intolerable, with his wife forced to support his writing by working as a seamstress. Later that year he decided Berlin might be better and decamped.[3] Bunin meanwhile seemed to be forever wallowing in his longing for the landscape of his aristocratic, landowning family in Voronezh: "Was it all so long ago—the power, the richness, the fullness of life—all that was ours, our home, Russia!" he lamented. He was one of the fortunate few to be published quite soon after arrival; in 1921 his collection of short stories, *The Gentleman from San Francisco*, was translated into French, its iconic title story would be considered the benchmark of Bunin's craft and heralded Bunin as one of the most skillful short story writers of the early twentieth century. A natural cosmopolitan, he was well received by the Paris press. But he constantly worried that his writing days were over, that he was out of touch, locked into a past that had no relevance now.[4]

As the writing community in exile took root in Paris in the early twenties, two personalities resumed their self-appointed position of preeminence from the literary salons of old St. Petersburg days. In the late summer of 1921, Dmitri Merezhkovsky and his wife, Zinaida Gippius, both now in their fifties, returned to the apartment they had acquired on rue Colonel Bonnet in the 1900s. They were amazed on their return to turn the key in the lock and find everything—"books, kitchenware, linen"—exactly as they had left it.[5] Which is just as well, as this otherworldly couple had little connection with the practicalities of everyday life. They were, without doubt, the most idiosyncratic, eccentric pair, admired in equal measure with the derision targeted at them behind their backs by their supposed friends and fellow writers. There was no mistaking the pretentiousness of "the abominable Merezhkovsky couple."[6] He was small, bearded, and thin—like a "dessicated mummy," thought the singer Vertinsky— with a bent spine that became more pronounced as he aged. He had an odd falsetto voice and a natural deathly pallor that was disconcerting, if only because his lips and gums were bright red. "There was something frightening about this. Vampire-like," thought Teffi (who herself had organized the very first émigré salon in her modest hotel room in Paris in 1920). She made fun of the fastidiously dressed Merezhkovsky and his shoes with pompoms. Writer Alexey Remizov thought him "a walking coffin" and his wife "all bones and springs—a complex mechanical apparatus" whom it was impossible to think of "as a living human being."[7] With a mass of thick red hair and green eyes ("a witch out of a German fairy tale," thought one writer), Gippius had once been a great beauty, but now was very deaf and increasingly bony and decrepit, though she had fine legs, according to Nina Berberova, and liked to show them off in short dresses.[8] She had poor eyesight and wore a signature lorgnette that she loved to raise to her eyes inquisitorially when inspecting guests, as if they were "insect[s] under the microscope"—when she wasn't dandling one of her fine cigarettes in her hand.[9] Zinaida Gippius dominated proceedings at her salon as a high priestess of art, speaking in a mannered style that was born of a wish "to astound, to impress."[10]

Leaving aside their difficult and often obscure writing, "each could have been the central character in a long psychological novel," wrote Teffi. The Merezhkovskys' "almost tragic egocentricity" was the product of an "utter detachment from everyone else" and an absorption in their own religious and metaphysical preoccupations; they had no time for the "small talk of the petit bourgeois." "They both lived in the world of ideas, and they were unable to see or in any way understand either people or life itself," wrote Teffi. Such was their level of almost childlike naivete about practical things that they "were always irritated, astonished, even sincerely outraged by the need to pay bills."[11]

Although Merezhkovsky had enjoyed considerable acclaim in Russia as a controversial decadent poet, essayist, and critic at the center of the St. Petersburg literary scene, his obscure mystical doctrines preoccupied with Nietzschean philosophy and religious messianism seemed out of place in this new émigré colony. What interest did impoverished Russians working long and exhausting days for minimum wages have for his convoluted philosophical theses and antitheses? Merezhkovsky seemed oblivious, channeling his erudition into a succession of inaccessible religious-philosophical works.

The rest of his time was spent in endless, excruciating philosophical discussions.[12] It was only in his commitment to his Russian literary roots that he *did* convey a message that resonated with émigrés. Like Bunin, he was passionate about preserving the prerevolutionary tradition of Russian literature in the diaspora: "For those of us who have lost our country Russian literature is our final homeland, everything that Russia was and that Russia will be," he said, declaring his sacred mission to ensure its survival. "Russian literature is our Holy Writ, our Bible—it is not books, but the Book, not words, but Logos. The logos of the national spirit."[13]

In artistic terms, Gippius was the greater talent, as an admired exponent of the symbolist school of poetry, but she shared her husband's apocalyptic religious visions, and her life in Paris was equally preoccupied with arcane aesthetic debate. "Art should materialize only the spiritual," she declared rather grandly.[14] Together she and Merezhkovsky encouraged a new form of Christianity that vehemently rejected Bolshevism and looked to the Second Coming of Christ. From Paris they set out systematically to undermine the despised new communist state in Russia at every opportunity. The anti-Bolshevik struggle that they envisaged was a fundamental, mystical battle between darkness and light, good and evil, and it found its focus at the influential literary-philosophical gatherings they held at their apartment on Sunday afternoons. Here the Merezhkovskys maintained strict control over what was discussed, and all papers had to be submitted for their approval prior to being read at meetings. Their salon was, however, an important forum for aspiring young Russian writers and poets—so long as their work was suitably spiritual and serious—and Gippius was at pains to encourage them to master and write in their native Russian rather than adopting French.[15]

Émigré writer Vasily Yanovsky thought Zinaida Gippius far more independent of thought and more intelligent than Merezhkovsky, who played the prophet rather too much. He was far too fond of his own voice, "an actor of genius, inspired by other people's texts—and by applause." Despite his revered status, to Yanovsky he was a grandiloquent, pretentious fraud who fell upon an idea "like a shark attracted to the scent and the convulsions of the wounded victim," who squeezed the last drop of life out of an idea until he arrived at a "sophisticated conclusion." Like Teffi, Yanovsky noted Merezhkovsky's similarity to a vampire: "As a matter of fact he looked like a bat that feeds at night on infants' blood."[16] More disturbingly, he betrayed his reactionary tendencies in an admiration for Mussolini. With the rise of Hitler, Yanovsky noted that he "fluttered toward the Nuremberg light with the fervor of a young butterfly." After all, Hitler was fighting communism, and in Merezhkovsky's view "whomsoever faced the dragon must be an archangel, or, at least, an angel. Marxism was the anti-Christ."[17]

In exile, Zinaida Gippius became great friends with Bunin, despite his showing not the least interest in the recherché intellectual preoccupations of the Green Lamp, the literary and philosophical society that she and Merezhkovsky founded in 1926. As a confirmed atheist, he had no truck with their messianic Christian message; "she has given birth to all kinds of literary junk," he told Vera. While he remained always courteous in conversation, he shied away from the kind of abstract themes that the Merezhkovskys fixated on, along with their interest in Russian symbolism, instead "stubbornly pursuing his dialogue with what lodged in his memory—oak copses, birches and skylarks." Bunin was, Yanovsky sadly concluded, "a proud dinosaur condemned to extinction."[18] Gippius too remarked on the extent to which he was living in the past, perpetually consumed by the melancholy of this "valley of tears" that was emigration.[19]

The painful reality was that Merezhkovsky, Gippius, and even Bunin might have been literary celebrities in Russia before the revolution, but in Paris nobody was interested in their work other than their own narrow émigré circles. "No one paid attention" to them, Bunin confided to his diary on January 1922; "we're just poor Russians." He was lonely, and morbid, convinced that his life was over. "Spring, nightingales, and Glotovo [the family estate]—this is all so far away and finished forever." English journalist Stephen Graham, who visited Bunin in Paris, found him "very bitter," though he "could make the most acrid remarks in the sweetest way and stab with a smile."[20]

Bunin found consolation for the loss of the old world by drinking and reminiscing with émigré aristocrats such as Grand Duke Boris at meetings of General Wrangel's White veterans in Paris.[21] As for his literary reputation abroad, he still had his admirers. One such was the young English short story writer Katherine Mansfield, who had long revered both Bunin and Chekhov as masters of their art. In January 1922 she had come to Paris to be treated by Prince Gavriil Romanov's TB doctor, Ivan Manukhin, who had been allowed to leave for Paris, thanks to Gorky's intercession, and who had set himself up offering his special TB therapy at a clinic at the Trocadero. Mansfield had been suffering from TB since 1917 and had been rather seduced by the idea of meeting, through Manukhin, émigré Russian literary celebrities in the Paris community such as Kuprin, Merezhkovsky, and especially Bunin: "To think one can speak with somebody who really *knew* Tchekhov," she enthused.[22] But the meeting with Bunin had been a disappointment: his patrician face seemed tired and drawn. He had complained bitterly of not receiving any royalties from Russia or any fees for the translation of *The Gentleman from San Francisco*, just published in English; but worst of all, Bunin had been rather dismissive of Mansfield's hero Chekhov, no doubt disappointed that she showed so little interest in his own work:

"Aha—Ah—oui, j'ai connu Tchekhov. Mais il y a longtemps, longtemps." *And then a pause. And then, graciously,* "Il a décrit des belles choses." *And that was the end of Tchek-hov.*[23]*

Dr. Manukhin's radical and painful treatment had not come cheap for Mansfield: fifteen sessions at three hundred francs each—4,500 in all. In a letter she admitted her "sneaking feeling that he is a kind of unscrupulous impostor." She endured it for three months but cut short the remainder of her treatment in October and transferred her loyalties to an another recent Russian exile—the fashionable guru George Gurdjieff, but died during therapy at his communal settlement near Fontainebleau four months later.

One of the first émigré writers to decamp from Berlin to Paris in the early 1920s had been Ilya Ehrenburg. His return to Russia after the revolution in 1917 had been unhappy. Having fallen afoul of the new government with his anti-Bolshevik journalism and barely scraping together a living, he had managed to get a much-sought-after new Soviet passport to travel abroad on "artistic assignment" as a foreign correspondent for the Soviet press.[24] Unfortunately the French—without explanation—expelled him from Paris when he returned there in March 1921, and he had settled in Berlin. But he found the city depressing and was disturbed by the "first shots of the fascists." Like fellow literary exiles Alexey Remizov and Marina Tsvetaeva, who were also in Berlin at the time, he remained aloof from German life and was quite unable to adjust; he "parted from Berlin without regret" when the authorities allowed him to return to Paris in 1925.[25]

Berlin had proved to be a place of transition, a temporary refuge for numerous Russian writers: "we are being tossed through life like snowflakes in the wind," one friend wrote to Bunin:

---

* "Ah yes, I knew Chekhov. But that was a long, long time ago. . . . He described beautiful things."

We've put in at Berlin... Why there?... I don't know. It might as well have been... Persia, Japan, or Patagonia... When the soul is dead and the body is the only concern, there's not much to get excited about... The only thing alive for me now is our literature.[26]

Alexey Tolstoy, who had transferred to Berlin from Paris in hopes of an improvement to his literary prospects, had remained restless and gloomy. "You'll see, no literature will come out of the emigration," he told Ehrenburg. "Emigration can kill any author within two or three years." Greatly depressed by his relentless life of privation, in 1923 Comrade Tolstoy (as he was derided by his erstwhile friends) crept back to the Kremlin for his thirty pieces of silver.

Alexey Remizov too was unable to adjust to life in Berlin, and in 1923 transferred to Paris. He was perhaps the most eccentric of all the émigré writers. Short and fat, with a "long inquisitive nose and lively, twinkling eyes" behind thick pebble glasses, he had enjoyed success in Russia with his quaintly archaic and very ethnic folk tales. Ehrenburg thought him "the most Russian of all Russian writers," and Berlin had never felt welcoming. It had never been part of the Russian family of cities, Remizov said, nor was it entirely foreign either—it was "the stepmother of Russian cities."[27] And so he moved to Paris with his snub-nosed doll-like wife, Serafima—who, with her rolls of fat, looked like the archetypal peasant woman. They lived in a small flat on rue Boileau in the 16th arrondissement much as they had in Berlin: often cold, often hungry, always in debt. Remizov would sit at home huddled up like a babushka in a woman's shawl, and in the process developed a hunched back from hours spent drawing at his table in this position. Like some strange little monkey, he scratched away through the night in his beautiful, elaborate old Russian script on odd, supernatural stories that no one would ever buy. He had had great difficulty getting anything published in Russia even before he left; in Paris his situation was worse, "because the émigrés did not crave to read books in peasant Russian."[28] Nevertheless, many of the Russian writers in Paris revered him and beat a path to his door, where Serafima was always ready with an enormous pot of tea and a plate of stale rolls "as hard as stone."

Vistors were struck by Remizov's weird, reclusive life, how he was locked into a strange fantasy world. "He lived on the earth, even underground, like a sorcerer or a mole, found inspiration in the roots of words and indulged in oddities rather than in involved abstractions," wrote Ehrenburg.[29] His room was piled high with books, talismans, abstract drawings, and cuckoo clocks and decorated with strange, cut-out paper chains of monsters and devils, hung alongside fish bones, seaweed, and starfish.[30] He liked to "feel at the bottom of the sea," he told a visitor. "Down there you find the light of fairyland." He spent his days creating and living out the fantasies of his mysterious society—the Great and Free Chamber of Monkeys—and talked of apes and imps and goblins (the manifestation of probably suppressed sexual fantasies, thought Nina Berberova) and clung to memories of the Russia he had left behind—treasuring the "three handfuls of Russian earth" that he kept in a box and had brought with him to Paris.[31] Some thought it was all a pretense, a fraud to win sympathy and gifts of money—that poor Remizov had had a raw deal. "He had been harmed, cheated, shortchanged" by life and was deserving of pity—it was a characteristic of what Vasily Yanovsky saw as a habit of mendacity, a mindset—the "general émigré misery." But nobody came away from meeting him without finding Remizov the most intriguing of the émigrés: a sorcerer, a mystic—an irreplaceable one-off.[32]

When Ehrenburg had arrived back in Montparnasse, he was struck by how much it had lost its provincial village atmosphere and had become the magnet of the new bohemian Paris of the Jazz Age. The streets were lined with new apartment buildings; thousands of cosmopolitan tourists now inhabited the cafés where Russian artists and revolutionaries had once congregated. But the grand dukes and their kind had, of course, vanished. The once famous Tournée des Grands Ducs was now referred to by Parisians as La Tournée des Américains, the Americans having "stepped into their patent leather shoes." As journalist Basil Woon observed: "In former days a Parisian cocotte who could attract the attention of a grand duke was a queen indeed. Now she would not deign to glance at him."[33] Many of Ehrenburg's old drinking companions had gone: Modigliani was dead; so too was Apollinaire; Rivera had gone back to Mexico; and Picasso and his Russian ballerina wife had "moved to the Right Bank and had grown cool to Montparnasse."[34] Even Soutine had moved on and, thanks to a new patron, was now living "the life of a rich derelict" in a succession of hotels in the 14th arrondissement "which he would leave, one after the other, filthy and uninhabitable." He had taken to avoiding his Russian friends, not wishing to be reminded of his previous impoverished life in Paris or his even more humble roots in Vitebsk.[35]

Even at the Rotonde, Ehrenburg's old haunt, things had changed. "It seemed the Rotonde would last forever—the unshakeable bedrock of our Paris life," recalled writer Andrey Sedykh, but then in December 1922 the proprietor Victor Libion had announced he was buying the two premises next door and extending into a bigger, new-style café with dancing, a bar, and a restaurant, offering jazz upstairs and champagne downstairs. The Russian-émigré clientele were horrified at the transformation: their favorite dark, shabby back room where before the war writers and artists and poets had read and debated till the early hours, their last drink long since drained, was now transformed. "A new, huge and uncomfortable hall appeared with marble walls" and mirrors and electric lighting, recalled Sedykh, and a long terrace was created outside, "illuminated like a circus arena." The waiters changed their black jackets for suave white smoking jackets, and "the price of a coffee doubled." The Rotonde had become bourgeois.[36] Ehrenburg and many of the other Russians decamped, some to the Select and the Napoli, Sedykh to the Chameleon, where they could carry on holding their literary gatherings and still feel that old sense of émigré solidarity in poverty.

Elsewhere, those émigrés with no interest in or little time for rarefied debates over literature sought escapist release in nostalgia—the Russia of gypsy choirs, dancing Cossacks, and balalaikas—and gravitated to the Russian cabaret-restaurants that were now opening up all over Paris. The Caveau Caucasien, set up in the heart of Pigalle in October 1922 to cater to the craze for Russian exoticism and gypsy choirs, soon became legendary, as too the Yar on la Pigalle—inspired by its namesake in Moscow where Rasputin had dined—and the Troika on rue Fontaine, these three forming a "Russian triangle," where their vibrant culture thrived.[37] The most expensive Russian cabaret—the Persian-style Kazbek—later opened on avenue de Clichy; Prince Chervachidze set up the Bistrot Russe, another very popular restaurant-cabaret on rue Fromentin, and the Shéhérazade. The latter was decked out like a sheikh's harem, inspired by Bakst's designs for the Ballets Russes, and debuted performances by jazz violinist Django Reinhardt to patrons including the visiting kings of Spain, Sweden, Norway, and Denmark.[38]

Many émigrés took great comfort in drowning their loneliness and homesickness at the Russian cabarets. It only took a brief refrain from a beloved gypsy melody to transport them back to their roots and start spending the little money they had. But the big spenders in the Russian cabarets during the 1920s were the Americans, whose dollar bought them twenty-five francs at the time. As the artist Konstantin Kazansky recalled, it was difficult to resist the Russian cabaret and its seductive ambiance and "difficult to have a good time without spending all the money that one has."[39] The Caveau Caucasien, with three separate floors of entertainment, became adept at marketing Slavic-style spectacle to pull in the tourists—Russians too, when they could afford it. Kazansky watched many a Russian recklessly spend the last of what little money they had on expensive champagne. But how could one resist the ethereal voices of Nastya Polyakova and her gypsy choir, or Nico Bouika's orchestra featuring a Romany—Nitza Codolban—on the cimbalom, or Rufat Khalilov leading fifteen Cossack dancers in a *lezginka* with daggers in their mouths, swirling and whirling to an enthralled audience of rich Americans, who threw banknotes at them. It was these cabaret stars, wrote Kazansky, who now took the place of the tsar and princes of old imperial Russia.

Any military émigré who had held on to his Cossack uniform or could play the balalaika could get work front of house, singing or dancing, or waiting tables. George Orwell's Russian friend Boris, who had come from a military family and been a captain at twenty, "talked of the war as the happiest time of his life." But in Paris he had had to work in a brush factory, as a porter at Les Halles, and then as a night watchman. He had even had to resort to scrubbing floors and dishwashing before working his way up to be a waiter. Like all Russian waiters in Paris, as Orwell quickly discovered, Boris dreamed of becoming a maître d'hôtel, of saving fifty thousand francs, so he could "set up a small, select restaurant on the Right Bank."[40] But right now all that he had of his former life, the only things the revolution had left him, were "his medals and some photographs of his old regiment; he had kept these when everything else went to the pawnshop." "Ah, but I have known what [it] is to live like a gentleman, *mon ami*," he reassured Orwell. Boris advised him to give up writing; it was "bosh" and he would never earn a living at it. But he would make a good waiter if he shaved off his mustache, he told him, and he could earn a hundred francs a day: "if ever you are out of a job, come to me."[41]

American tourists certainly enjoyed being served by real live Russians such as Boris, who remembered one particular stroke of luck he had enjoyed:

Once when I was at the Hôtel Royal an American customer sent for me before dinner and ordered twenty-four brandy cocktails. I brought them all together on a tray, in twenty-four glasses. "Now, garçon," said the customer (he was drunk), "I'll drink twelve and you'll drink twelve, and if you can walk to the door afterward you get a hundred francs." I walked to the door, and he gave me a hundred francs. And every night for six days he did the same thing; twelve brandy cocktails, then a hundred francs. A few months later I heard he had been extra-dited by the American Government—embezzlement. There is something fine, do you not think, about these Americans?[42]

The émigré waiters learned how to seduce customers with tales of their fallen glory, turning on their ex-military charm and swash-buckle, even more so if in their former lives they had been admi-rals, counts, or princes, and had once seen the tsar! The tourists lapped it up. In the clubs of Paris nothing could be more evocative of Russia than the performances of the hugely popular singer Alex-ander Vertinsky, who, having left in the evacuation to Constanti-nople, had toured in eastern Europe and Germany before working in the Montmartre cabarets, especially the Kazbek. You could also find Count Mikhail Tolstoy, a son of the famous writer, playing piano and singing Russian folk songs in a trio with Madame Nina Spiridovich (wife of General Alexander Spiridovich, the former chief of the emperor's guard) and Prince Alexey Obolensky (who had escaped Russia "with only his Stradivarius violin and a string of pearls").[43] Since all three had been tutored in music as children, it had seemed only logical to Count Mikhail that this would be the best way to support their families:

> My situation, like that of my two friends, is a mystery to no-body. I have been ruined since 1919, when I left Russia. I have seven children in school in France. I love music, so why shouldn't I attempt to live by it? The memory of my father forbids me writing—so I'm going to sing and play the piano.[44]

One of the most colorful Russian entertainments in Paris in the 1920s was the Théâtre de la Chauve-Souris (the Bat), a private after-theater revue transplanted from Moscow by larger-than-life show-man Nikita Balieff after a stint in Constantinople. It opened in Paris in December 1920 at the Théâtre Femina on the Champs-Élysées. Featuring a mix of Russian song, dance, mime, and vaudeville, per-formed in highly stylized and colorful traditional costumes, it em-ployed former actors from the Russian imperial theaters. Here was a homegrown Russian alternative to the French frivolities of the Folies Bergère (where some of the dancers from Ballets Russes performed in Madame Komarova's cancan troupe), and a poignant reminder of the kind of satirical theater Russians had known and enjoyed in Moscow and St. Petersburg before the revolution. It also employed some of the artists, such as Sergey Sudeikin,* who had worked with Ballets Russes, to design and paint its stunning sets and costumes.

For émigré dancers and singers such venues were a lifeline providing work as entertainers and hostesses—although the pressure to "stimu-late gayety—and champagne consumption" among the clientele could

---

* Unfortunately for Sudeikin, his beautiful blond wife Vera, who worked as a costume de-signer and painter for the Chauve-Souris, met Igor Stravinsky when he visited the club. He fell madly in love with her, and she became his long-term mistress until his invalid wife died in 1939 and they were able to marry.

be trying and the long night shifts were exhausting. The work was vulgar, at times degrading, but it was a living; by 1928 a hundred or so Russian restaurants and cabarets had opened in and around Montmartre, prompting French singer Henri Fursy to remark:

In truth, I was the one who felt like an emigrant, in among these Caveau Caucasiens, these Troikas, these Yars, these Moscows or these Petrograds. In a word the only Frenchman in Montmartre was me.[45]

After giving up on the Rotonde, Ilya Ehrenburg had begun patronizing the Parnasse, a new café that had opened close by, where he was delighted to find his old friend from Rotonde days, Marc Chagall, who had returned from Russia, after a stopover in Berlin, in September 1923. On his return to Russia Chagall had initially been full of enthusiasm for the revolution: "Lenin turned [Russia] upside down the way I turn my pictures," he had remarked with amusement. In September 1918 he had accepted Anatoly Lunacharsky's invitation to be a commissar of culture in Vitebsk, but his sense of fun had quickly evaporated with the imposition of new artistic constraints in Soviet Russia. The ban on abstract painting in 1922 was the final impetus for him to leave Russia a second time. Thanks to some good connections at the Kremlin, Chagall wangled a visa and, with his wife, fled back to Paris, which seemed once more a haven of grace, even though the 150 canvases he had left at La Ruche had all disappeared. But luckily he was returning to an already established reputation and the promise of lucrative commissions. Chagall soon became estranged from his old impoverished bohemian life in Montparnasse and moved out to Boulogne-sur-Seine, where he could better concentrate on his work.

By now two new stars had taken their place in the Russian artistic emigration in Paris, which had mourned the death of Bakst in 1924:

the leading avant-garde painters Mikhail Larionov and his partner, Natalya Goncharova, had taken a studio on rue Jacques Callot. Goncharova had already spent time in Paris in 1914 when she had worked on a primitivist set design and costumes for the Diaghilev opera-ballet *The Golden Cockerel,* and Larionov also designed sets for Ballets Russes during the 1920s. For a few years Goncharova took commissions as a designer for the French fashion house Maison Myrbor, producing Slavic designs favoring embroidery and appliqué work that were then so in vogue.[46] Her major work for Diaghilev came in 1923 with the folkloric designs for *Les Noces,* a new ballet scored for piano, percussion, and voices by Stravinsky. This had opened at the Théâtre Gaîté-Lyrique in June, an ensemble piece choreographed by Nijinsky's sister Bronislava, with echoes of *Rite of Spring* in its representation of a Russian wedding fable. The press had loved it as an "aesthetic revelation." Four days after the premiere on June 13, Gerald and Sara Murphy, a wealthy, influential couple from America, who were eager patrons of Diaghilev and the production, held an extravagant party on a converted barge moored in front of the Chambre des Députés that was attended by all the usual glitterati. Diaghilev was there, as was his key patron, Winnaretta Singer; Jean Cocteau; and various American celebrities, notably the Broadway composer Cole Porter and his wife, Linda, who were regular guests at "Aunt Winnie's" salons.[47] The Porters had frequently socialized with Diaghilev; indeed Linda had tried to get him to commission the score for a ballet from Cole, and had even asked Stravinsky to give him lessons in musical composition.

By 1923 Ivan and Vera Bunin (they had finally married in 1922) had begun dividing their time between Paris and Grasse in the South of France, where they rented the Villa Belvedere on a cliff in sight of the Mediterranean, only seventeen miles from the Russian émigré community at Nice. It was tatty and run-down but provided the

peace Bunin needed to get back into his writing, a place also where
he could welcome émigré friends.[48] Separation from Russia, although
painful, had not dimmed his vision, the refuge of Grasse producing
two Russian novels, *Mitya's Love* (1924) and *The Life of Arseniev,* a
semi-biographical novel written over many years, which confirmed,
as Zinaida Gippius wrote, that "Bunin is Russian in bone, flesh, and
blood; he is truly 'a writer of the *Russian* land.'"[49]

Being able to reconnect with his writing had prompted Bunin
in 1924 to deliver a lecture in Paris, "The Mission of the Russian
Emigration," in which he emphasized that the Russians in France
were "émigrés . . . not exiles . . . people who have voluntarily left
their homeland . . . [and who] could not accept the life there." He
conceded that "the word 'mission' has a lofty ring about it," "but
we've chosen this word, fully conscious of its meaning. . . . Some
of us are very tired . . . we're ready to give up the cause . . . we see
our time abroad as useless and even shameful." But now was not
the time to capitulate, for "one of the blackest and most fatal pages
of history is now being written in your annals"—the establishment
of a communist state in Russia.[50] Full of fire and brimstone, Bunin's
speech attacked the degeneracy and moral bankruptcy of Lenin and
the corrupting force of the new Soviet regime on art and literature,
which was bent on destroying their most treasured artistic traditions. But worse was to come. On October 28, 1924, France gave
formal diplomatic recognition to the Soviet Union. "I cannot think
without shuddering that a red flag will fly over the embassy," Vera
wrote the following day.[51] The sense of despair this brought was
made worse by the fact that the Western writers whom the émigrés
sought to attract to their work—for support and patronage in their
fight against the communist suppression of freedom of expression—
were largely fascinated by the new, and politically fashionable, socialist experiment in Russia and keen to champion what they saw as
its progressive policies.

Everywhere they turned, Russian émigré writers had to battle against a tide of indifference that was finding them and their work, produced on a small scale on shoestring budgets, as rooted in the past and reactionary. Nevertheless, they clung to their determination to preserve the literature of the diaspora from destruction by alien cultural pressures: "The cup of Russian literature was thrown out of Russia," wrote Zinaida Gippius, "and everything that was in it was scattered in fragments across Europe." It was their duty to retrieve the pieces. This sentiment was also voiced by Nina Berberova, who in a poem declared:

> *I say: I'm not going into exile,*
> *I don't seek out earthly paths,*
> *Not into exile, but on a mission,*
> *It's easy for me to live among people.*
> *And my life—it's almost simple—*
> *A double life, and when I'm dying*
> *In some great city I will return to my ancient home,*
> *To whose doors at times*
> *I cling, perhaps like*
> *The leaf to the branch before the storm,*
> *in order to remain whole, in order to survive.*[52]

Having spent time traveling between Paris, Berlin, Prague, and Italy, Berberova and her partner, the poet Vladislav Khodasevich, had settled in Paris for good in 1925, when their money ran out. But Paris was not at all where they had wanted to end up: "All was alien, comfortless, cold, cruel-seeming, threatening," Berberova wrote of her first impressions on arrival.[53]

They found a room with a tiny kitchen at the Pretty Hôtel on rue Amélie. They had no money at all; took walks by night after the summer heat had subsided "through the narrow and stinking streets of Montmartre," visited cheap vaudeville theaters, sat in cafés haunted by prostitutes, where Khodasevich resisted the offers of five sous to go "upstairs." Gradually they became acquainted with the émigré literary community; all their fellow writers were slightly underfed like them and "did not know fully what they would do the next day, how and where they would live, and instead sat in front of a cup of coffee on a café terrace."[54] Everything was alien; even the French Berberova heard in Paris "suddenly seemed not at all like the one taught to me in childhood" in Russia. Khodasevich—one of the finest poets of his generation—found it particularly difficult to settle; but he was now on a list of proscribed writers in Russia and they couldn't go back. "*Here* I cannot, cannot, I cannot live and write, *there* I cannot, cannot live and write," he insisted. He couldn't exist without his work; but outside of Russia, Khodasevich could not disguise his bitterness at having reached a "poetic dead-end" in Paris.[55]

The constant battle between a longing for the inspiration of Russia and the need to be free exercised everyone in the writers' colony. "Zina, what is dearer to you," Berberova had asked Gippius:

> "*Russia without freedom or freedom without Russia?*"
>   *She thought for a minute:*
>   "*Freedom without Russia,*" *she would answer,* "*and that is why I am here and not there.*"[56]

Like so many who had opted for freedom above all, Khodasevich and Berberova's life in Paris was unbearably bleak at first; they had to "divide every earned kopeck in half, share insult and injury, insomnia." They would sit on their bed late into the night and drink tea, "talking endlessly, debating," unable to decide what to do: scared of the present and unwilling to think about the future. [57] They scraped together a living writing articles for the two major anti-Soviet émigré journals, she for the most widely read daily, *Poslednie novosti,* he for the newspaper *Dni* (Days) and the traditional "thick journal" *Sovremennye zapiski* (Contemporary Notes), which also favored the work of Remizov and Gippius.

During his work for the émigré press, Khodasevich vented his frustration in often cruel and merciless criticism of the work of others. Berberova, meanwhile, struggled to hold things together; she tried doing cross-stitch needlework, earning sixty centimes an hour. But it was not enough to pay for their room, so she took a commission to inscribe messages in Christmas cards: "A thousand times I wrote 'Ah, mon doux Jésus!' for which I received ten francs." It was just sufficient for "three meals, or one pair of shoes, or four Gallimard books." Eventually they moved to a slightly better flat, acquiring two bedsteads without mattresses (they couldn't afford them) and no change of bedclothes, plus two chairs, a frying pan, and a broom. Nina's wardrobe amounted to two hand-me-down dresses. Beyond their door the Paris of the roaring twenties was in full swing, but it was totally beyond their means; expenditure on anything but necessities "left a gap in domestic arithmetic which it was impossible to fill in any way, save by actually walking through the city for weeks."[58]

Khodasevich drained her energies: he preferred the company of cats to people, having a great distrust of human relationships. In the evenings they would go and sit for hours in the Rotonde over a single *café crème*, after which he would write all night while she slept. Always, Berberova recalled, there was this terrible feeling of "constraint," of being free but not free, of living out of Russia and suffering the intellectual stagnation that went with that separation; and beyond, remorselessly, "there always stood, like a watchman of my every step, poverty."[59] This was made worse by Khodasevich's perpetual problems with his health—a nasty infectious condition, a kind of eczema that affected his skin, particularly his fingers. None of the injections and pills the doctors gave him helped. But at least he could still hold the cards well enough with his bandaged fingers for games of bridge in the basement at Le Murat, about which he was fanatical, and which he played for relatively high stakes.[60] Despite all his despondency, in Paris he produced his best poetry in his fifth collection, *European Night*, published in 1927, but it is one pervaded with the gloom of exile, of a life, as Soviet poet Nadezhda Mandelstam later wrote, "that was one of negation and non-acceptance":

> *No panther leaping in pursuit*
> *Has driven me into my Parisian garret*
> *And there's no Virgil at my shoulder.*
> *There's only Loneliness—framed in the mirror*
> *That speaks the truth.*[61]

When they were living in Prague, Berberova and Khodasevich had met probably the greatest poetic talent of the Russian emigration— Marina Tsvetaeva. She and her husband, the poet Sergey Efron (who had fought with the Whites in southern Russia), and their two children had previously lived in Berlin, before transferring to Prague and then Paris, where they moved in with Russian friends at 8 rue Bovet. The culture shock hit Tsvetaeva immediately, as she complained to a friend:

> *The quarter in which we live is horrifying, it looks like a London slum out of Dickens' time. There is an open sewer and the air is polluted by the smoke of the chimneys, not to mention the soot, and the noise of the trucks. No neighborhood to go for a nice walk, no parks. . . . Nevertheless we walk—along the canal with the dead, taint water. . . . The four of us live in one room, and I can't manage to write in peace.*[62]

Efron could not find work, and all the family had to live on was Tsvetaeva's small pension (awarded by the Czech government to Russian émigré writers), plus any money given by sympathetic friends and admirers. Everyone in the émigré community recognized her enormous talent; but they could also see how emotionally fragile Tsvetaeva was, how proud and how desperately rooted in perpetual nostalgia for her lost Russian homeland. This was repeatedly echoed in her poetry and prose. It was as though she had a duty to keep that old way of life alive: "I want to resurrect that entire world, so that all of them should not have lived in vain," she said, "so that I should not have lived in vain."[63] Vasily Yanovsky thought her "inordinately lonely, even for a poet in emigration." In Paris she seemed "one against all" and "even took pride in it."[64] She had come to the city hoping to build a wider readership, but instead had to endure intense poverty, though she was far from alone in that experience. But there was no missing the enormous irony of the fact that from Russia—"a country where her poems were needed, like bread, she had ended up in a country where nobody needed her or anyone else's poems. Even Russian people in emigration ceased to need them," Tsvetaeva said, "And that made Russian poets miserable."[65]

When one looks back over the literature of the Russian emigration in Paris it is hard not to be left with the impression of so many stunted careers, inhibited by an intense hardship that never allowed its exponents to flourish, chained as they were to menial work in order to survive. Their émigré readership was in the main too poor to buy books, and print runs for even the most celebrated writers such as Bunin never amounted to more than about 500–800 copies. So many would-be émigré poets in particular came and went with little more than a flicker of interest beyond their own very tight circuit of cafés, clubs, and literary societies. This narrow, incestuous world felt safe, but inspiration was too often starved by privation. Sophisticated Western tastes, while still admiring of the Russian greats such as Tolstoy and Dostoevsky, had moved on. It was the Berlin colony that would produce the greatest writing of the emigration: the novels of Vladimir Nabokov.

By far the most successful genre in Paris, tailored by necessity to the brevity demanded by the émigré press, was the short story, and in this regard Teffi enjoyed the largest number of weekly readers. But the short stories of the emigration were, inevitably, distillations of the grim realities of everyday life in Paris, of unremarkable people living insignificant lives. Nina Berberova proved a master at depicting "life's little tragedies," the only one of her community to produce an entire collection of stories about the uncertainties of life for ordinary Russians in the working-class suburb of Billancourt.* Teffi, who had an instinct for the tragicomic akin to Chekhov, tired of being labeled as merely a humorist; Don-Aminado also tried to keep the Russian humorous tradition alive in his short journalistic pieces, but his satires of the vulgarity of "our little émigré life" too often struck a nerve, and the laughter became painful. "Anecdotes are funny when you tell them," said Teffi. "But when you live through them it's a tragedy. And my life is one big joke—in other words, a tragedy."[66]

In the end, all roads lead back to the master of the telling moment—Ivan Bunin, who, like Teffi, wrote often of aging, solitary people in emigration. He was able to strike a chord of devastating poignancy in stories such as "In Paris," about an old and friendless Russian, his eyes with their "look of dry sorrow," whose wife had left him in Constantinople and who had "lived with a wound in his soul" ever since. In a small Russian restaurant in Passy, he had

---

* A great deal of material—memoirs and press coverage in particular—about émigré life focuses on the experiences of the former aristocracy and members of the cultural and intellectual elite. There is sadly a real shortage of documentation of how ordinary Russians fared in Paris, such as those at Billancourt.

BOULOGNE-sur-SEINE - Parc des Princes
Résidence de S. A. I.
Le Grand Duc Paul de Russie

The beautiful house near the Bois de Boulogne, bought by Grand Duke Paul, where he and his wife Olga built up an impressive collection of paintings and objets d'art. They took many of these back to Russia with them on their ill-fated return in 1913. Their son Vladimir, Prince Paley, can be seen standing on the front steps. (*Courtesy Archives Municipales de Boulogne-Billancourt*)

Grand Duke Paul and his elegantly dressed wife Countess Olga von Hohenfelsen, later Princess Paley, made Paris their permanent home from 1904. Olga returned here, widowed and impoverished in 1921, but the house had to be sold to pay off debts. (*Public domain*)

Grand Duke Kirill and his wife Grand Duchess Victoria Melita, taken in 1923. From exile in Coburg in August 1922, he declared himself to be Curator of the Russian throne. In 1924 Kirill proclaimed himself Emperor of All the Russias and moved to Brittany. (*Smith Archive/Alamy Stock Photo*)

Sergey Diaghilev (left), director of the Ballets Russes, which enjoyed enormous acclaim in Paris, particularly in the years up to World War I; seated next to him is his favorite collaborator, Igor Stravinsky, who composed the music for *The Rite of Spring* and other Diaghilev ballets. (*Album/Alamy Stock Photo*)

The Jewish émigré artist Chaim Soutine, seen here in 1927, lived in abject poverty till rescued later by a wealthy patron. He remained in Paris through the Nazi occupation, in hiding, but many of his fellow Jewish artists such as Chagall fled to the US. (*Unknown photographer, Courtesy Klüver/Martin Archive*)

Dancers in the 1913 production of Diaghilev's most controversial ballet, *The Rite of Spring*, premiered in Paris. They found it difficult to dance in the cumbersome costumes designed by Nikolay Roerich. Marie Rambert (second left) who was trained in eurythmics, was called in to help teach the dancers the complicated rhythms. (*Public domain*)

TOP LEFT: Grand Duke Nikolay Nikolaevich, better known as "Nikolasha," de facto leader of the White Russian army in exile, on board the British destroyer HMS *Marlborough*, which evacuated him and other Romanovs from Crimea in April 1919. (*Charlotte Zeepvat/ILN/ Mary Evans*)

TOP RIGHT: The French fashion designer Coco Chanel, with her then lover, the handsome and charming Grand Duke Dmitri Pavlovich. The couple enjoyed a brief affair during 1921–23, but Dmitri, who was very much down on his luck in Paris, later found a wealthy American wife. (*Public domain*)

An example of the severely overcrowded conditions in which Russian civilians and the remnants of the White Army were evacuated from Crimea in 1920—some on French and British naval vessels, but many, as in this case, on ill-equipped cargo boats. (*American National Red Cross photograph collection/LOC*)

A promotional advertisement for Grand Duchess Maria Pavlovna's fashion label Kitmir, one of several couture labels created by exiled Russians in Paris in the 1920s. Sadly, all of them suffered badly in the economic downturn in the fashion industry in the 1930s. *(Public domain)*

Grand Duchess Maria Pavlovna (left) enjoyed considerable initial success supplying Russian-style embroidery to Chanel before establishing her own label, Kitmir; she is seen here presenting one of her own evening gowns. But despite her best efforts, the business failed and she emigrated to the United States in 1928. *(Classicpicture/TopFoto)*

Many of the old Russian aristocracy arrived in Paris virtually penniless. This former princess, who sadly can't be identified, was forced to sell newspapers on the street in order to scrape a living. Note that she is wearing carpet slippers. *(IMAGNO/Austrian Archives (S)/TopFoto)*

Prince Felix Yusupov and his wife Irina (center) set up their own fashion label, Irfé, in 1924, where the beautiful Irina often modeled their designs. They are seen here promoting their perfume, of the same name, but they too ran into financial difficulties and the business folded in 1931. *(Public domain)*

Impoverished émigrés in Paris gravitated to cheap canteens to keep warm. Here a group of unemployed Russian workers huddled round a stove are seen on the front cover of the popular émigré weekly *Illustrated Russia*. (*Provided by Ghent University Library, Source: coll. La Contemporaine (Paris) 4 P 2780of*)

The celebrated Russian writer Ivan Bunin (center), despite his fame and distinguished career in Russia, suffered considerable financial hardship in exile. Seen here arriving in Stockholm in December 1933 to collect his Nobel Prize for Literature. (*Unknown photographer; Leeds Russian Archive. MS 1066/1686. Reproduced with the permission of Special Collections, Leeds University Library*)

The sumptuous interior of the popular Russian restaurant and gypsy cabaret Shéhérazade. The decor was inspired by the designs of Bakst for Ballets Russes and it was one of the popular "Russian Triangle" of venues where émigré Russian music and culture thrived. (*Roger-Viollet/TopFoto*)

The poet Marina Tsvetaeva, despite her prodigious talent, struggled to make ends meet in Paris. Worn down by poverty and literary rejection, she made the fateful decision to return to the Soviet Union, where she committed suicide in 1941. (*ITAR-TASS News Agency/Alamy Stock Photo*)

Writer Nina Berberova and her partner, poet Vladislav Khodasevich, in happier times just before they emigrated to Paris in 1925, where they endured grinding poverty for many years. Berberova achieved considerable publishing and academic success later in the United States. (*Public Domain*)

The poets Zinadia Gippius and Vladimir Merezhkovsky owned a flat in Paris, to which they fled in 1919. In exile they became leaders of the émigré literary community with their Green Lamp literary society. (*Provided by Ghent University Library, Source: coll. La Contemporaine (Paris) 4 P 2780of*)

Automobile workers, among them many Russians, leaving the huge Renault factory at Boulogne-Billancourt. The French motor industry was a major employer of émigré Russians in the 1920s and 1930s. *(Courtesy Archive A. Korliakov (France), Russian Emigration in photos, 1917–1947—Towards success—by Andreï Korliakov, YMCA-Press ed., France 2005, "VERITAS-2006" Prize)*

Russian taxi drivers became ubiquitous, if not legendary, in Paris of the 1920s and '30s. Here two Russians take a break sitting on a Renault G7, the most popular make of taxi in those decades. *(Courtesy Archive A. Korliakov (France), Russian Emigration in photos, 1917–1947—Towards success—by Andreï Korliakov, YMCA-Press ed., France 2005, "VERITAS-2006" Prize)*

Pavel Gorgulov, the Russian émigré who assassinated French president Paul Doumer on May 6, 1932, pictured here shortly after his arrest. He was guillotined at Paris's La Santé prison four months later. *(Courtesy of Bibliothèque Nationale de France)*

Prima ballerina Mathilde Kschessinska (left), a star of the imperial Russian ballet and former lover of Nicholas II, married Grand Duke Andrey in 1921 and with him settled in Paris, where she set up her own successful ballet studio in 1929. (*Roger-Viollet/TopFoto*)

Mother Maria Skobtsova (bottom right) and members of her staff at her refuge for destitute Russian émigrés at rue Lormel in Paris. During World War II she helped and sheltered French Jews but she and her son Yuri, next to her, were arrested by the Gestapo and perished in the concentration camps. (*Courtesy of Jim Forest, Fr Hildo Bos, Helene Arjakovsky*)

The funeral cortege of Russian opera singer Feodor Chaliapin pausing outside the Paris Opéra en route to his burial at the Batignolles cemetery. Chaliapin made a spectacular debut in Diaghilev's Saison Russe in Paris in 1907. After leaving Russia for good in 1921 he settled in Paris but always longed for Russia. The whole of the Russian community turned out for his funeral in April 1938. (*Courtesy Team of the site "History of Russia in Photographs"*)

found a consoling friend in a young waitress, only to collapse and die not long afterward on the Paris Métro, his words encapsulating the plight of the émigré: "Yes, from year to year, from day to day, in our heart of hearts there's only one thing we wait for—a meeting that will bring happiness and love."[67]

———✧✦✧———

CHAPTER 9

"Emperor Kirill of All the Russias"

J ust after Christmas 1923, the Paris correspondent of the London *Daily Express* broke a story that, while it left the Western press bemused, was already having repercussions within the Russian diaspora. Behind the shuttered windows of a private house in Saint-Cloud owned by his brother Boris, forty-six-year-old Grand Duke Kirill had secretly proclaimed himself "Tsar of All the Russias."* The reporting was, however, inaccurate; the *Western Mail* clarified that invitations had been sent out for a convention of monarchists held at Boris's house, at which the cabinet of a secretly formed provisional government had made a "formal and solemn declaration" that Kirill was the rightful tsar.[1]

Kirill had in fact already declared himself to be curator (*Blyustitel*) of the Russian throne the previous August. This secret ceremony in Paris appears to have been recognition of that fact, in Kirill's presence, by loyal monarchists in the émigré community, he having come to Paris from spending the winter season in Nice.[2] But

_____

* The press misreported Boris as Kirill's cousin. The house in question was probably Boris's house Sans Souci, in the Paris suburb of Bellevue, in Meudon.

it had sadly lacked any Romanov grandeur. The press dismissed it as somewhat "pathetic." "There were 10 women present, with nobles who formerly held high office in the Russian Court," reported the *Daily Express,* adding somewhat dismissively that these erstwhile aristocrats "are now working as waiters, valets, taxi drivers, waitresses, and domestics."³ So intent was Kirill on regaining the throne that he had gone as far, the press reported, as to send an agent to Moscow when he heard that the Bolsheviks were reported to be selling off the Russian crown jewels, "with the intention of securing the crown of Monomakh, prototype of all the Russian crowns, with which the Czars must be crowned by law."⁴

Why, the press wondered—six years after the revolution and the fall of the Romanov monarchy—should the Russians think it remotely possible that there could be a restoration? And what useful purpose could such an act have in a rapidly changing postwar world that had already seen several other European thrones fall? In fact, from the moment the surviving members of the Romanov family had fled Russia, there had been considerable controversy within the then largest émigré colonies of Paris, Berlin, Rome, and Constantinople about the possible restoration of the monarchy, and who was the legitimate heir to the Romanov throne. Even now, with the new regime in Russia still unstable, some White Russians nursed the idea that a restoration was the only hope for their beloved, abandoned Russia, which was now being dismantled by the virulently anti-tsarist Soviets. But was there honestly a place now, in the twentieth century, for the kind of benign despotism of the tsars; was this really the best option for Russia's anarchic and largely peasant population? Tsaritsa Alexandra had always believed in it; and so too did Kirill's wife, Victoria Melita. Like her sister-in-law,* she had always nursed great

---

* Victoria Melita was first married to Alexandra's brother Ernst, Grand Duke of Hesse and by Rhine. They divorced in 1901, much to the disapproval of the Tsaritsa Alexandra

ambitions for her family and mourned the loss of power and position. It was Victoria Melita's determination and tenacity that pushed the weaker and often vacillating Kirill into taking a stand, much as Alexandra had dominated Nicholas. Indeed, in 1917 it had been Victoria Melita who, sensing the danger, had insisted they get out of Russia fast while their relatives prevaricated, to their ultimate cost.

For much of their first years in exile, although they had an apartment in Paris, Kirill and Victoria Melita had lived mainly in Coburg at the Villa Edinburg, left to her by her mother, the former Duchess of Coburg. Thus by default they had greater support within the Berlin and Munich émigré Russian communities. It was from Coburg therefore that, on August 8, 1922, Kirill had declared himself "Curator of the Russian Throne," as the nearest surviving male relative of his first cousin, Nicholas I. The Russian law of succession was by primogeniture in the male line, and there was no disputing that technically Kirill was the rightful heir, as third in line after the tsarevich Alexey and Nicholas's brother Mikhail, both of whom most Russians now accepted had also perished in 1918. However, many émigrés, particularly those in the Supreme Monarchist Council created in exile in 1921, were hostile to Kirill's claim on moral grounds. They had not forgotten his self-serving action, as they perceived it, in March 1917, when he had rushed to declare his allegiance to the Provisional Government the day before Nicholas abdicated. To confirm this, Kirill had marched his Guards Equipage from Tsarskoe Selo to the new seat of government, the Duma, at the Tauride Palace in Petrograd. Worse, in so doing he had abandoned Tsaritsa Alexandra and her five sick children at the Alexander Palace, in breach of his solemn oath of loyalty to the sovereign. It was a precipitate act that many were never able to forgive, nor Kirill to live down.

---

in particular. Despite a degree of Romanov opposition, in 1905 she married Grand Duke Kirill.

Kirill had not, in fact, been the only candidate for the throne. Grand Duke Dmitri Pavlovich, his cousin who was fifth in line, had also been favored. While Dmitri Pavlovich himself might have fantasized about this possibility on the pages of his diary and how he would rule a modern-day Russia as an enlightened emperor, he never took the suggestion very seriously. He certainly had some devoted followers who would have championed his claim, but to pursue it would have required a level of energy and commitment that the effete, perennial playboy Dmitri patently lacked. In any event, many monarchists refused to entertain him as a candidate because of his involvement in killing Rasputin, arguing that a murderer could not sit on the throne of Russia.*

Interviewed by *Le Figaro*, Kirill insisted that in making this declaration he was "obeying the aspirations of the Russian people" to overthrow Bolshevism. "A reconstructive action must be exercised," he urged, "of which I, in virtue of my lawful rights, am designed to be the chief."[5] In an attempt to counter Kirill's claim, on July 23, 1922, the makeshift Assembly of the Land was hastily convened in the Priyamursk region near Vladivostok by General Mikhail Diterikhs of the White Army, at which Kirill's uncle, Grand Duke Nicholas Nikolaevich, was nominated, in his absence, as emperor. Popularly known as Nikolasha, the grand duke neither accepted nor refused this rather empty gesture. In any event, the Whites were routed two months later.

Not long after Kirill's August 8, 1922, declaration, the controversies over the Romanov throne had first filtered through to the Western press. In typical tabloid style, the *Daily Herald* ran a banner headline: "Nick and Cyril in Race for Crown—Each Wants to Be the New Tsar—Monarchist Plotting—White Lights Shine in

---

* Some even discussed the possibility of Grand Duke Mikhail's young son George as the "true successor"; he was now being educated in England but showed no interest in the idea. Tragically, he died in a car crash in the South of France in 1931 when he was only twenty.

Secret Meeting." The article described how a recent meeting held near Salzburg had brought together leading White Russian émigrés who sought to oust the Soviet regime in Russia and bring the country "back to Tsardom." At the meeting it was agreed that Nikolasha "would issue an appeal to the soldiers in the Red Army, admonishing them to restore the glorious days of Tsarist rule," although "considerable ill-feeling was evinced on the choice of a Tsar." But at this juncture at least, the press concluded that Nikolasha had won the "contest" to be tsar "by a nose."[6]

The difficulty remained, however, that many monarchists were still nervous about accepting any nominated successor until absolute, irrefutable evidence was provided that Nicholas II; his heir, Alexey; and his brother Grand Duke Mikhail were all dead. The practicalities of exactly how the Russian people would be encouraged to rise up against their Soviet oppressors remained extremely nebulous. Kirill realized it was foolish to envisage some kind of military intervention from outside, and Nikolasha too insisted that "the future of the structure of the Russian state" could be decided "only on Russian soil, in accordance with the aspirations of the Russian people."[7] Kirill's desire to be the latter-day savior of Russia left many unimpressed; Grand Duchess Maria Pavlovna asserted that his following was "never large as he did not succeed in finding a formula which would make him acceptable to the greater number of royalists . . . who put Russia's interests before the re-establishment of a monarch." She felt that Kirill and his supporters—known as the Legitimists—were unrealistic, that they "still clung to past traditions as the only consolation in a shattered world." Kirill was "a figurehead upon which to fasten their hopes"; equally, although Nikolasha commanded greater respect in the émigré community, his faction was, noted Maria Pavlovna, "hardly more fruitful of important results" than Kirill, for he was "surrounded by a wall of old-timers whose ideas had not broadened in the slightest," despite the revolution.[8]

In August 1924 Kirill decided that having waited six years, it was now time to proclaim himself as emperor and his son Vladimir as his heir. He composed a declaration in booklet form, "Who Shall Be the Emperor of Russia?" timed to accompany a manifesto of August 31 declaring his assumption of the title of Emperor of All the Russias. Kirill had become very concerned about events in Russia since the formal establishment of the Soviet Union in 1922. "Russia is perishing. In deep anxiety the country is waiting for its deliverance," he declared, adding that he now considered it his duty as "Eldest Member and Head of the Imperial House" and guardian of the imperial throne to urge "the reunion of all Russians—true to their Oath and loving their Country—around the same and only banner of legality, under whose protection there can be neither quarrels nor dissension."[9] In declaring all this, he was, nevertheless, deeply apprehensive about the reaction of the émigré community; "Nothing can be compared with what I shall now have to endure on this account," he told Grand Duchess Xenia, "and I know full well that I can expect no mercy from all the malicious attacks and accusations of vanity."[10]

A hostile response came shortly afterward when, from exile in Serbia, General Wrangel, former leader of the White Army, voiced his concern that Kirill's declaration would provoke conflict in monarchist circles. Wrangel refused to put the veterans of his army at Kirill's disposal, instead, on September 1, 1924, forming them into the Russian All-Military Union (the Russkii Obshchiy Voinskiy Soyuz, known by the acronym of ROVS), dedicated to purging Russia of the Bolsheviks. After consultation with fellow émigré White commanders, Wrangel urged Nikolasha, who till now had remained "obstinately in the background," to offer himself as a unifying figure.[11] The ex-military within the Paris colony were very much pro-Nikolasha; as former commander in chief of the Imperial Army, he was already viewed as the de facto leader of the Whites in emigration, especially as Kirill continued to live mainly in Coburg at that time. While Wrangel did not consider Nikolasha to be a contender for the throne—any more than Nikolasha did himself—the émigrés wished to see him take command of their forces, which in 1925, taking in the members of ROVS and other veterans in exile, amounted to around forty thousand men.[12] In response to these pleas, Nikolasha moved from his then residence in Antibes on the Côte d'Azur to the Château de Choigny, a modest and rather run-down country house forty miles south of Paris. Here he lived a quiet and somewhat reclusive country life, insisting that anyone seeking his advice or influence in émigré politics should come to him. Eventually he built a small Russian Orthodox chapel in the grounds, where a priest came from Paris to hold services and the loyal Cossacks he employed as bodyguards sang in an impromptu choir. It was not long before the grand duke's home became an unlikely focal point, with many loyal émigrés begging him to play a more visible role: "If your voice were heard Russians would forget their quarrels and unite."[13]

On September 25, 1924, with the opposing sides becoming entrenched, Sandro issued an appeal to Russians to stand with his nephew Grand Duke Kirill; upon which Dmitri Pavlovich announced that he had no political ambitions for himself. Privately the Supreme Monarchist Council, anticipating the elderly Nikolasha's demise, had asked Dmitri to be prepared to assume the leadership of the monarchist movement, and he had adamantly refused. His decision was also no doubt influenced by a stern visit he had received in Paris from Victoria Melita, who had insisted to him that Kirill was the rightful tsar. Disturbed by the vehemence of the pro-Kirill faction, Dmitri Pavlovich insisted that the law of succession should prevail, although claims to the throne on his behalf persisted. "I have made up my mind to join the party of Grand Duke Cyril," Dmitri declared. Thereafter he spent more and more time away from Paris, tripping around the South of France from one party to the next, flitting in and out of the social round of London, seeing and being seen at the polo and other swanky events. He continued to risk what money he had in high-stakes gambling, and in so doing drifting further and further away from those Russian émigrés who had seen in him the last hope of a charismatic leader who would save their country.[14]

By 1926 Dmitri really only had one remaining objective in life: to find himself an extremely wealthy wife who could sustain him in the lazy, hedonistic lifestyle to which he had become accustomed. In Biarritz he found the answer to his dreams: a rich and beautiful American heiress named Audrey Emery, whose father was a property millionaire. They married after only a two-week engagement at a ceremony in Biarritz attended by many members of the exiled Russian aristocracy; but the marriage was morganatic, thus putting paid to any claim Dmitri might have had on the Russian throne. Kirill did, however, bestow the title Princess Ilyinsky on Audrey.

The opposition to Kirill, meanwhile, intensified in October 1924, with the dowager empress Maria Feodorovna, the most revered and highest-ranking Romanov, stubbornly refusing to endorse him. From her home at Hvidøre in Denmark, she wrote an open letter to Nikolasha expressing her pain at the news. Kirill's proclamation was "premature," she declared; she would not, could not, accept that her beloved sons Nicholas and Mikhail were dead. "There is still no one who could ever extinguish in me the last ray of hope," she insisted, and indeed this remained the case till her dying day.[15] Kirill's action was also seen as a betrayal of an unspoken agreement that nobody would make a claim to the throne while the dowager was still alive; to do so would be to destroy all hope of a concerted opposition to the Bolsheviks. In reporting on the controversy, the Washington *Evening Journal* was critical of the dowager's stand: "in denying the claims of all successors, especially of Grand Duke Cyril, she talks of the divine rights of rulers as if the world were plunged back into the Middle Ages."[16]

Kirill was greatly pained by the Dowager's response; on October 11, he wrote to her from Villa Edinburg that he considered it "my sacred duty to stand at the head of a united movement to save our Country" and that he would do all in his power "to find your sons for you, if they're still alive." He was scathing in his condemnation of Nikolasha, who with his wife had been supporters of Rasputin and had, according to Kirill, contributed to his undermining of the prestige of the Romanov family.[17] Despite this, in November 1924 Nikolasha assumed supreme command of all Russian forces in exile, including those of ROVS in Serbia, on the principle that he sought to reestablish law and order in some future, democratically led Russia. He certainly had the charisma and the authority to lead, but such a military intervention was, of course, a chimera.

The reaction within the émigré community in Paris to all this claim and counterclaim was bitter and divisive. Sandro, who stuck by Kirill's claim, dismissed Dmitri and Nikolasha as having both fallen "victims to the boundless enthusiasm of their supporters" and described how the byzantine workings of the various arguments had "left unbiased observers thoroughly perplexed."[18] It was all rather laughable in Sandro's view: Soviet Russia showed not the least sign of collapsing, thus making the "three-cornered battle of the Pretenders . . . highly premature, to say the least." "They ran around; they congregated; they intrigued," and

> *true to the old Russian custom, they talked each other into a state of stupor. Ragged and pale, they flocked to the meetings of monarchists, to the stuffy and smoke-filled halls of Paris, where the relative merits of the three Grand Dukes were being discussed almost nightly by orators of prominence.*
>
> *One heard lengthy quotations from the fundamental laws of the Russian Empire confirming the inalienable rights of Cyril, recited by an elderly statesman clad in a Prince Albert*

coat and looking like an upright corpse held from behind by
a pair of invisible hands. One listened to a much-decorated
major-general shouting that the "large masses of the Russian
population" were insisting on seeing Nicholas, the former
Commander-in-Chief of the Imperial Armies, on the throne of
his ancestors. One admired a silver-tongued lawyer from Mos-
cow defending the rights of the youthful Dimitry in a manner
which would have been certain to squeeze tears out of the eyes
of a jury.[19]

In addition, as Sandro so rightly pointed out, all this was going on while Parisians sat happily enjoying a drink on the grand boulevards of Paris "utterly oblivious of the importance of electing a Czar of Russia."[20] One might add that the vast majority of hardworking émigré Russians stuck in their taxis for twelve hours a day or sweating on the assembly lines out at Billancourt had little time either for such rarefied preoccupations, and the vast majority of the influential literary community wanted no truck at all with the monarchists.

Undaunted, Kirill and his wife proceeded to play out the roles of emperor and empress with the confident and well-organized Victoria Melita effectively running proceedings as the real power behind the throne. In October 1924 she had protested their reluctance to take this "definite step" to her sister Alexandra, which "would rob us once and for all of our quiet and peace of mind," but shortly afterward her ambitions nevertheless took her on a lecture tour to the United States to promote the monarchist cause.[21] Although she and Kirill preferred Germany, where Victoria Melita had lent her enthusiastic support to Hitler in the early 1920s, they now needed to be closer to the heart of the monarchist cause in Paris. They had always loved Brittany, which they had visited for holidays, and in 1925 they bought a house at the fishing village of St. Briac, where the golf-mad Kirill could enjoy the local links. After renovations were completed, they settled there permanently from Coburg in 1927, naming the house Ker Agonid (Victoria's name in Breton) and adding an Orthodox chapel.

Here, from his ground-floor study, Emperor Kirill of All the Russias conducted a minicourt and dreamed of returning to Russia to claim his rightful inheritance. He certainly looked the part; he was tall like all the Romanov grand dukes, very handsome and dignified, and took his self-proclaimed role very seriously, though not without a degree of pomposity. Some thought the theatricals of the court at St. Briac absurd. "It isn't even theater," sniffed one Russian. "It's a puppet show."[22] But Kirill was determined; he was at his desk every day from nine to six, issuing proclamations and doling out directives, as well as dealing with voluminous amounts of incoming mail from Russian émigrés all over the world. It was, as Sandro noted, something of a challenge trying to rule over "subjects driving taxis in Paris, serving as waiters in Berlin, dancing in the picture houses on Broadway, providing atmosphere in Hollywood, unloading coal in Montevideo or dying for Good Old China in the shattered suburbs of Shanghai," and in truth, amid the comedy, he found an aching pathos in it all. Keeping the "fires of the Monarchist Idea burning" was an onerous burden, a sacred duty. "I am working for the salvation of our country," Kirill assured him. The swing of the pendulum of history might at any time turn the other way, and Kirill was teaching his son Vladimir to be ready to follow in his steps.[23]

In the meantime, the Soviets, who had spies everywhere in the émigré colony in Paris, were delighted to sit back and watch the cracks in the monarchist camp deepen as a result of the succession controversy, while hopes for the fall of the Soviet regime faded. That particular quarrel was still ongoing when, in the mid-1920s, another controversy threw the exiled Romanov family into further conflict. It came over the claims of a mysterious woman named Anna Tschaikovsky, a failed suicide fished out of the canal in Berlin in

1920, that she was Grand Duchess Anastasia, youngest daughter of Nicholas II, who by a miracle had escaped the massacre at Ekaterinburg in 1918. By April 1927 the whole of Paris was "up in arms" about her, as the monarchists took sides for and against in what became the "burning issue" of the émigré community.[24]

The dowager's stubborn longing for the miraculous reappearance of her two lost sons had shown over the years since 1917 that there was still a desperate, lingering hope, earnestly prayed for in front of the icons and at church on Sunday, that somewhere, somehow one of the murdered imperial family had survived against the odds. Such hope was endemic in the White Russian community, with rumors of sightings regularly surfacing, only for raised hopes to be smashed. Although the claimant herself remained for most of that time an invalid, living largely in Germany and Switzerland at the various homes of her indulgent supporters, the impact of her claim was felt throughout the émigré communities of Europe. In Paris various Romanovs, ex-courtiers, and former government officials fell into two camps. In February 1928 Kirill's brother Grand Duke Andrey had made a special journey from his villa at Cap d'Ail on the Riviera to meet the claimant at the Palais Hotel—an encounter arranged by another false-Anastasia supporter, the Grand Duke of Leuchtenberg. Andrey was beguiled by the "mysterious invalid" and her claims and soon after announced his "unshakeable" belief in their veracity. Kirill was furious, dismissing her as "an adventuress," and declared that his brother was being used by the Tschaikovsky camp.[25]

Nevertheless, this was a story that would run and run—and nobody then could have anticipated for exactly how long. On February 10, 1927, the *Western Mail* reported that Russian monarchists in Paris were "amazed at the revival of the story," thinking that it "had been exploded long ago." In a statement to the press, Alexander Krupensky, president of the Russian Monarchist Council, said that he thought Grand Duke Andrey had made a mistake in his positive identification. The claimant was a Polish peasant girl whose real name was Franzisca Szankowska, and her story had "absolutely no foundation."[26] The dowager empress, her daughter Olga, and Felix Yusupov all equally adamantly rejected Tschaikovsky, Yusupov going so far as to call her a "sick hysteric and a frightful playactress."[27] Before long, Grand Duke Andrey relented and withdrew his support; Tschaikovsky's disappointed supporter Mrs. W. B. Leeds—aka Princess Xenia of Russia, a daughter of Grand Duke George, murdered in 1919—whisked her protégée off to New York in hopes of a more favorable response there.*

The Paris colony would not be taken in again. When another, far less convincing claimant (real name Eugenia Smith) had the temerity to turn up there in 1936 (having immigrated to the United States in 1929), she found no supporters. Baroness Sophie Buxhoeveden, who had been a close friend of the former empress Alexandra for many years, came from Brussels to inspect the false claimant at the Paris home of the Russian diplomat Nicolas de Basily. "At last a taxi stopped before our door," recalled de Basily's daughter Lascelle:

A small foot in a high-heeled slipper descended. The baroness sighed: "That is not my Grand-Duchess," she murmured sadly. It seems that Anastasia had rather large feet and could never have worn small shoes with high heels.

The baroness, "with all the chilly hauteur of the Russian court," quickly sent the imposter packing.[28]

---

* In the face of unrelenting opposition in Europe and an excruciating case lasting thirty-seven years in the German courts, Tschaikovsky decamped for good to the United States in 1968, where she married and lived out her delusions as Anna Anderson till her death in 1984. The solitary visit that this false Anastasia made to Paris in 1928 in pursuit of her claim was later the basis for the 1956 Hollywood film starring Ingrid Bergman, the plot hinging around a tearful meeting between Anastasia and the dowager empress, at the end of which the aging Romanov accepts her as indeed her granddaughter.

No sooner had the first false Anastasia been seen off in 1928 than another scandal exploded, which caused a great deal of distress in the Paris émigré colony. This was the appearance of Felix Yusupov's attention-seeking memoir *Rasputin: His Malignant Influence and His Assassination*. Published in 1927 by the Dial Press in New York (and in French in 1929 as *La Fin de Raspoutine*), Yusupov's book recounted his part in the murder of Nicholas and Alexandra's spiritual guru and healer, and was no doubt prompted by financial pressures. The Yusupov fashion house Irfé was running into difficulties, and the proceeds of the sale of the family jewels were practically extinguished. Unfortunately, Yusupov took no account of the outraged feelings of Rasputin's daughter Maria, now eking out a living as a cabaret dancer in Montmartre, who sued him in the Paris courts for damages of $800,000 and dragged Yusupov's co-conspirator, Dmitri Pavlovich, into the proceedings. Dmitri was appalled; he had long since broken off his friendship with Yusupov, telling him in 1920 that the murder would "always remain for me as a dark stain on my conscience . . . I consider that a murder is a murder and always will be." He insisted that he never wished to talk about it and that in terms of their old friendship, "an abyss now separates us."[29] Yusupov paid a heavy price; as he himself admitted in his later memoir, *En exil,* the book's appearance raised part of the Paris colony against him and unleashed an "avalanche of insulting letters and even threats—most of them anonymous."[30]*

In his memoirs, the singer Alexander Vertinsky observed that the Paris community largely lived in groups by profession and that

---

* Maria Rasputin's claim was dismissed, but in retaliation she published *My Father* in 1934. The case aroused sufficient interest in the story for Hollywood to film a very loose version of Yusupov's book as *Rasputin and the Empress,* upon which Yusupov took M-G-M to court for defaming his wife, Irina, in its portrayal of her. In the ensuing high-profile court case in London, Yusupov was awarded £25,000—equivalent to £1.8 million ($2.5 million) now—and never had to worry about money again.

there was "no common Russian center in the city." All attempts to organize clubs that would unite these disparate elements of the emigration "failed at the very start." The reason for this, Vertinsky added, was the "diversity of political convictions. All circles hated each other, taking advantage of every opportunity to settle personal scores." Indeed, through all the adversities of exile and the sheer grind of earning a living, "the only place where Russian émigrés converged, regardless of their political convictions was the Russian church on rue Daru."[31] On Sundays, the Alexander Nevsky Cathedral, not far from the Champs-Élysées, became the hub of the émigré community. It operated as a "discreet forum" for the exchange of anecdotes, gossip, letters, and even for doing business, all of which happened both inside—in whispers—and outside the church during divine service.[32] To cater to the growing need of the community, another thirty small local churches were built in the Paris suburbs during the 1920s, gradually taking the place of hastily improvised churches in garages, sheds, or cellars created by émigrés at their own expense and in their spare time. But the Alexander Nevsky Cathedral remained the focal point. On weekdays it was the venue for funerals, memorial services, prayers, weddings, and christenings, but the real life of the Russian community hummed on Sunday mornings when the colony turned out in force for the divine liturgy.[33]

For many lonely émigrés suffering the loss of the homeland the church was an important cultural link to Russia, to their national traditions, and to Russian history itself. Their religion also created a protective barrier from French life that many did not wish to breach. They felt safe within their own observant religious community, and many of the older generation had no wish to integrate.[34] The cathedral on rue Daru was the hub of their social life, "the heart of Russia-out-of-Russia," so much so that even those émigrés who had despised the old tsarist system and the church in Russia as instruments of oppression and reaction now found solace and succor in the church in exile and became regular worshippers. The Orthodox service, the magnificent choral music, the incense, the icons in flickering candlelight—all created "an atmosphere reminiscent of home" and contributed to a resurgence of faith among Russian émigrés. Even Zinaida Gippius admitted to the spiritual uplift she received there; she loved the Alexander Nevsky's "dark spaciousness and its pious and pensive atmosphere."[35]

At Easter the cathedral would be bursting at the seams; the whole émigré community turned out for the late-night vigil, converging on rue Daru in a "hushed, exalted throng." All the surrounding roads were parked bumper to bumper with the vehicles of Russian taxi drivers. Seventeen-year-old Lesley Blanch (later a distinguished author and traveler) remembered being ushered inside to watch this profoundly moving service on her first visit to Paris in 1921. Within the cathedral, all was "dark, anguished, still, as priests and people alike await[ed] the moment when Christ is risen." She inched her way forward to leave her lighted candle "before one of the loveliest, oldest of the miraculous ikons." Just before midnight, the "church doors swung open and in a flood of color and candlelight the glittering procession emerged to circle the building three times"—a ritual that was an "expression of the hesitation, the doubts of the Disciples, finding Christ vanished from the Sepulcher." She remembered the night air smelling damp and fresh, "the scent of the early lilac in the courtyard overcoming the wafts of incense that floated from the church along with snatches of muffled chanting." Outside, the long tapers carried by the priests

sparkled on the sumptuous brocaded vestments and the diamond-studded crowns of the Metropolitan and high clergy. Gold-coped priests and acolytes swung censers and carried the banners and ikons, all glowing out from the darkness. At last with measured tread, grave in their joy, they re-entered the church, there to announce to the waiting throng that Christ was Risen. We heard a sudden burst of singing, rapturous music, and the bells rang out overhead.

The words "*Kristos voskres — Voistinu voskres!*" ("Christ is risen — In truth He is risen") united the congregation in joy as, with one great cry, they crossed themselves, prostrated themselves on the ground, hugged and kissed each other with the triple kisses of the Trinity, and even embraced passing strangers.[36] After the service, émigrés would go off to eat an enormous celebratory Easter breakfast. Even on ordinary Sundays, there was an incredible vibrancy to the area after the church service finished, as crowds of people, all babbling in Russian, poured out of the church and into the nearby Russian cafés and pastry shops or stopped at the myriad of little stalls set up in the churchyard offering favorite Russian *zakuski*. Old friends — and even relatives — separated in the chaotic flight from Russia often rediscovered each other at rue Daru; others would sit for hours after service over coffee or vodka reading the Russian newspapers and reminiscing about the old days. Noticeboards close to the church offered jobs to newly arrived Russian émigrés and advertisements for jobs wanted by others, not to mention announcements of births, weddings, and funerals in the colony.[37]

Yet, even here in Paris, the Russian Orthodox Church was fraught with conflict in the 1920s, with Russian Paris becoming an "ecclesiastical battleground" after the break between the Moscow patriarchate and Russian parishes abroad.[38] After the revolution, in 1918 the synod of the Russian Orthodox Church in Russia had been dissolved and the ancient patriarchate in Moscow was restored; but because of the continuing persecution of the church by the Bolsheviks, the new patriarch, Tikhon, granted autonomy to the émigré dioceses for as long as that situation prevailed. Bishop Evlogii in Berlin was appointed head of the Provisional Administration of the

Russian Parishes in Western Europe in 1921, while in Serbia émigré Orthodox bishops founded the "Karlovtsy Synod," or Russian Orthodox Church Abroad. These factions inevitably undermined the unity of the Russian Orthodox Church. Evlogii moved his headquarters from Berlin to Paris in 1923 as Metropolitan of Western Europe, and Metropolitan Anthony remained in Serbia as Metropolitan of the Church Abroad. Thereafter, as the church within the newly formed USSR slipped further under Soviet control, frequent rejoinders were issued to Evlogii not to publicly express hostility toward the Soviet state, as church members within Russia were already being subjected to considerable intimidation and persecution.[39] In 1928 Evlogii broke off any communications with Moscow, and in 1931 he split from the other émigré factions by placing the Western parishes under the authority of Constantinople, thus provoking further conflict within the diaspora, with three ecclesiastical jurisdictions now competing for the loyalty of the Orthodox faithful in exile. Nevertheless, ultimately, whatever their religious or political loyalties, for most émigré Russians the Church remained an important emblem, a spiritual home. Orthodoxy and opposition to the Soviets were "essential components of genuine Russian patriotism" and the cornerstone of émigré life, and the Russians in Paris were at least united in this.[40]

Another aspect of émigré life fostered by the church was the shared aspiration to look after their own poor, sick, and elderly in the community. In the mid-1920s an unlikely benefactor stepped forward to fund the establishment of a home for elderly Russian émigrés out at Sainte-Geneviève-des-Bois, fifteen miles south of Paris. It came about thanks to the friendship of émigré philanthropist Princess Vera Meshcherskaya, a director of the Russian Red Cross, with an Anglo-American heiress and racehorse owner, Dorothy Paget. Dorothy was the daughter of Lord Queensborough and his wealthy American wife, Pauline Payne Whitney, who when she died in 1916 left Dorothy a $2 million fortune (in the region of $50 million today). Something of a rebel and having been expelled from numerous schools in England, Dorothy was sent to a finishing school at Auteuil in Paris that had been set up by Princess Meshcherskaya, who had fled Russia in 1917. Vera was Dorothy's tutor and formed a lasting bond with her. She was already active in charity work, running a workshop where émigré women were taught needlework that was then sold in the shop. Through Vera, Dorothy became closely involved with the Russian émigrés in Paris and regularly donated large sums for welfare among them.

In 1926 Dorothy purchased an eighteenth-century farm, the Château de la Cossonnerie, for Vera and her sister Elena Orlova to convert into a "house of retreat" for elderly émigrés. It cost four hundred thousand francs, and Dorothy insisted on remaining anonymous and not being named in any official documents.* The establishment became known as La Maison Russe; a Russian landscaped its gardens and it had an Orthodox chapel built in Novgorod style on the grounds. It originally accommodated indigent members of the Russian nobility, but admission was quickly extended to all.[41] With the addition of several chalets on the grounds, it housed around two hundred residents, their soup "cooked by two former generals, the potatoes peeled by the widow of a famous statesman." Dinner in the evening was "taken with all the elegance of Petersburg society" of prerevolutionary days. Dorothy Paget even ensured that the residents were served with turkey and plum pudding at Christmastime. "Those of us who are here are so much more fortunate than the young," remarked one contented resident. "At least we can keep our memories unspoiled, but *they* have to face a changed world."[42]

---

* Three wealthy American ladies—Mrs. Rodman, Whitehouse, and Loomis—later financed the construction of an annex to the Maison Russe with far less discretion than Dorothy Paget, naming it the Los Angeles Lodge. The Maison Russe was known in English as "The Russian Home for Aged and Disabled Refugees."

When Russian ambassador Vasily Maklakov had been relieved of his duties in Paris in 1924 with France's recognition of the new Soviet Union, he donated all the embassy furniture, including Romanov portraits and other imperial memorabilia, to the Maison Russe. And so the dining room there boasted portraits of Alexander II and Nicholas II, while the salon "where samovars gently burbled . . . for countless servings of tea" was dominated by a portrait of the dowager empress. It all exuded an old-world, prerevolutionary Russian charm, where refined etiquette prevailed and gave it "the atmosphere of a dacha at Tsarskoe Selo."[43] French journalist Jean Delage could not help noticing that there was no discrimination in how the rooms were allotted: a chambermaid was as comfortably accommodated as a lady-in-waiting from the Romanov court. The same applied in the growing and preparation of food. You would find a professor cultivating the garden, an elderly mining engineer working at carpentry, and a prince serving the tea. In his book *La Russie en exil*, Delage noted the names of some of the residents: Count Nieroth, deputy minister of the court; Princess Galitzin, widow of the grand huntsman of the imperial court; Admiral Kolchak's widow, Anna; Baron Knorring, a former general of division; Prince Gagarin, master of the imperial court. When he visited some of the residents' rooms, Delage was moved by the few precious mementos that they had been able to bring with them on fleeing Russia: one or two favorite books, a decorated box, a framed photograph—the sum of a life now past, and forever lost. Everywhere he went, he encountered calm and smiling old faces, but "on which so many miseries had left their mark."[44]

One of the most distinguished residents of the Maison Russe had been the senior lady of the imperial court, Princess Elizaveta Naryshkina, the tsaritsa's Mistress of the Robes. When she died at the Maison Russe in 1928, she was buried in the nearby cemetery.[45] But calls were by now growing that deceased residents of the Maison

Russe, as well as others in the émigré community, should have their own Russian Orthodox burial ground. Further money was quietly donated by Dorothy Paget to buy land from the existing cemetery to create one, and other benefactors later paid for a chapel to be erected there in the 1930s.[46]

There is no greater pervading sense of Orthodoxy in exile than at the now famous Russian cemetery at Sainte-Geneviève-des-Bois, which today contains the graves of more than ten thousand émigré Russians, including Ivan Bunin, several Romanovs, Prince Yusupov and his wife, Dmitri Merezhkovsky and Zinaida Gippius, and Princess Vera Meshcherskaya. Together with the Maison Russe and its chapel, the complex at Sainte-Geneviève effectively became a whole Russian religious center—a "mini Zagorsk" (after the famous religious center in Russia) that remains a place of pilgrimage today for those wishing to see the last resting place of the many famous Russians buried there (most notably, the ballet dancer Rudolf Nureyev). The presence of the Orthodox Church in Paris also encouraged the establishment of the St. Sergius Theological Institute, where leading theologian and philosopher Father Sergey Bulgakov surrounded himself with émigré scholars and intellectuals such as the historian Georges Florovsky and philosopher Nikolay Berdyaev, both of whom had been deported from Russia as "undesirables" by Lenin in 1922.

The Russian Orthodox Church in Paris became involved in numerous important community projects. Youth groups, schools, and church centers, as well as much-needed charitable and philanthropic groups targeting those most in need of financial and practical assistance, sprung up everywhere, supplementing the help already offered by the International Red Cross, the League of Nations, and the YMCA. Grand Duchess Maria Pavlovna recalled how she would spend "hours sitting on committees, visiting organizations, planning charity performances, selling tickets, begging for money":

Around myself I saw nothing but need, such need and sorrow
as to make one's blood freeze. It was beyond human power
and ingenuity to come to the aid of all who required it, and this
helplessness often drove me to despair.[47]

Sadly, the same old "class suspicion and distrust" that had preceded the revolution, and which the flight into exile had still not
effaced, often thwarted her best efforts. The "naïve enmity of progressive intellectuals toward the former aristocrats, based upon old
prejudices and preconceived ideas, made it almost impossible to
work together." Even here in exile in Paris people grouped along
the old political lines, and even though they were equally virulently
anti-Soviet, they still found it "almost impossible to work together."

There was good reason for so much philanthropic activity in
the colony: there was a worrying incidence of ill health among the
émigrés, many of whom were ex-military men between the ages of
eighteen and forty. This group in particular suffered a high mortality
rate, debilitated in many cases by years of fighting with the Whites
and enduring battle wounds, disease, and malnutrition. In response
to such needs, several of the Romanovs and other former aristocrats
contributed to charitable causes, among them Countess Shuvalova
(Shouvaloff), who founded the Hôpital Franco-Russe at Villejuif
in 1922, which developed into a fine surgical hospital with modern
equipment, and Mariya Maklakova (sister of the ambassador), who
did much relief work at the embassy among poor émigrés.[48] American reporter Kenneth Roberts recorded her devotion in 1921: "The
first time that I walked into the embassy a long line of [refugees] was
waiting to see her. A young woman had just collapsed from hunger.
Every woman who was waiting wore mourning, and not one of them
had enough money to buy food for herself or her children on the
following day." A committee run by Mariya sent men to a school in
Paris where they could train to be electricians and mechanics; in the

same school women learned "dentistry, photographic retouching and weaving." She also helped found the Paris Russian Lycée on rue Docteur-Blanche in the 16th arrondissement for two hundred boys and girls.[49]

Grand Duchess Vladimir's daughter Elena was another important philanthropist; she used the money raised from the diamonds she had inherited from her mother to rent a château in the Paris suburbs at Saint-Germain-en-Laye, where she set up an orphanage known as Le Pecq. It was her way, she said, of memorializing her mother. Princess Paley's eldest daughter, Irina, established the Brunoy school at the Château de Quincy for young Russian girls from destitute families, which she and her wealthy second husband financed.[50] This was an offshoot of one of the largest and most influential organizations of White Russians in Paris, if not in Europe—Le Comité de Secours des Émigrés Russes (Committee to Aid Russian Émigrés), which was founded by Irina's mother in 1925 and taken over by Irina after her death in 1929. The committee held a considerable database of the Russian diaspora in France—effectively a census of all the Russians who had fled the Bolsheviks. Knowing that its files contained much useful information on potential anti-Soviet activists abroad, the Soviet secret police—the OGPU, which had succeeded the Cheka in 1922—tried to infiltrate it many times; sympathetic Russians within Russia with links to the émigré communities were also watched for displays of anti-Soviet sentiment.[51] By the beginning of the 1930s, with the Whites now better organized as an expatriate political force, such had been the growth of their subversive activities that the Soviets began plotting countermeasures and took their first steps to silence them.

CHAPTER 10

"Ubiquitous Intriguers," Spies, and Assassins

B ritish secret service agent Oswald Rayner was no stranger to the byzantine workings of the Okhrana—the former tsarist secret police—or its Bolshevik successors the Cheka and, from 1922, the OGPU. He had had firsthand experience of Russia, having been implicated in the plot to remove Rasputin that had culminated in his murder in December 1916. But trying to work out the machinations of the various Russian émigré political groupings now vying with each other in Paris was proving to be quite a problem. With his specialist knowledge of Russia, it was Rayner who had been called on to vet an intelligence report entitled "Proposed monarchist coup against Soviet Russia" received at the British Foreign Office on June 28, 1923. Rayner was only too familiar with the culture of intrigue and denunciation within the various White groups and advised that "All that can be gleaned from the conflicting stories recounted in this paper, is that dissension is everywhere rife among the Russian émigrés."[1]

In describing the three major Paris groupings behind Nikolasha, Grand Duke Kirill, and Grand Duke Dmitri, as well as the various rival republican groups, Rayner outlined the mass of inconsistencies:

> *Some are desirous of securing foreign aid, others eschew such intervention. Some are pro-German, others spurn all contact with the Germans whom they regard as responsible for Russia's fate. Some are willing to respect the Polish frontiers as at present constituted,* others wish to extend them; others again wish to reduce them. To all this must be added the significant information that the remnants of the Wrangel forces are disorganized and unreliable.*

"The general impression given by a perusal of these documents,"Rayner went on, "is that the paper wars discussed in them are examples of the wish being father to the thought." In summary, he could suggest only that "it is probable that the Bolsheviks themselves, through their intelligence service, are the greatest authorities on the progress of movements of this kind."[2] Never a truer word was said: dissension, as the Soviets knew only too well, was a breeding ground for leaks and a facilitator of infiltration, which they were now busy achieving across the Russian diaspora. Bolstered by the official recognition given it by Britain, France, and Germany, the Soviet government in Moscow had been emboldened to intensify its monitoring of the machinations of the Russian émigrés, particularly those "ubiquitous intriguers"—the Whites. Even the French looked upon them as troublemakers obsessed with petty intrigues. Their base in Paris was considered to be the hotbed of anti-Bolshevism, and the Soviets had moles watching their every move.[3] Indeed, Soviet subterfuge went further: plans were now being discussed in

---

* The recent Polish-Soviet war of 1919–20 was a dispute over the borders of Ukraine and Belarus and rumbled on until after World War II.

Moscow to attempt the kidnap and return to Russia of key military and political figures in the emigration, such as Nikolasha, the head of the Russian army in exile. For nothing would better suit the Soviet propaganda machine than a big show trial of a member of the hated former aristocracy.[4]

In 1924, after Wrangel had persuaded him to assume command of the White forces in exile, Nikolasha and his cohorts had taken over much of the movement's administration through ROVS at its headquarters in Paris. Members paid a small subscription, which kept them in touch with fellow exiles, and links were maintained with White military groups dispersed across Europe. Together the Whites were the only group likely to pose any kind of threat to the Soviet Union, and while they may have lacked unity of politics or doctrine, they had at least saved the old Imperial Army from disintegration in exile, and within their cadres there remained a core of experienced, proactive officers ready to be called on.

In response to this, the Soviets had been busy creating their own group of provocateurs to infiltrate and spy on them in Europe. After the Russian Civil War came to an end, and with it also the Russo-Polish conflict, in 1924 the OGPU set up a counterintelligence unit, known as the Trust, a group of operatives posing as promonarchists, whose objective was to infiltrate and encourage émigré groups seeking the overthrow of the Soviet regime. One of the Trust's objectives was to win the confidence of key figures and lure them back to the Soviet Union and there arrest and interrogate them. Under cover of their new embassy in Paris, in a grand mansion named the Hôtel d'Estrées, the Trust set up a network of agents in France. Some worked as cultural and commercial officials from out of the Paris embassy, the consulate, and the new Soviet trade delegation; others, posing as journalists, businessmen, and artists, moved covertly within the Paris émigré community. Reports from agents on military matters were collated and assessed within the trade delegation;

at the embassy, second secretary Lev Borisovich Helfand clandestinely headed OGPU operations to infiltrate ROVS and organize agents to take them out.

A clever program of provocation by the OGPU to dupe the Whites in Paris was now set up by a man named Alexander Yakushev, a former civil servant in the tsarist Ministry of Communications, who contacted the monarchists in Paris and Berlin, the objective being to convince them and Nikolasha of the existence inside the Soviet Union of a powerful (but in fact mythical) resistance movement that wished to collaborate with them. This bogus "Monarchist Union of Central Russia," was supposedly bent on overthrowing the new Soviet state. The members of ROVS in exile would thus be lured into believing that a collaboration between the two groups could orchestrate the downfall of the Soviet state; to achieve this, ROVS in Paris would need to hold covert meetings with activists from Russia. But first the Monarchist Union required financial assistance as well as details of existing White networks — names, addresses — so that they could work with them.[5]

With Nikolasha's sanction, General Alexander Kutepov, formerly Wrangel's second in command, moved from Serbia in 1924 to help create an anti-Bolshevik underground in Paris; he did so even though Wrangel opposed the idea.[6] As a military man, the iron-willed Kutepov was formidable: strong, energetic, and determined. His strict disciplinary principles had held the evacuated White army together at Gallipoli and on the island of Lemnos, when his men had been detained, stripped of their weapons, and left on starvation rations after the evacuation from Russia. But he was primarily a combat officer and inexperienced in the subtleties and double-dealing of spying. Nevertheless, Kutepov set about recruiting and running his own intelligence section at ROVS headquarters in Paris, code-named "The Inner Line," a fighting group of two dozen or so people, dedicated to fostering anti-Bolshevik activities inside Russia. Kutepov began liaising via coded messages with the Trust, little knowing they were OGPU agents, and was rapidly sucked into their lie.[7]

Such subversive action was dangerous and risked acts of retaliation; Nikolasha was the Kremlin's ultimate target, either for assassination in France or for kidnap and interrogation back in the Soviet Union, although Soviet spies in Paris were always on the lookout for other vulnerable targets in the White Russian community. Intelligence within Russia had revealed that of all the Romanovs now in exile, Nikolasha was the one whose popularity had not waned and who still enjoyed some support among surviving monarchist groups.[8] Security measures at Nikolasha's home at Choigny had to be increased, with help from the French secret service. Kutepov took personal responsibility for maintaining a high level of vigilance among the grand duke's Cossack guard there, who were constantly patrolling the grounds.

Soon even Grand Duke Dmitri was drawn into the intrigue, for the Trust saw him as the key to getting close to Nikolasha at Choigny. With Lenin sidelined increasingly by severe physical decline triggering a series of strokes (the underlying cause not officially admitted to being neurosyphilis of the brain), in the final two years of his government (1922–24), Stalin was angling to take over. But Stalin became jittery that Nikolasha might be able to spark sufficient anti-Soviet support for a restoration of the monarchy. Nikolasha, for his part, hoped that a counterrevolution could be triggered in Moscow by buying the loyalty of the military and bureaucracy, backed up by strikes in major industrial centers. It was his hope that the assassination of "prominent leaders of the Soviet regime" would start a domino effect across other major cities; the peasants would then rise up, and Nikolasha's White army would enter Russia from the Polish borders to wrest control. But first the Russians had to liberate themselves; the Whites would only move in afterward, to consolidate the new order.[9]

With the Soviet Union undergoing a period of economic renewal under Lenin's New Economic Policy of 1922–24, which had relaxed state controls of industry and agriculture (and which the Trust claimed as evidence of their successful undercover work), it was suggested that now might be the only opportunity for a seizure of power; the Russian people once more sensed the possibility of freedom from the draconian controls brought in by the Bolsheviks. Such dreams of rediscovered liberty had to be nipped in the bud by the OGPU, who proceeded to round up and suppress monarchist and anti-Bolshevik groups inside Russia. For even the stubbornly hostile peasantry who had resisted Bolshevik domination from the start were talking of Nikolasha returning as tsar and still had a lingering respect for him, especially former soldiers.[10]

Recent research in Russian archives has revealed that the rather grand schemes projected against ROVS by the Trust boiled down to several small-scale penetration operations. Nevertheless Kutepov was sufficiently convinced by the Trust that a vigorous terrorist campaign would so destabilize the Soviet system that the people in Russia would rise up that he began sending agents into the Soviet Union, with funding provided by Nikolasha. These agents included Kutepov's own niece, Maria Zakharchenko-Schultz, and her husband, who in 1925 helped smuggle British agent and anti-Bolshevik agitator Sidney Reilly back into Russia, where, instead of working underground with the Trust as he had expected, he was arrested, interrogated, and executed. Reilly's capture would be the Trust's biggest coup, but with his killing the whole bogus edifice of the Trust was essentially blown. It was a while before the full extent of how the Whites had been duped filtered through, but by the time it did the seeds of distrust had already been sown. After the debacle of the Reilly arrest and murder in Russia, Wrangel became increasingly suspicious of the Trust, but Kutepov nevertheless kept faith with it. He remained convinced that a well of sympathy still existed inside Rus-

sia for the anti-Bolshevik cause and took energetic steps to rebuild
confidence in ROVS, determined to step up terrorist operations inside Russia. In June 1927 three of his agents succeeded in throwing
two bombs into a history seminar being held at the Central Party
Club in Leningrad, seriously injuring thirty-five people, and managed to escape back to Finland. But three other agents on a mission
to blow up the headquarters of the OGPU in Moscow were caught
when their bomb failed to detonate, and were summarily executed;
these included Kutepov's niece, Maria.[11]

With Kutepov cranking up his anti-Soviet activities, it was inevitable that the OGPU would retaliate with a spate of arrests in Russia; several ROVS agents, often disguised as peasants, were caught
by patrols when trying to enter via the Polish-Russian border and
taken to Moscow, interrogated, and shot. Years later, a defecting
Soviet diplomat, Gregori Bessedovski, reported that Kutepov's
activities were far from clandestine and had been "as clearly visible to us [the Soviets] as if we were watching them under a glass
bell."[12] But, like it or not, by the end of the 1920s Kutepov had
become the unchallenged—though far from universally liked—
head of ROVS and White anti-Soviet operations and was even now
plotting to assassinate Stalin and other OGPU leaders in Moscow.
It was inevitable that the OGPU, having failed through the Trust
so far to persuade Kutepov to visit the Soviet Union, where they
could seize him, would target him in Paris. As Sidney Reilly had
prophesied: "there are two or three people during whose lifetime
the Bolsheviki will never sleep in peace. General Kutyepov is one
of them."[13]

In April 1928 General Wrangel had died in Brussels after a long
illness, and less than a year later Nikolasha followed him. The grand
duke's death on January 5, 1929, in Antibes, at the age of seventy-
two, had been a huge blow, not just to the members of ROVS but
also the Romanov family, for only four months previously the

dowager empress had died in Denmark.* Ivan Bunin went to pay his respects to Nikolasha's body as it lay in state, dressed in the Cossack *cherkesska* in an "inordinately long" coffin draped with the Russian flag. He was impressed by the sight of the grand duke's "huge fist grasp[ing] a cyprus cross, like a cudgel. Splendid! What a tsar-like corpse!" Bunin's wife, Vera, was overwhelmed by the collective sense of loss: "There was a feeling that we were burying old Russia. You live on as if all your wounds have healed, and then you bump into something and the wounds are reopened, and it's painful, very painful," she wrote in her diary.[14] Surviving Romanovs and senior Whites gathered for the funeral at the Russian Orthodox Church in Cannes; Nikolasha's coffin was subsequently interred in the crypt.[15] After the funeral, Kutepov was besieged by reporters anxious to know how Nikolasha's death might affect the policies of ROVS; his response was that they were determined to keep the grand duke's work alive. He insisted that the Russian people on Russian soil must decide the fundamental forms of their future government and, beyond that, ROVS had "no political aims." Bolshevism would not evolve into "something more reasonable"; the only hope was that under the Red Army's "thick red coating was ripening a Russian national consciousness." What he didn't tell the reporters was that through its program of subversion inside Russia, ROVS intended to make that happen.[16]

By the early 1930s the ROVS headquarters on the second floor at 29 rue du Colisée was buzzing with activity as the organization extended its tentacles beyond Paris and across Europe. *Pravda* correspondent Mikhail Koltsov disguised himself as a French journalist

---

* Maria Feodorovna had expressed a wish that her burial in Denmark in October 1928 be only temporary and that she should eventually join her husband, Alexander III, in St. Petersburg. It would be seventy-eight years before this became possible, after the fall of the Soviet Union, when her coffin joined Alexander's at the Peter and Paul Cathedral on September 28, 2006. Nikolasha and his wife's coffins were returned to Russia in 2015.

in order to infiltrate this supposed hive of counterrevolution. The atmosphere, he recalled, was "sour, with the scent of aniseed, sealing wax and dust," with "books, files, folders and piles of old papers stacked on wooden racks along the walls." The rooms were hung with portraits of Nicholas II, Nikolasha, Kolchak, and Wrangel. "Distinguished gray haired gentlemen were shifting books and papers around on the tables." These were colonels, secretaries of staff, sorting through issues of Soviet journals such as *Planned Economy, Red Star, Bulletin of the Air Fleet*. These elderly colonels had a lot of work, Koltsov noted: "they scribble papers, draw up circulars, dictate them to typists," but it all seemed rather futile. He could not help wondering how many years had passed since the Soviets had "defeated, dispersed and thrown out the White army and had scattered its remnants to the wind, while here, on rue Colisée, they still tried to control human destinies that had been irrevocably broken."[17] Deprived of their homeland, the members of ROVS still waited in the wings, with the idea forever drummed into them that they might be called up again on campaign, that they might one day stand together under the banners of the White regiments.[18]

With Nikolasha's death, however, the threat of a monarchist attempt against the Soviets receded dramatically, for nobody in the emigration had his charisma. But there was still Kutepov. On the morning of January 26, 1930, the OGPU finally caught up with him. That Sunday, Kutepov was seen by several neighbors leaving his house on foot—for some reason the usual taxi driven by one of his officers was not waiting outside to pick him up. It was later reported that he had chosen to walk to divine liturgy at the Church of the Association of Former Gallipoli Veterans on rue de Mademoiselle.[19] He lived at 26 rue Rousselet, next door to a Catholic hospital, and one of the nurses witnessed what happened; how "a car drove up, a man in uniform, impersonating a French policeman, got out, arrested Kutepov and drove away with him." Other accounts suggest Kutepov was lured from his home on the pretext of a meeting with two anti-Bolsheviks from Russia; some reports spoke of him being bundled into the car by "two tall and burly men in yellow overcoats."[20]

When it was clear that Kutepov had been kidnapped, the leading émigré dailies demanded that the French government break off diplomatic relations with the Soviet Union, and a crowd of émigrés threatened to storm the Soviet embassy on rue Grenelle. In response, the French government launched a full inquiry, and four hundred agents of the Paris and security police were seconded to search for him. Meanwhile, the outraged French press denounced the Soviet government for having orchestrated such a brazen act of kidnapping on French soil.[21]

The precise sequence of events remains unknown, but it would appear that Kutepov, who was a huge bear of a man and very strong, had had to be sedated. He was then rolled up in sacking and driven to Cabourg in Normandy and taken out by motor launch to a Soviet freighter, the *Spartak*, that was anchored off the coast.[22] Kutepov seems to have died en route to Russia—either of a heart attack (he suffered from a heart condition) or from an overdose of the anesthetic used to tranquilize him during the kidnap. Either way, he was dead before the *Spartak* reached Novorossisk. Several commentators have argued that his subordinate, General Nikolay Skoblin, and his wife, Nadezhda, were OGPU agents and had organized the kidnap.[23]

General Evgeniy Miller, who succeeded Kutepov as head of ROVS, was far less efficient and experienced in his leadership. But he cut a good military figure and looked suitably distinguished with his splendid handlebar mustache, broader even than that sported by Kutepov. The size of his mustache matched Miller's "preposterous ambition"; he became notorious for his "bizarre enterprises and plans that were invariably inept in execution." He naively moved into new offices without a thorough check, little knowing that they had already been bugged by the OGPU, and put the already-suspect Skoblin in charge of counterintelligence.[24] But Miller knew he was a marked man, and seven years later, on September 22, 1937, when he was still dreaming of Russia rising up against the communists, he too was kidnapped—this time by NKVD agents, the successor to the OGPU—again in broad daylight in Paris, and probably with the connivance once more of Skoblin.

Against his better judgment, Miller had agreed to a meeting with two secret "German agents" at a rendezvous point near the Bois de Boulogne; but prior to leaving the ROVS office, he had left a note expressing his apprehension, to be opened if he did not return as expected. Miller was later seen with Skoblin near the Soviet villa on boulevard de Montmorency, and then he vanished. This time the NKVD agents were careful not to overdose him before the seventy-year-old Miller was hidden in a wooden crate and transported by a gray truck owned by the Soviet embassy to a merchant freighter, the *Maria Ulyanova*, docked at Le Havre.[25] The French prime minister, Eduard Daladier, was apparently informed of this fact but chose not to send a French naval vessel to intercept the freighter; political tensions were high in the run-up to war, and he did not want to antagonize Stalin.[26] Skoblin, meanwhile, had vanished—apparently making his way to the safety of Spain. His wife, a popular singer named Nadezhda Plevitskaya, was arrested on suspicion of being an accomplice in the kidnap, after French police uncovered secret codes, fake passports, and other evidence at their home. She was tried and condemned to twenty years' hard labor in December 1938 but died in jail in 1940. Stalin had been planning a big show trial in Moscow for Miller but, fearing a diplomatic crisis with France, changed his mind. Recent evidence suggests Miller was held for nineteen months in solitary confinement in Moscow, during which he was interrogated by NKVD head Nikolay Yezhov. He was shot on May 11, 1939, in the Lyubyanka, having yielded up little or no useful intelligence to the Soviets. Such had been their comprehensive penetration of ROVS that the kidnap of Miller had ultimately proved fruitless.[27]

During the 1920s and 1930s, many of the younger generation of Russian émigrés had found little to identify with in any of the older generation White groups and had looked elsewhere for inspiration—some to Russian Christian movements, the YMCA, or to youth movements linked to nationalism in Mussolini's Italy. The most notable of these was émigré aristocrat Alexander Kazembek's radical-right youth group known as Mladrossi (Young Russia), which originated in 1923 as a group that venerated Russian Orthodoxy and the Romanov monarchy. With groups in Paris, Berlin, Prague, and Belgrade, in its patriotic fervor it gained the support of Grand Duke Kirill and also Dmitri Pavlovich. The movement capitalized on the bitterness and disillusion of many young émigrés from formerly eminent Russian families, who were seeking a new identity for themselves in emigration. From the outset, Mladrossi manifested anti-Semitic sentiments and, with its uniform and military discipline, became increasingly drawn toward Italian fascism (with Kazembek aspiring to be a Russian *Duce*). By the mid-1930s it had about eight hundred members in France, but it had become increasingly pro-Soviet, with the OGPU even attempting to recruit Kazembek. Ensuing rumors that he and his membership were in the pay of the Soviets and being used to create friction in the émigré community further alienated Mladrossi from its old-guard supporters in the former Russian aristocracy. It was not long before it lost the patronage of Dmitri Pavlovich, who for a while had been chairman of its council, particularly once it openly expressed an admiration for Hitler and national socialism.[28]*

---

* Dmitri Pavlovich also voiced his concern at his cousin Grand Duke Vladimir's flirtation with fascism in the run-up to World War II. Kazembek was later accused of being a Soviet agent; he escaped to the United States in 1940; in 1956 he defected to Moscow.

For those ex-military still itching for a cause for which to fight, Spain seemed the answer during 1937–38, when a hundred or more Whites—almost all from the Paris colony—crossed the Pyrenees on foot and in secret to volunteer for the Franco-led nationalists during the Spanish Civil War. For the war offered a chance of some hands-on experience in fighting in the Spanish "Crusade against Communism," as well as perhaps—to those with more fertile imaginations—providing "an opportunity to set in motion a grand if wildly romantic, plan to regroup the White Volunteer Army scattered in exile."[29] Once again, fanciful dreams resurfaced that "after delivering a decisive blow to the Bolsheviks on the Iberian Peninsula a regalvanized Imperial Russian army would be ready to return and recapture the Russian Motherland." Unfortunately, the Spanish did not share in this aspiration; they did not recognize the military ranks of the numerous former Russian officers who made their way to Spain and were suspicious of their motives, being under the misconception that all Russians were Reds. Consequently, the Russian volunteers, forced to serve as ordinary soldiers irrespective of their former rank, had a hard time of it. The experience was a humiliating one, with the nationalist leaders showing no interest in their Russian military traditions or their fighting experience in the Russian Civil War. Meanwhile, the Republican side welcomed the arrival of Soviet forces and hardware, in the shape of T-26 tanks and I-15 aircraft from Russia.[30]

The machinations of ROVS and the Soviet moles in Paris in their quest to undermine each other's political agenda were but one aspect of a climate of political schism among the Russian émigrés that formed an unwelcome backdrop to the everyday struggle to exist. The average émigré had no time for or interest in politics, but for those who did every faction across a wide political kaleidoscope from hard-left socialists to right-wing German-fascist sympathizers could be found in the colony. They were all hamstrung, however, by having no outlet in a parliament or government of their own; their forums, beyond meetings and debates, were the émigré Russian press. In this respect, Paris was the ideal center for organizing and propagandizing through this medium.

Much of the émigré press was run by exiled politicians who had had varying levels of experience in the state Duma of 1905–17 and the short-lived Provisional Government that had followed it. Long after the revolution and the end of the civil war, resentment still festered about the failings of the Provisional Government, ousted after only eight months by Lenin's Bolsheviks; the recriminations and arguments were often heated and dragged on for years, particularly over the failure to save the Romanov family.[31] Within the émigré community in Paris, there was little love lost for the two leading figures of that failed government, both of whom, unlike the imperial family, had escaped with their lives.

One of the most vociferous in defending his honor had been former prime minister Alexander Kerensky, who as early as 1921, in response to an article in *Le Figaro*—"Qui est responsable de la mort de Nicolas II?"—published an article blaming the failure to save the Romanovs on the British government.[32] A "mediocre St. Petersburg lawyer" before becoming justice minister in the newly formed Provisional Government, Kerensky had ordered the arrest of Nicholas and Alexandra in March 1917, supposedly for their own protection. True, in August he had arranged their removal to what was then the safer location of Tobolsk in Western Siberia, but he had fled Russia—ignominiously, in the view of many—prior to Lenin's coup. Kerensky was striking in appearance with his chalk-white, square-jawed face and his close-cropped crew cut and had been renowned in Russia as a magnetic speaker. During his heyday he had "strut[ted] before vast audiences with an air of command; hammering out staccato phrases of liberty in a military manner," a man once "acclaimed the man of the hour," but who had failed to contain the Bolshevik threat and had subsequently taken neither side during the civil war. Kerensky now was something of a pariah in Paris and frequently "execrated as a coward and a traitor."[33] In 1926 he had transferred the weekly newspaper, *Dni,* that he had set up in Berlin to Passy in Paris and through it clung to the hope that Bolshevism could not and would not last. In 1927 he published *The Catastrophe*—his account of the Russian Revolution—in the knowledge that most émigrés detested him, yet remaining unassailably confident that he had been in the right—this in a storm of British indignation for once more blaming them for his own failures.[34]

In Paris, Kerensky had once again met up with colleagues from the Provisional Government such as former foreign minister Pavel Milyukov; at that time they had been bitter opponents, but now at least they were united in their belief that any attempt at armed intervention in Russia would be sheer folly. Bolshevism had to be "undermined and overthrown by progressive forces from within"; in this belief they were at odds with those who still held on to romantic hopes that Russia could be delivered from without by the émigrés.[35] Although he was now in his seventies, Milyukov had lost none of his vigor as the influential editor of the most widely read émigré newspaper, *Poslednie novosti,* noted for its powerful editorials in which he lambasted the monarchists and the Bolsheviks in equal measure, advocating that a future Russia should be a democratic republic.[36] Aside from his frequent editorials, Milyukov was also a scholar who was equally at home writing about "Greek architecture or Italian art of the Renaissance or Russian music" with a great depth of knowledge.[37] But his manner was cold, detached, and professorial. He did not engage at a popular level with ordinary Russians in the emigration with "his vision of a republican Russia, organized as a parliamentary, democratic federation with Socialists very much to the fore."[38] Locked away in the bubble of his editorial office, working late into the night, Milyukov had few admirers. He advocated the creation in Paris of some kind of "inclusive governing body for the emigration" that could present a united front against Bolshevism; but it proved impossible to bring so many opposing factions and divergent views into line to share a single platform. Nevertheless, Milyukov's paper was undoubtedly the Soviet Union's chief critic in the emigration, and several hundred copies a day of *Poslednie novosti* were dispatched to Moscow by OGPU agents in Paris in order for the Soviets to keep tabs on their most vocal Paris critics.[39] Milyukov also provided a showcase for the best of émigré writing in his Thursday literary pages, when he published stories and extracts from the works of writers such as Bunin, Teffi, and Remizov. He also provided an outlet for young poets, notably the hugely promising Boris Poplavsky, and for the feuilletons of Don-Aminado and the literary criticism of Vladislav Khodasevich. More important, Milyukov kept his journal going as the voice of the literary emigration until hours before the German occupation of Paris in June 1940.[40]

There were many, however, who rejected the ardent republicanism of Milyukov's newspaper and opted for the more conservative *Vozrozhdenie* (Renaissance), which alongside news published many émigré writers. The other leading voice of the emigration was the review journal *Sovremennye zapiski*, which modeled itself on the old nineteenth-century Russian literary journals; of all the émigré publications, it had the most impressive list of literary contributors. Under its principal editor, Mark Vishniak, and three coeditors from the social democratic side of the emigration, it accepted contributions from essayists, philosophers, writers, and poets across the political spectrum and published the early work in emigration of novelist Vladimir Nabokov, writing then under the pseudonym Sirin. The journal faced the constant threat of financial crisis, but across the seventy volumes of its lifespan from 1920 to 1940 helped keep the flame of émigré Russian literature burning.[41]

On Sundays at rue Daru copies of the émigré newspapers and journals were displayed for sale outside the churchyard. Across the street, the Russian bookshop carried many military and naval periodicals as well as specialist Cossack publications, while the popular monarchist (but violently anti-Semitic) journal *Double-Headed Eagle* was brought in regularly from Berlin. Some émigré publications were little more than a single sheet or two produced on a shoestring, and were thus often short-lived.[42] But they were full of information and help for émigrés in finding cheap places to live, getting medical and legal assistance, and obtaining passports and identity cards. They also regularly carried appeals from desperate Russians needing money to put their children in school or start a business, or anxious notices asking the whereabouts of lost relatives and friends from whom they had been separated. *Poslednie novosti* even ran a regular feature called "Hungry Friday" urging readers "to go hungry for two meals on Good Friday and send the amount thus saved to a fund for destitute children."[43]

But in fact there was one fundamental thing readers of the émigré press in Paris wanted to know above all else: they were desperate for news of home. And so they devoured the imported Soviet newspapers, searching for news of friends and relatives back in Russia, noting accounts of their persecution and imprisonment, the attacks on religion and the destruction of churches, searching always for "flaws in the Bolshevik armor, for indications of the usurper's impending downfall, for even the faintest ray of the dawn of the Day of Return."[44] Unrealizable, idealistic hopes for Russia refused to die down among the émigré community in Paris, but in 1932 they were severely damaged by the violent act of a madman.

On May 6 that year Paris was rocked by a horrifying event that would bring serious consequences for the Russian colony's standing in France. Hostility against so many Russian émigrés had been building among the French public, ever since the aftereffects of the 1929 New York stock market crash had begun filtering across to Europe, bringing a rapidly deepening recession. But the attitude of the French, once welcoming to Russian refugees, changed dramatically on that day in May, when a disturbed thirty-seven-year-old Russian emigrant named Pavel Gorgulov assassinated French president Paul Doumer.

The night before, Gorgulov, who had traveled up from Monaco and had no residence permit to be in Paris, went and prayed in Notre Dame Cathedral; he then hid out in a cheap hotel, drank a liter of wine, fired himself up with hatred, and "spent the night writing curses on the Communists, the Czechs, the Jews, the French"—all of whom variously had thwarted his own political ideals.[45]

On the afternoon of the sixth, having obtained an invitation to a charity book fair raising funds for French war veterans, Gorgulov made his way to the Hôtel Salomon de Rothschild in Paris and fired five shots from a small pocket pistol at the seventy-year-old president when he arrived at 3 P.M. as guest of honor. Two of the bullets hit Doumer; he was rushed to the hospital but had lost too much blood and died the following day.

Gorgulov was quickly seized and taken away. Details of his background subsequently emerged. He was a Cossack, born in the Kuban and had been studying medicine before World War I, when he was called up. During the Russian Civil War he had fought with the Whites before settling in Prague in 1921, where he became involved in the émigré political circles advocating terrorist methods and founded a Russian fascist party.[46] He completed his medical training in Prague in 1926 but had run into trouble for practicing illegal abortions. A political fanatic, when questioned by the French police, Gorgulov claimed to be president of the "Peasant All-Russian People's Green Party"—the Greens being a peasant group of mainly deserters that had fought both sides during the civil war and had massacred Reds and Whites indiscriminately.[47] Their program, a mix of Russian populism and Mussolini-inspired fascism, was violently anti-Semitic, and the solution it offered to all problems was war: "War is the only escape for the Russian émigrés dispersed all over the world," Gorgulov insisted; it was his mission to bring down the Bolsheviks. After moving to Billancourt in March 1931, he had married a Swiss girl but had been forced to decamp to Monaco when proceedings had been begun against him for illegally practicing medicine. It was in Monaco that he decided to kill the French president, hoping that in so doing he could provoke France into taking military action against the Soviet Union.[48]

Gorgulov had also fancied himself as a poet and writer, and was known to émigré literary circles in Paris, who all agreed that he was "not normal." One editor went so far as to regard him as "a dangerous lunatic, and that he was so violent that it was unpleasant to be in his company." He had no money and, according to Ilya Ehrenburg, although banned from practicing medicine, secretly treated fellow Cossacks who had caught gonorrhea and used the money to publish poetry and a couple of novels under the pseudonym Pavel Bred.[49] *Bred* is the Russian word for "delirium," which in itself seems appropriately Dostoevskyan; indeed, Ehrenburg, who covered Gorgulov's trial for the Soviet daily *Izvestiya*, wrote that in court, "before me was a man whom Dostoevsky could have invented in his sleepless hours."[50]

The writer Vasily Yanovsky had met Gorgulov at a literary meeting; he vividly remembered the reaction of those gathered in the back room of the café when it was Gorgulov's turn to read:

Gorgulov rose to his full, epic height, and those sitting close became scared. This was a giant, a weight lifter who could easily grab one of the heavy benches and smash us all to pieces. And yet how ridiculous, how incongruous: a model of physical fitness

with an obvious flaw in the brain. Why in the world was he
writing poetry?[51]

Gorgulov's trial, which began on July 25, lasted four days, during
which witnesses in the box were constantly interrupted by shouts
and interventions from the accused "roar[ing] incoherently of moon
rockets and peasant masses" in unintelligible French; at every opportunity, Gorgulov tried to harangue the court with his political
thinking; he even attempted to read his poetry.[52]

A search of Gorgulov's home had revealed a set of detailed documents charting a bizarre plot by Gorgulov's organization—"The
Green Brothers"—to foment an uprising in Russia, with himself as
the "Great Green Dictator" leading agitators wearing a uniform designed by him and carrying his specially designed banners. He also
fantasized about assassinating German president Paul von Hinden-
burg and Czech president Tomáš Masaryk.

In his defense, which was confused to say the least, Gorgulov
explained his motives in the killing. He had shot Doumer not because of who he was but because he represented France, and France
had not done anything to support the Russian émigrés against the
Bolsheviks but had gone ahead and recognized the new Soviet state.
"France, listen to me! I am the apostle of my Idea," he declared,
"My crime was a great protest in the name of the miserable ones
who wait 'over there' [in Russia] . . . My Idea is more precious than
my life. Take my life, but save my Idea."[53]

Commentators agreed that Gorgulov was most decidedly unlike
the French. As a Slav suffering from "fantasies, fanaticism, mysti-
cism and cruelty," his difference was played on by the French pros-
ecutor. A psychiatric evaluation, argued by the medical expert for
the prosecution, ruled out insanity, putting Gorgulov's extremist attitudes down to his ethnicity and pointing out the obsessive traits of
Russians portrayed in works by Dostoevsky: "He is Russian. Like

all Russians, he has an intellect different from ours."[54] People in the Russian colony were distraught as this condemnation of Gorgulov as a Slav. It rubbed off on all of them as Russians: "all has collapsed, all that we have done here for ten years, all has gone to the dogs," said one young reporter in despair.[55] There were fears that this assassination could become another Sarajevo moment; indeed, Gorgulov had used the same model of pistol to kill Doumer as that used by Gavrilo Princip to assassinate Archduke Franz Ferdinand in 1914, sparking World War I. Fearing deportation and anxiously awaiting inevitable acts of retribution, émigrés went out of their way to express their loyalty to France. Two dozen of the leading members of the Russian colony sent letters of condolence; hundreds more wrote to the widowed Madame Doumer and sent flowers; a memorial service was held in the Alexander Nevsky Cathedral. One former Russian officer, a proud Don Cossack now working in Paris as a waiter, committed suicide by throwing himself from a sixth-floor window, so overwhelmed was he by the dishonor that Gorgulov had brought on his people. In retaliation, the leading French paper *Le Matin* was already demanding that politically active foreign nationals be expelled.[56] "How we get on all their *nerves*," declared a friend of Nina Berberova:

> *Christ! How they are fed up with us! If I were in their place, I would long ago have chased all the émigrés to the Sandwich Islands, with all their claims to unemployment benefits, to free education of children, to old-age pensions. You'll see: when war comes . . .* [57]

It was clear that Gorgulov was deranged, and desperate; in court he described his fixation on murder as "a hypnotic obsession." The prosecution responded by cranking up hysteria, referring to him as a "wild beast" and "the Rasputin of Russian Refugees." Gorgulov's defense lawyer, Henri Géraud, decided the only possible line to take was mental instability—his client had after all suffered a serious head wound in the war.[58] The defense of insanity did not, however, convince the jury or the judge. Found guilty, Gorgulov was sentenced to death. On August 20 his appeal was rejected.

Gorgulov was publicly executed just before dawn on September 14, 1932. Accompanied by his two defense lawyers and a Russian Orthodox priest, he was brought to the boulevard Arago outside the wall of La Santé prison in Paris to face the guillotine. About two thousand people had gathered through the night behind the police cordons to witness this ghoulish spectacle; local bistros had stayed open and did a roaring trade. Only a few hours before, the guillotine—popularly known as "The Widow"—had been assembled in position "by hand and spirit level"; it was French tradition not to inform the condemned person in advance of the day of their appointment with her.

Gorgulov was woken from a deep sleep at 5:30 A.M. with the offer of a cigarette and a double tot of rum. As he was led out, his hands and feet heavily manacled, and with his shirt pulled down to his chest, baring his neck and shoulders, he said that he was dying "for his country, for his idea." He said he forgave everyone as the official executioner, Anatole Deibler—popularly known as "Monsieur Paris"—in his signature derby hat and assisted by his son-in-law, laid Gorgulov down on the *bascule* (bench). There then followed a hideous pause as Deibler struggled to get the condemned man into the correct position: "Gorgulov's huge body had not fitted the guillotine," recalled Yanovsky, "the Cossack's neck had been too big for the frame beneath the blade." Before the guillotine eventually fell, Gorgulov's last distinct words, in French according to Deibler, were "Oh Sainte Russie!" His body was then taken to the cemetery at Ivry and buried in a common grave known as "The Square of the Damned" alongside twenty-eight other executed murderers. His pregnant widow, Anna, later reclaimed it and buried him elsewhere in the Paris suburbs; Monsieur Deibler collected his usual fee of three thousand francs.[59] In the United States, United Press reporter Mary Knight claimed a scoop: disguising herself as a man, she had been the only woman to get inside the special enclosure for officials and journalists, she said, to witness seeing Gorgulov, "looking like a great monster in the light of early day" and with an "unholy smile" on his face, "lose his head."[60]

It was later revealed that while waiting for his victim that day, Gorgulov had bought three books at the bazaar and had inscribed them: "Paul Gorgulov, chief of the Russian Fascists, who has just killed the President of the French Republic."[61]

The general consensus in the press was that he was clearly demented; even his wife had said as much. But there were also claims that he was a Soviet agent and had used the murder to provoke an anti-socialist, reactionary election stampede, for the killing came the day before elections to the French Constituent Assembly. Gorgulov had certainly hoped to provoke a backlash against the left wing, which had recently seen a surge in support in France, but the killing had no such effect, and indeed the left were returned to power with a majority and reacted to the Doumer killing with demands to "Throw out the White Guards." The Russian émigrés were accused of colluding with the French right "as the nucleus of a vast anti-Soviet warmongering conspiracy" and were demonized as being "all Fascists, or the dupes of Fascists."[62]

In the émigré press, *Vozrozhdenie* condemned Gorgulov as a "semiliterate neurasthenic" and also insinuated that he had in some way been involved in the kidnap of General Kutepov; a day later it went so far as to openly state that he was "a Soviet commissar."[63] Milyukov at *Poslednie novosti,* however, was more measured, anxious not to further inflame French hostility toward the Russian community. There was now, in his view, an urgent need to impress

upon the French the "indissoluble ties" that bound the Russian émigrés to Europe and European civilization.[64] Thanks to Ivan Bunin,
Russian Paris would soon be celebrating a major cultural triumph
that, for a while at least, relegated Gorgulov's hideous and senseless
crime to the shadows.

CHAPTER 11

"A Far Violin Among Near Balalaikas"

I n the years since leaving Russia, Ivan Bunin had dwelt increasingly on the past in his writing, on a Russia not founded on the
reality of the new and greatly changed Soviet state—to which
he had no physical or emotional connection—but on the memory
of Russia as it once was, before the revolution. The Soviets had inevitably castigated him for becoming "arid and boring," a victim of
"counterrevolutionary obscurantism." To them Bunin seemed preoccupied with ruin and decay, with "the rot and dust of the centuries," while stubbornly remaining "alien to all that is new in Russia."
A Soviet critic concluded that the once revered Russian author had
become an irrelevance: "no one needs an invalid who lives abroad,
rejected by living, laboring Russia. . . . Bunin is a man of the grave."[1]

That, however, was not the view of the Paris community, who
continued to revere Bunin as a literary father—their "first figure."
"We have not had a writer like you since Tolstoy," writer Mark Aldanov assured him. In 1930, at the annual commemorative gathering in
Paris to celebrate the birth of Pushkin, Bunin took center stage. Tall,
cavernous, graying, with kind but intensely sad eyes, in his nobility
he seemed to embody the tragedy of exile, the "irreparable mistake" of

having abandoned his homeland.[2] Here was a man whom the mainstream of European literature had passed by; perhaps it was his own doing for remaining too detached from what was going on in the literary community; after all, he spent most of his time in the south, in Grasse. His readers were still loyal, though, still "bewitched" by his elegiac and evocative style, thought Zinaida Gippius, but he was "not a teacher, or a leader."[3] Nevertheless, ever since 1923 literary circles in Paris had been arguing that Bunin had a serious chance of winning the Nobel Prize in Literature. Indeed, that year moves had been made to submit a joint nomination of Bunin, Merezhkovsky, *and* Alexander Kuprin. The latter, alas, once a popular short story writer in Russia, had little chance. Since settling in Paris he had retreated into loneliness and alcoholism; "his immense public had gone."[4] There were rumors too that Maxim Gorky, who had remained in the Soviet Union, was a favorite. In the event, none of the Russians were nominated. Nevertheless Bunin continued to hope that the prize might eventually be his. He was constantly complaining, as in a letter of February 1927, of being "worn out by perpetual want and perpetual anxiety . . . My literary earnings are paltry, despite my 'fame.'" "I am not for the masses," he had admitted, and because of that he simply wasn't making enough money. Even *The New York Times* noted that "the Russian writer who conquered the literary elite of America and England with such works as *The Gentleman from San Francisco* and *The Village*, has become for Paris the tragic example of a great author who is more praised than read."[5]

Once again, at the end of 1930 the names of Bunin and Merezhkovsky were being bandied about as "serious contenders" for the 1931 Nobel Prize. Mark Aldanov urged Bunin to put his name forward and write the necessary letters: "Now it's becoming a mathematical certainty," he told him, "if only Gorky would quit the competition." Supporters rallied round to encourage Bunin, telling him "there was an enormous wave of sympathy for him in Paris."

As ever, the financial problems that would be solved by such a win were pressing: "this year we've gone about as absolute beggars," Vera complained to her diary. "Even a young person has never earned so little money."[6]

At the end of January 1931 confirmation came that Bunin's name had been put forward as a candidate; Merezhkovsky wrote to him suggesting each should support the other's candidacy and whoever won could share the prize money. Once again disappointment prevailed; of forty names submitted that year, the prize for literature in the end went, posthumously, to a Swedish poet, Erik Axel Karlfeldt. Bunin was in despair: "Winning this award has been the goal of my entire life. The prize would have forced the world to pay attention to me, to read my works, and to translate them into all the languages of the world."[7] He felt that if it didn't happen this year, then it never would. But . . . but . . . everybody was telling him: his haunting, introspective novel *The Life of Arseniev* was a masterpiece, a book of "Proustian recollection" that echoed *À la Recherche du temps perdu*, melding poetic descriptions of nature with elements of Bunin's own autobiography and his early years as a young writer. Steeped in literary references, the novel also was a paean to the traditions of Russian literature and its great writers, particularly Turgenev. Bunin would "undoubtedly receive the prize next year."[8] There followed a behind-the-scenes battle between warring camps as the Soviets, supported by the Germans, lined up Gorky for the 1932 prize; the English publisher Hogarth Press came on board for a translation of *The Life of Arseniev* and things looked hopeful. But yet again the prize went elsewhere—to the English novelist John Galsworthy. Vera recorded in her diary that they were now so poor, that Bunin "can't buy warm underwear for himself."[9]

At long last, on November 9, 1933, a telegram arrived from Sweden confirming that the now sixty-three-year-old Bunin had been awarded the Nobel Prize in Literature—"for the strict artistry with which he has carried on the classical Russian traditions in prose writing."[10] He was the first Russian to achieve that honor and undoubtedly it was the single most important event in the cultural and literary life of the Russian emigration. The prize, worth 170,000 Swedish krona (or 400,000 francs, equivalent then to $36,000), bought him immediate respite from debt. Bunin generously set up a fund to share a quarter of the money with his fellow writers; the begging letters were, of course, legion. Down in Grasse, the Villa Belvedere was under siege. At last, celebrity beckoned; he was courted by the international press, with letters and telegrams of congratulations pouring in from all over the world. Suddenly the French press, whom Bunin felt had ignored him, wanted to know all about "Monsieur Bounine," aside, that is, from the communist-run *Humanité*, which sneered that there was "something comic in the fact that this award has been given to a relic of that old world that has been swept away by the proletarian revolution."[11] The Soviets were furious, having hoped, even expected, their proletarian literary hero Gorky to win, and forbade the domestic press from reporting Bunin's triumph. But the Paris colony celebrated with a grand dinner and a thanksgiving service at the Alexander Nevsky Cathedral.[12]

On 10 December Bunin attended the ceremony in Stockholm to receive his prize from the king of Sweden. He found it all bewildering—"I feel like a tenor who's scored a big hit," he told a friend. Pale and solemn, he took the podium for his acceptance speech, given in French, in which he admitted that during his past thirteen years in exile his sorrows had "far exceeded my joys."[13] He spoke of his gratitude to France for giving him, a Russian refugee, a home. The prize was affirmation of the exiles' cause, their suffering, and the precious gift of independence of creative thought that life in France provided.[14] Vasily Yanovsky, however, was disappointed in what he thought was a "flat and colorless speech." On the podium in Stockholm with the world watching, Bunin had had a chance "to stand up to his full height, to cry out some truths about the Bolsheviks, about the war, about the heroism of the emigration, about freedom, real and conventional." But no, he had said nothing about any of this; all he could do "was impress Europe and America with his elegant tails and courtly bow."[15]

Other émigrés disagreed; they saw Bunin's win as righting the injustice of neither Tolstoy nor Chekhov ever having been nominated. The choice of the émigré Bunin, who had had the courage to leave Russia, over a modern Soviet writer, whose creativity was restricted by state censorship, seemed significant: for them the award proclaimed "the superiority of 'gentry' literature over 'proletarian' writing." It also was a gesture of compassion and solidarity, for it had "gone to a man without a country." In fact, as Vera Bunin later noted, the diploma presented to the winner usually bore the flag of the winner's home country, but "out of sympathy for [the stateless] Bunin, all the flags were removed from the diplomas" that year.[16]

Bunin's Nobel laureateship injected a degree of much-needed optimism in the Paris colony in 1933. The life of the émigré was "so gray, boring, and burdensome"; if Bunin could rebuild his life in exile, then why shouldn't they, particularly now that word was filtering through from the Soviet Union of the bullying of writers and artists into the straitjacket of socialist realism, of harsh political repressions and increasing economic suffering. As one critic affirmed that November, "Bunin's winning of the Nobel Prize acknowledges the value of the free émigré word." Yes indeed, confirmed Zinaida Gippius, "is not our Russian language the only treasure we have left? . . . Bunin personified for émigrés the last and most valuable part of a Russia which can never be taken away from us." But did he really take any comfort in the award, aside from the much-needed money? When young writer Vladimir Nabokov met Bunin shortly afterward, he found him "terribly preoccupied with the passage of time, old age, and death."[17]

Behind the scenes, an air of bitter jealousy circulated in émigré literary groups that soured Bunin's win. People squabbled over the share out of monies via the committee Bunin had set up. Several of them, notably Merezhkovsky and Gippius, had not attended the celebration of Bunin's victory at the Théâtre des Champs-Élysées in November 1933. Zinaida Gippius was furious that the Nobel had not gone to her husband, and the couple made no attempt to disguise their longstanding, seething jealousy of Bunin. Marina Tsvetaeva too had been highly dismissive, having favored Gorky to win. "Gorky is an epoch, Bunin is the end of an epoch," she declared; "Merezhkovsky deserved it more than Bunin": "for if Gorky is an epoch, and Bunin the end of an epoch, then Merezhkovsky is an epoch of the *end* of an epoch."[18]

By 1930 in Paris at large, the charm and seductive romance of "Russianness" had begun to wear thin. Only a year or so before, the Russian humorist Don-Aminado, familiar for his journalistic pieces in the émigré press, had published a satirical piece on the Russian "takeover":

> What is going on, what is going on!
> The French hold up their hands and gaze with apprehension
>   at the Eiffel Tower.
> It is the only thing left that has not been captured by the
>   Russians.
> Everywhere else the conquest is complete.
> In the Champs Élysées the Don Cossack are singing.
> Around the corner on the right Platov's company is appearing.
> Around the corner on the left, horseback riders are per-
>   forming.

On the Grand Boulevards balalaikas are playing.

In the dressmaking shops—Russian hands.

In the ballet—Russian legs.

At Worth's and Paquin's—Russian figures.

At the Place Pigalle a regular Caucasian hurricane, and for ten
    years now it smells of genuine shashlik and onions. . . . [19]

But this was the Russian Paris of the tourist trail. For most émigrés, their existence remained one of stoic endurance, of a working
life of drudgery and menial jobs. Some had never felt comfortable
in Paris; they felt neither really Russian nor really French and had
sought little or no contact with their French hosts. This sense of
rootlessness was defined by Vasily Yanovsky, who looked upon his
generation of young émigré writers in the interwar years as "The
Unnoticed Generation"—unnoticed by the French and even other
Europeans.[20] Their parents had, in a way, endorsed this; they kept
reminding their children that "one day Russia will have need of you.
You must be prepared to serve her on the day when the return becomes possible." With this in mind, émigrés resisted assimilation and
fought for their cultural survival by trying to teach the younger generation the importance of their Russian language, its literature and
history. Zoé Oldenbourg recalled how those born after 1925 threw
off their parents' tendency to wallow in the past. They wanted to be
part of French popular culture and tended to speak French rather
than Russian; nor did many of them know how to read and write
it. Naturalization, which many of their parents refused to pursue,
therefore seemed a sensible option and certainly made it a lot easier
to get a job. But the older generation would tell them "You're still
Russian in your hearts, whether or not you have French papers."[21]
Zoé and her family, who had arrived in 1925, found the earlier Paris
émigrés quite alien; her mother thought them "fanatical, limited, ridiculous." She was also angry: they had escaped Soviet rule, whereas

she and her family had lived under it for seven years: "You cannot hate the Bolsheviks as we do—you didn't know what it was like," she insisted. For this reason she referred to herself as "Soviet," not Russian; the émigrés had no concept of the moral resistance of those back home, whom she considered to be "the only authentic representatives of Russia—not the émigrés."[22]

By 1930, according to French journalist Jean Delage, there were 43,250 Russians living in the twenty Paris arrondissements, with another 9,500 in the outer suburbs.* Of these, the vast majority worked in car manufacturing, construction, and industry and about 2,400 were taxi drivers.[23] Few Russian emigrants had been able to find work in France that matched the professional expertise they had gained in Russia, and economic decline in France during the 1930s reduced the need for foreign labor. This triggered calls for the number of foreign workers entering the labor market to be controlled, for there were now three million aliens working in France.[24] Work was becoming extremely hard to find for many émigrés. George Orwell recalled traipsing the streets of Paris with his Russian friend Boris in search of work during the Great Depression. Boris had by now fallen on hard times, having lost his lucrative waiting job due to a leg injury that had left him with a limp:

> *All the clothes he now had left were one suit, with one shirt, collar and tie, a pair of shoes almost worn out, and a pair of socks all holes. He had also an overcoat, which was to be pawned in the last extremity. He had a suitcase, a wretched twenty-franc cardboard thing, but very important, because the patron of the hotel believed that it was full of clothes—without that, he would probably have turned Boris out of doors.*[25]

---

* It has been impossible to find any two sources agreeing on the exact number of Russians in Paris at any given time, though Delage seems the most reliable. Estimates vary between 100,000–175,000 Russians living in France as a whole in the interwar years.

Together the men had spent hours, as did many others, hanging around outside hotels and restaurants in the hope of a few hours' work. Walking was agony for Boris; yet one day they covered fourteen kilometers of Paris's pavement in search of work; on another, they crossed the Seine eleven times in their quest. "Tomorrow we shall find something, *mon ami*, I know it in my bones," Boris told Orwell. "The luck always changes. Besides, we both have brains—a man with brains can't starve."[26] But nobody wanted to hire "a lame man, nor a man without experience." When Orwell found a sou dropped on the pavement, they gorged themselves on boiled potatoes. It was only by pawning both their overcoats for fifty francs that they were able to keep going until they finally found menial work in a hotel (Orwell as a *plongeur*, washing dishes). Through it all Boris continued to dream of a change in his fortunes and of "wearing a tail coat once more."[27]

With so many émigrés struggling to support themselves, the welfare bill was escalating rapidly by the end of the 1930s; by 1937 unemployment in Paris alone was costing the French taxpayer 80 million francs. French resentment had in fact been building since the end of World War I; the accusation that *ces sales Russes* (these dirty Russians) were stealing French jobs was heard at every turn. "Whenever we had to get papers at the Prefecture it was a real drama. We were treated like dogs," remembered one émigré. "There were many uneducated Russians—soldiers, for example—who did not speak French, so they were bounced from one counter to another, yelled at, treated in the worst possible manner. . . . The people in the street . . . bore a grudge against us for their lost money."[28] Old resentments had indeed died hard; French people had not forgotten how tsarist Russia had received a big loan from France before the revolution that had never been repaid. Many who had bought Russian bonds at the time had lost their money, which had impacted directly on their savings. With work permits harder to obtain, the

French minister of the interior ordered those Russians who did not have one to be expelled, forcing some to cross back into France, in secret, and take up illegal residence.[29] A few sympathetic deputies in the French parliament lent their support to émigré concerns, and the new socialist government of Léon Blum in 1936 righted some of the wrongs and introduced some social benefits. Nevertheless, a xenophobic backlash against the émigrés grew during the late 1930s, when the Paris colony had to contend with denunciations by right-wing, nationalist French politicians of their community of *apatrides* (refugees) as being a drain on resources at a time of economic hardship: "Not only do we not clean our own doormat," declared an editorial in *Le Matin,* "but we even hold it out to the muddy of the whole world so that they might come and wipe their feet on it."[30]

A volatile period of strikes and demonstrations in Paris, followed by food shortages, brought painful reminders of revolutionary Russia, and fearful Russian émigrés prepared for another Armageddon. The printers at *Vozrozhdenie* went on strike, and writers (including Teffi) who wrote for it regularly weren't paid and were hit with further reductions in their piece rates when it resumed.[31] "We are living on a volcano," Teffi wrote to Bunin "and everything is flying . . . in the wrong direction." Writers' already-paltry fees were going backward, and Teffi was finding herself in extreme difficulties, with *Vozrozhdenie* paying so little now for her work. Writer friends like Khodasevich were having their fees cut in half; one had fallen sick with malnutrition and died; journals were going bust, and even the leading ones were struggling to keep going.[32] Every writer Teffi knew was angry and worried, not just about their own survival but the very survival of Russian literature abroad. Some were trying hard to adapt by including French subjects and topics in their work, including Teffi in her short stories; but she knew she could not penetrate the inner life of the French. The only way to begin to do so was to write in French rather than Russian and seek a wider audience.

"Young people are gradually leaving Russian literature for European [literature]," she wrote; "young Russian writers are no longer inspired by Tolstoy and Dostoevsky, but by André Gide and Marcel Proust."[33] This was the case with the émigré Lev Tarasov, who as Henri Troyat established a brilliant and prolific career for himself from the mid-1930s, writing about a wide range of subjects in French; Nina Berberova also turned to writing in French, as did Zoé Oldenbourg and Henri Kessel; even Vladimir Nabokov produced the occasional work in French. It was only those Russian novelists and poets who adapted in this way who were accepted into the mainstream of French literature. Troyat recalled a strange schizophrenic existence: being in France at school and speaking French; then returning home to Russia and speaking Russian at the end of the day — an existence lived between real-time Paris and the memory of Moscow.[34]

It wasn't just the writers who were struggling: the Paris fashion industry that had been such an important employer for émigré Russian women when they first arrived without money or the means of earning a living was now suffering a major recession. Through dint of hard work, Grand Duchess Maria Pavlovna had made a success of her Kitmir business and had adapted to the need, for the first time in her life, to work in order to live. "It is not necessary to feel sorry for me," she had said. "I do not believe that idle women are happier than those who work." Unlike so many of her class, she had faced reality and got on with it: "you have to build something new and fruitful," she had insisted."[35] But Kitmir's success had demanded greater outlay at her expensive premises near the Champs-Élysées, and she had been forced to sell more of her rapidly shrinking collection of Romanov jewels, for well below their true value; then she lost money on an investment in a Dutch consortium. By the late 1920s Kitmir was struggling; fashion was a fickle business, and the trend for Slavic-style fashion was waning. With the discovery of the tomb of King Tutankhamen and all its fantastical artifacts, ancient Egyptian was now all the rage. For a while, Maria Pavlovna was able to adapt her embroidery to the new Egyptian themes.[36] But embroidery was falling out of fashion, and in 1928 Kitmir went bankrupt and she sold out to the firm of Fritel & Hurel.[37] Undaunted, she decided to go into perfume production and spent time in London creating her own signature fragrance, "Prince Igor." It was a flop. The grand duchess was left with one asset to fall back on: her memoirs, which she began writing in 1928. She also made a trip to America, where both the fashion house Bergdorf Goodman and the cosmetics company Elizabeth Arden made clear their interest in hiring her services.

In the summer of 1929, Maria Pavlovna decided that her future lay in America. After winding up her affairs in Paris and selling her house in Boulogne-sur-Seine, she sailed to New York with "three hundred dollars in cash, a travel typewriter and a Russian guitar" just as the crash was taking hold. "Here there will be a place for me, here I will succeed," she wrote in her diary; "Here flows such a stream of energy, that everything seems possible."[38] Soon afterward, Bergdorf Goodman on Fifth Avenue hired her as a "style adviser." In 1930 the first volume of her memoirs, translated from her Russian manuscript, was published. So successful was it, with French and Spanish translations also, that when volume 2 came out in 1932, Maria Pavlovna gave up her job at Bergdorf Goodman to write full time.

Over in Paris, other Russians in the fashion trade in Paris fared badly too: various smaller establishments specializing in Slavic-style decorative beaded, appliqué work and embroidered fabrics went under during the late 1920s, such as Countess Orlova-Davydova's label Mode, which employed 125 Russian home-based workers.[39] The Tao label created by Princesses Trubetskaya, Annenkova, and

Obolenskaya closed down in 1928 when Obolenskaya moved to New York. Prince Gavriil Romanov's wife, Antonina, had also had to close down her business, the House of Bery, in 1936 due to declining sales. Betty Hoyningen-Huene kept her fashion house, Yteb, going a bit longer, introducing a perfume, Yteb no. 14 — an obvious dig at Chanel — and dramatically adapting her house style to suit changing tastes. Fashion was rapidly moving away from exoticism, with an increasing emphasis on women's everyday wear; the frivolous dropped waistlines of the Jazz Age were now being supplanted by sleeker, longer styles. Yteb's elegant lines remained popular into the 1930s, but recession inevitably forced the company to cut back on its sewing staff and mannequins, and by now their wealthy clients were also feeling the economic downturn.[40]

Over at their own fashion house Irfé, the Yusupovs had also been struggling. They had overreached themselves, based on their initial success, by setting up branches in Le Touquet, London, and Berlin and moving to bigger, swankier premises on rue Duphot. Practically all their employees were Russian émigrés, but no one at Irfé seems to have had much of a head for business, least of all the Yusupovs themselves. Nevertheless, the fashion house traded well on Felix's name and notoriety.[41] In 1926 they had introduced their own exclusive perfume, Irfé, but soon financial difficulties loomed and the Yusupovs were forced to sell their house in Boulogne-sur-Seine to cover their debts.[42] And then the Wall Street crash deprived them of a lot of well-heeled American clients. It was at this point that Yusupov suggested that his own failing business should join ranks with Yteb in an attempt to stay afloat, but the venture ended in bankruptcy. Irfé folded in 1931, and Yteb in 1933. A rare Russian survival was the House of Hitrovo, patronized by film stars such as Rita Hayworth. It continued to produce lingerie through the Second World War and the German occupation, but it too was finally forced to close down—but not till 1956, when its fine silk lingerie was superseded by the advent of the new and much cheaper nylon.[43]

Although the Ballets Russes had continued to perform in Paris throughout the 1920s, they also appeared in London and Monte Carlo and regularly went on tour. Diaghilev had remained very much a presence in the cultural life of the city—albeit now an absent one. But the company had never quite repeated the artistic successes of the pre–World War I years. Even a stunning new production of *The Sleeping Beauty* in London, starring Lyubov Egorova in 1921, had resulted in huge financial losses.

By 1928 Diaghilev was a very sick man, suffering from severe diabetes; he lived long enough to witness the success in Paris of a new neoclassical ballet, *Apollo*—choreographed by George Balanchine to music by Stravinsky. It received its premiere on June 12, 1928, at the Théâtre Sarah Bernhardt. A year later, not long after Stravinsky had enjoyed a successful revival of *The Rite of Spring* in Paris and Berlin, Diaghilev died in his room at the Grand Hotel des Bains de Mer on the Venice Lido at the age of only fifty-seven; he was buried in the famous Russian Orthodox section of the cemetery on the Isle of San Michele. A month before his death, Diahgilev had affirmed the importance of *The Rite* in his life's oeuvre. "At last these imbeciles have come to appreciate it," he wrote to a friend. "The *Times* says that *The Rite* is for the twentieth century what Beethoven's Ninth was for the nineteenth!"[44]

Diaghilev was dead, but many of his dancers were still trying to earn a living, for with his death Ballets Russes was disbanded. Several of the former prima ballerinas of the company had taken up teaching ballet, among them Pavlova and Karsavina in London, and Lyubov Egorova in Paris. A former dancer at the Mariinsky Theater in imperial St. Petersburg, she had competed for roles with Tsar Nicholas II's former lover Mathilde Kschessinska, and Diaghilev had brought her to Paris to dance with Nijinsky in the original production of *The Sleeping Beauty* in 1918, revived in 1921. Married to Prince Nikita Trubetskoy, she and her husband had settled in Paris, where from 1923 Lyubov had run the Ballets Russes school on the top floor of the Olympia Music Hall on boulevard des Capucines. Here she attracted pupils such as writer James Joyce's daughter Lucia, who deemed her "a pitiless teacher," and in the summer of 1928 and spring of 1929 Zelda Fitzgerald, wife of the American writer Scott Fitzgerald, when the couple were living in Paris.

Zelda was obsessed with the idea of becoming a ballet dancer and was recommended to Egorova for ballet lessons by Diaghilev patrons Gerald and Sara Murphy. Egorova found her difficult and half mad (she was at the time heading for mental breakdown), but she persevered. Zelda practiced relentlessly—to the exclusion of her husband and child—and to the point of physical collapse and injury for eight hours a day, paying Egorova a generous three hundred dollars a month. She was convinced ballet would bring her spiritual transformation and drive out the devils that were tormenting her.[45] She invited the Murphys to watch her train at Egorova's studio. "There was something dreadfully grotesque in her intensity," Gerald later remembered. "One could see the muscles stretch and pull; legs looked muscular and ugly. It was really terrible. One held one's breath until it was over."[46] Was it all worth it, wondered her husband. Privately, Scott Fitzgerald asked Egorova's verdict: Zelda was good enough to attempt a professional career, she told him, but because she had taken up ballet late, she could never be a first-rate star. Soon after, she completely broke down and was committed to a psychiatric hospital. But she wrote up the experience of Lyubov Egorova's rigorous training in her 1932 novel *Save Me the Waltz*, in which her teacher appears as "Madame."[47]

In 1929 Egorova's erstwhile dancing rival Kschessinska had also set up a ballet school in Paris. After fleeing Russia with her partner,

Grand Duke Andrey, and his mother, Grand Duchess Vladimir, she and Andrey had married and settled on the French Riviera, but later financial difficulties forced them to move to Paris. They found a small house and studio in the 16th arrondissement.[48] Friends rallied round with loans to enable Kschessinska to set up a dance studio, where she was able to draw on her considerable past fame in Russia, attracting several pupils who would later themselves become prima ballerinas of distinction: Margot Fonteyn, Alicia Markova, and Tamara Toumanova among them. By the mid-1930s she had over a hundred pupils and could afford to enlarge her studio.[49] She mourned the loss of Diaghilev, even though they had quarreled in the past, and, in 1931, that of another Ballets Russes star, Anna Pavlova. Pavlova, who died in The Hague of pneumonia at the age of only forty-nine, had never settled happily in England. She had missed Russia to the point of "insomnia, tears, headaches, to despair!" she told the singer Alexander Vertinsky. London, where she had a beautiful house at Golder's Green, was "cold and alien." She would give everything, she told him, "for a small cottage with our Russian grass and birches somewhere near Moscow or Petrograd."[50] The ballerina Tamara Karsavina, who had married a British diplomat, Henry James Bruce, and had settled not far from Pavlova, in Hampstead, was also eaten away by the same sense of longing, asking Vertinsky after a concert in Paris, with "tears streaming down her face": "Will we ever return to our homeland?" She had finished writing her memoirs, *Theater Street,* the day she heard of Diaghilev's death; her closing words of remembrance summed up his loss to the world of ballet: "His ruthlessness belonged to Art; his faithful heart was his own."[51]

So many stories of the Paris emigration are those of artistic talent never allowed the chance to breathe and flourish—stunted by adversity, sickness, poverty. Success stories are few; disappointments are many. One of the most touching is that of the poet Irina Knorring, who with her family had been evacuated to Bizerta in Tunisia and in 1925 settled in Paris. The family lived in desperate poverty; Irina was an aspiring poet and married another poet, Yuri Sofiev. Poetry simply didn't pay, and Yuri was reduced to washing windows to earn some money. Even though the revered Russian poet Anna Akhmatova recognized her talent, the odds were against Irina. She found life in the West suffocating. Her fate, her life, her inspiration were all inextricably linked to her homeland, but emigrant life had brought only the "merciless collapse of hopes," as fellow emigrant Yuri Terapiano noted. Her diary-like poems, published in the émigré Paris journals, reflected everyday experiences, particularly of loneliness, exacerbated by the severe diabetes from which she suffered, which caused her to be hospitalized several times and prevented her from taking part in the literary life of the Russian colony. In her isolation she wrote spare, unbearably sad verse about the harshness of émigré life, such as one of her best known: "The Dining Room Window":

How many weary minutes
Have I passed here in silence!
How much pain has been reflected
In its dark glass.

How many words and lines are clear
And nights without sleep
Have died at the frame
Of this window.

In the distance—the hum of Paris
(At night—hear it).
I only see the world
That's in my window.[52]

Knorring's work has passed almost unnoticed in the history of the Russian literary emigration, although her poetry's plangent echoes encapsulate so much of the heartache of exile. There was, however, one literary émigré who often caused a stir and got himself noticed, though ultimately for all the wrong reasons. Boris Poplavsky was undoubtedly the *enfant terrible* of the young Paris poets and his rise was as meteoric as his downfall was ignominious. Fellow poet Georgiy Ivanov wrote that he behaved "like a hooligan" who tried people's patience to the limit; Yanovsky thought him demonic, because of his notorious bad behavior and his "aesthetic fascination" for evil. Poplavsky had extremely poor eyesight and always wore dark glasses, which immediately "gave him the air of a mystical conspirator"; indeed, the writer Irina Odoevtseva was convinced that he deliberately cultivated the manner of a blind person; Nina Berberova agreed that it was an affectation.[53] Poplavsky was rude, confrontational, swore a lot, but, conceded Yanovsky, his "influence on Russian Montparnasse during the first half of the thirties was enormous," with many seeing his work as inspired by the French decadent poets Baudelaire, Rimbaud, and Apollinaire, although he never achieved their enduring fame.

Born in Moscow in 1903, Poplavsky had arrived in Paris in June 1921 via Constantinople and had settled in the Latin Quarter. After studying art, he took up history and philology at the Sorbonne. He spent days in museums looking at paintings; he immersed himself in philosophy and theology and amassed a huge book collection. It was all part of his dream of "becoming a professor of philosophy" back in a free Russia.[54] He haunted literary gatherings in the cafés, where he read his poetry and was soon nicknamed the "Prince of the Kingdom of Montparnasse." Undoubtedly an arresting presence, Poplavsky had "the smile of a fallen angel" that "lit up his ashen-pale inspired face with the dark wheels of its sunken eyes," recalled

Yanovsky.[55] He was desperately poor and lived in a gaslit apartment with his old parents at rue Barrault near the place d'Italie. Yet he always shared what little he had with his friends, who revered him as an ideological guru and mystic. For in addition to his devout Russian Orthodoxy, Poplavsky was drawn to a whole range of esoteric and semi-occult interests, to "Hindu mystics, to freemasonry, and to various forms of spiritualism," all of which helped distance him from the painful realities of his day-to-day life.[56] As Khodasevich later recalled: here was a man often tormented by hunger, with only the most rudimentary place to live, whose "daily budget averaged seven francs, three of which he gave to a friend. Next to Poplavsky, Dostoevsky was what Rockefeller is next to me."[57]

Merezhkovsky and Khodasevich both thought him one of the most gifted poets of the emigration; but his surrealist verse was difficult and there was a disturbing side to Boris Poplavsky. "Dark, saturated forces gathered around him," wrote Yanovsky; he was one of those extraordinary talents with a built-in self-destruct mechanism. Poplavsky's talent grew out of chaos: death was a constant presence in his thoughts: "The émigrés will express themselves, their voice may resound in golden ages," Poplavsky wrote, "only if they perish, die, disappear, dissipate." Indeed, artistic self-sacrifice was the cornerstone of his aesthetic and philosophy.[58] He would lock himself away for days on end, often sitting writing all night and then lying face to the wall all day on his bed. As a result, he developed a strange, unnatural pallor—the color and texture of his skin transformed by the heroin and cocaine to which he had become addicted. He had in fact been introduced to drugs very young—at the age of twelve—by his sister Natasha, who had discovered opium when traveling in the Far East and had predictably died young of her addiction. Through the vicissitudes of his impoverished Paris life and his isolation, drugs had become Poplavsky's refuge, bringing a psychedelic edge to the imagery in his verse, in the days long before LSD.[59] They also brought a tragic and premature end to his life at the age of thirty-two.

On October 17, 1935, Boris Poplavsky was found dead of a drug overdose in what initially appeared to have been a suicide pact with a "half-mad drug addict" of nineteen called Serge Yarko. It later appeared that Yarko had given Poplavsky an excessively large dose of a probably adulterated drug and that his death had been accidental; either that or it had been Yarko's intention to trick him into a joint suicide, for Poplavsky had not expressed any such intentions to his friends. His parents were utterly destitute and had no money to bury him; they appealed to their son's friends to help pay for a coffin and a burial plot, donations c/o *Poslednie novosti*.[60]

Khodasevich blamed the poet's death on the atmosphere of doom and hopelessness among the young Russian poets in Montparnasse. By his death Boris Poplavsky became "famous in a day," as Nina Berberova ironically observed. All the French newspapers wrote about him; but it was the first time that most of the Russians in Paris had even heard of him.[61] In his lifetime Poplavsky had published only sixty poems and nine chapters of a novel; he left behind a considerable amount of unpublished work, but had had no illusions about his legacy, as he told Vladimir Nabokov:

> *Fame? ... Don't make me laugh. Who knows my poems? A thousand? A thousand five hundred; at the very outside two thousand intelligent expatriates, of whom again ninety percent don't understand them. Two thousand out of three million refugees! That's provincial success, but not fame.*[62]

His work retained the adoration of a small cult of aficionados in Paris; but for the rest—indifference and silence. It took a while even for Nabokov, who had initially dismissed Poplavsky's work, to acknowledge his highly original style, prompting him to capture his gift as "A far violin among near balalaikas." He was, after all, "the first hippy," Nabokov later observed, "the original flower child."[63]

Nabokov himself had been a very late arrival on the Paris literary scene. He had lived and worked in Berlin since settling there with his family in 1920, though he had made frequent visits to Paris before moving first to the South of France and then permanently to the 16th arrondissement in October 1938, forced out of Germany by the rise in anti-Semitism that threatened the safety of his Jewish wife, Vera. Like so many other Russian émigrés, Nabokov found himself "leading an odd but by no means unpleasant existence, in material indigence and intellectual luxury, among perfectly unimportant strangers."[64] But he arrived at a period of cultural decline in the community, with many of the first-wave émigrés growing old and dying. The final years before the outbreak of war in 1939 brought a succession of deaths that added to an accumulating sense of loss among the older generation who had fled in 1919/20. In October 1938 Grand Duke Kirill died at Neuilly-sur-Seine outside Paris, having lost his wife, Victoria Melita, in 1936. Sandro too had died, in 1933 in the South of France. The monarchists now looked to Kirill's son Vladimir Kirillovich as head of the imperial house. But it was the passing of a great cultural rather than aristocratic figure that had a far more profound impact on the Russian colony of Paris, causing widespread grief. This was the death of Feodor Chaliapin on April 12, 1938; he was only sixty-five but had suffered from diabetes for some time and then had developed leukemia.

Chaliapin had left Russia for good in 1921 but was tormented by having had to do so. "How could I give up that country where I had not only compassed all that one can see and touch, hear and feel, but where I had dreamed dreams that enshrined my deepest longings, especially in the years that preceded the revolution? he asked in his 1932 autobiography, *Man and Mask*. But with Lenin's government

life had grown more "official," he said, "more arid"; the Soviets had
demanded money from him, assuming that his success meant that
he was "swimming in gold."[65] He had managed to get out of Russia
with his family but without a kopek, and had rebuilt his finances
during a successful career touring the United States and Europe. In
Paris he enjoyed the good life: he had a grand apartment on avenue
d'Eylau near the Trocadéro that was stuffed full of pictures, statues,
and antique furniture. Here Chaliapin had enjoyed the adulation
as the greatest male opera singer of a generation, but he was filled
with inconsolable sadness. The Russians had taken away his title
of People's Artist and his passport—"but they can't take away my
Russian blood," he told his friend Andrey Sedykh. His separation
from his lifeblood, the Russian theater, had, however, left him heart-
sick. "Why do I have to sing in Bordeaux or in Munich but not in
Saratov?" he asked.[66] He longed for his dacha at his home village of
Starovo and to swim and fish in the river nearby. "They've probably turned it into some kind of *kolkhoz* [collective farm] now,"
he mused. But at least he had had Paris; whenever he went on tour
he was always glad to return there—to the scene of his triumph in
the 1908 Diaghilev production of *Boris Godunov*.[67] Sedykh remembered visiting Chaliapin in 1937; he was not a happy man, despite all
his fame, all his success. Much like Bunin, he lived in mortal dread of
growing old, of losing his voice, and of being broke. "But there is no
joy in money," he told Sedykh. "Where is she, my beloved Russia?"
he asked him with tears in his eyes. "What is all this for? Why am I
here, and not in Moscow, or at my home on the Volga?"[68]

The whole of Russian Paris turned out for Chaliapin's funeral on
April 19 at the Alexander Nevsky Cathedral on rue Daru, with people spilling out into the surrounding streets. The French president
sent a huge wreath and the funeral service conducted by Metropolitan Evlogii was broadcast on French radio. Afterward, Chaliapin's
huge oak coffin, covered in a dark-red velvet catafalque embroi-

dered with gold, was taken to the Paris Opera, where the procession paused to hear the funeral lament "Eternal Memory" sung by Russians from the opera choir. From there it wended its way to the Batignolles Cemetery in the northern suburbs, where Chaliapin had chosen his burial plot years before—a modest choice that surprised people expecting something grander at Père Lachaise. At the graveside, Sedykh gave Chaliapin's widow, Maria, a packet of Russian earth to scatter on his coffin.*

By the late 1930s, and the longer their exile went on, many in the older generation of émigrés were suffering similar deep pangs of separation as those felt by Chaliapin. After he won the Nobel Prize, Ivan Bunin had wished only to retreat back to Grasse and write; but his newfound celebrity would not allow it. He reluctantly found himself the de facto "spokesman for 'Russia Abroad,'" and that brought with it obligations as a "cultural ambassador" for the emigration. When interviewed, he said how hard it had been to be separated from his Russian homeland: "Russia is in my soul. . . . This has not disappeared with the years"; Bunin, like Chaliapin, had remained a vagabond, a wanderer, as had so many of his compatriots, who even now dreamed of a return to "the Promised Land—to Russia."[69] The trauma of that separation ran very deep for some and caused untold psychological damage. Émigrés worried that the Russia they once knew was slipping out of their grasp: "We are forgetting the everyday life of our sunken Atlantis, our dear old life," wrote Teffi. "At times, our memory, just like the sea, unexpectedly tosses up some splinter, scrap, fragment from the drowned world, forever lost, and you begin to examine it with sadness and tenderness."[70]

---

* At the time of Chaliapin's death, the Russian Orthodox Cemetery at Sainte-Geneviève-des-Bois had only just been established. During the war years, Chaliapin's grave at Batignolles became neglected, especially after his family emigrated to the United States; his widow refused the offer to transfer Chaliapin's remains there. Instead, in 1984 Chaliapin was reburied in Moscow's Novodevichy Cemetery, with full Soviet honors, where he was later joined by Russian musical greats Prokofiev and Shostakovich.

As the 1930s progressed, Nina Berberova recorded with distaste
the increasingly shabby and wretched state of the émigré colony
and the insularity of the "concentrated but airless space in which
we lived."[71] A wave of despair and depression overtook some vulnerable émigrés, for whom suicide became the only answer to dealing with the wounds of separation and cultural disinheritance that
stubbornly refused to heal. Others, despite the uncertainty and the
danger, began making the decision to go back home, but to a very
different and in many cases unforgiving Russia.

CHAPTER 12

"I Forever Pity the Exile, a Prisoner, an Invalid"

In Paris during the economic downturn of the 1930s, there was an increasing need for charitable and philanthropic relief among the most impoverished members of the Russian colony. Many of the former aristocracy and better-off émigrés played their part, but none more so than Mother Maria Skobtsova. Born Elizaveta Pilenko in 1891 and originally from an affluent and noble St. Petersburg family, she was a talented artist and wrote plays and poetry, while pursuing a deep interest in theology and the spiritual life.[1] During the civil war she and her second husband fled Russia via Georgia and Yugoslavia, arriving in Paris in 1923. After their marriage broke up, Elizaveta approached Metropolitan Evlogii and begged to be allowed to become a Russian Orthodox nun. But she did not want to lock herself away in a monastery as Russian nuns normally did; she wanted to be a "nun in the world," to work in the community, among the destitute, to "share the life of paupers and tramps." Faith and religious practice were never her sole preoccupations—she was also a vigorous social activist. "At the Last Judgment," she insisted, "I will not be asked whether I satisfactorily practiced asceticism, nor how many prostrations and bows I have made before the holy table. I will be asked whether I fed the hungry, clothed the naked, visited the sick and the prisoner in jail. That is all I will be asked."[2] Evlogii agreed to her divorce in 1932 and to her taking her vows as Mother Maria Skobtsova; "the desert of suffering people's hearts" would be her monastery, he told her, and her work would be "in the heart of the world, in the center of the city."[3]

After two years in small make-do premises, Mother Maria found a large, derelict, three-story house at 77 rue de Lourmel. Located in the 15th arrondissement at the end of a lane "with a tiny court-yard and a few scraggly trees," she opened the premises in 1934 as a "House of Hospitality"—a homeless shelter and soup kitchen—on an open-door policy, but with very little funding. The house was "dusty, grubby, humble, unattractive," recalled one of her help-ers; it smelled of "cabbage, bedbugs, rotten floorboards," recalled Yanovsky, but all was "redeemed by its warm sense of shelter, secu-rity and gratifying huddling together in this salvatory Noah's ark."[4] The crumbling plaster was covered over with wall hangings made of Mother Maria's own beautiful embroidery work, including a re-markable depiction of the Last Supper, as well as many icons painted by her. The house was always full, and always noisy, day and night, with "the poor, ragged, unemployed, forgotten and abandoned" of the Russian émigré community, who were received and fed "with love and brotherliness," recalled Father Alexander Schmemann.[5]

At the center of it all was the larger-than-life figure of Mother Maria, the archetypal peasant babushka with her round beaming face and apple-red cheeks. She observed the rules of monastic pov-erty in her dress, wearing "a threadbare habit, a crude leather belt, torn sandals, and a faded black veil which never seemed to rest quite straight on her shorn head," remembered Hélène Iswolsky, whose father had been the last tsarist ambassador to Paris. Despite this drab appearance, so unlike the angelic images of the saints in icons, as

Iswolsky noted, "no other religious of the Paris Russian emigration reflected more of the spirit of Russian Orthodox charisma."[6] She was struck by how Mother Maria's "deep compassion for the poor, the sick, the prisoners and mentally disturbed" involved her in many projects that filled all of her time.[7]

Through it all, Mother Maria was always smiling, always busy knitting, or sewing, or "flitting about in some unstoppable, seamless action"—making soup in the kitchen from food she had begged from shopkeepers and on early-morning foraging trips to the market at Les Halles. Here, pulling her small two-wheeled cart, she piled it up with overripe fruit, root vegetables and greens slightly past their best, the occasional cheese, or meat bones—all donated willingly by stallholders.[8] Back at the hostel, she was forever sweeping stairs, painting icons on the damp walls of the chapel (which she had converted from some old brick stables at the back of the house), making stained glass windows, embroidering vestments, and in the evenings "sitting in the half-lit, sparse living room, greedily absorb[ing] a passionately debated lecture."[9] For in addition to her charity work, Mother Maria held regular and lively literary-philosophical salons at which political radicals, clerics, leading émigré philosophers, and academics such as Nicholas Berdyaev and Sergey Bulgakov held intense debates and exchanged ideas; in particular, she looked up to Berdyaev as a spiritual father.

Some of the nuns and clergy who worked at the hostel soon left, finding the atmosphere insufficiently "monastic" and lacking piety; Mother Maria's brand of *Pravoslavnoe Delo* (Orthodox Action), as she called it, seemed undignified. For when she wasn't at the hostel, she would go out on the streets and into the bars and cafés of Paris, seeking out those in need and offering help. "How could a nun be out in a bar, asking customers if they had a place to spend the night?" asked one of her staff. When challenged, Mother Maria told her critics that "foraging food at the markets at Les Halles was her morning prayer." She refused to give up her regular outings in search of the city's "drunk, despairing, useless" drifters, finding them slumped in all-night cafés or sleeping propped against the tables. "My feeling for them all is maternal," she said; "I would like to swaddle them and rock them to sleep."[10] At rue Lourmel, she eventually gathered a team of volunteers around her who were as dedicated as she was. She opened other hostels—one for families, another for single men—and established a part-time school and a sanatorium for people suffering from TB in a country house at Seine-et-Oise.[11] By 1937 the hostel had three dozen residents and its canteen served over one hundred dinners a day; those who did not receive dole money were fed for free.[12] Mother Maria exhausted herself in her many endeavors on behalf of her fellow émigrés but never turned anyone away; she often sat up through the night offering support to people in distress and sometimes even gave up her own bed to someone who needed it.[13] She also advertised in *Poslednie novosti* that she was willing to go to the homes of poor émigrés and clean; disinfect walls, mattresses, and floors; and exterminate bedbugs, cockroaches, and other parasites.[14]

As the years of their enforced emigration to France dragged on, there were still those in the Russian colony in Paris who clung, ever more faintly, to the hope of a dramatic change of regime and a return to Russia. This psychological mindset of "railway passengers sitting on their trunks and waiting for the signal to depart" became something of a syndrome among them.[15] It was hard to overcome this sense of perpetual longing, but the difficulties of life in the colony *were* occasionally enlivened by religious festivals, the annual commemoration of the birth of Pushkin—who had become the Paris emigration's figurehead—and other cultural gatherings. All these events were featured in the popular weekly illustrated magazine *Illyustrirovannaya Rossiya* (Illustrated Russia), which was an important forum for the more prosaic aspects of émigré life in increasingly uncertain times. As well as publishing human-interest stories about the Paris colony and émigré verse and stories, the magazine reported regularly on life in the Soviet Union. "With what pathetic eagerness the émigré readers study the pictures of city streets, of village life, of provincial towns with their familiar stuccoed houses, board fences, cobblestone streets and market places!" noted one observer. "Ah! Would that the narrow gauge / Ran straight from Paris to Yeletz!" mourned Don-Aminado in one of his popular poems.[16] There was good reason for the Paris Russians to be increasingly hungry for news: during the dark Stalin years of political intimidation, Soviet citizens became fearful of communicating with friends and relatives in the diaspora, and little news was filtering out about the true situation back home.

Illyustrirovannaya Rossiya performed a crucial function at this time, with its special pages for women and children's-interest material and a huge range of advertisements for every possible Russian-run business in Paris—from dress shops to schools to restaurants, hotels, garages, and even fortune-tellers, as well as ads for extras for films being made by the Albatross Film Company at the old Pathé studios at Montreuil, run by Russian émigrés.[17] In 1926 the magazine had introduced and sponsored the first annual Miss Russia contest under the original title Queen of the Russian Colony. The competition continued through the 1930s and drew on the considerable number of beautiful Russian émigrés already working in the Paris fashion industry and as photographic models. Entrants had to be between sixteen and twenty-five and of Russian descent; they must hold a Russian refugee passport and be of an "unstained reputation"; with so many émigrés in straitened circumstances, to win was to gain temporary relief from penury and considerable attention and acclaim. The lucky winner's photograph was circulated throughout the Russian diaspora as a popular postcard. She was then able to go on and take part in the Miss Europe and Miss Universe contests; many winners landed on the covers of magazines such as *Vogue* and *Paris Match*. Noted celebrities in the Paris colony were recruited as judges, including the writer Teffi, although she had disliked the humiliation of the selection process, when the twenty female finalists' bodies were inspected, their dresses pulled tight to show off the shape of their breasts and waist, and their skirts lifted above the knee. To her it seemed "senseless and immoral nonsense," but nevertheless the competition continued till 1939, when the last happy winner was seventeen-year-old Irina Borodulina.[18] One unhappy runner-up, in 1927, however, found it all too much and shot herself a few months later. For the naturally melancholic and volatile Russians, suicide became an increasingly present specter that haunted the difficult years of economic recession and despondency as war approached. Nina Petrovskaya, a young poet friend of Vladislav Khodasevich, who had arrived from Berlin utterly destitute, had succumbed to alcoholism. Unhappy in love and unable to fulfill her limited talents as a writer, she had shut herself in her shabby little hotel room and turned on the gas; novelist Ivan Boldyrev, equally despairing at his lack of professional success and the discovery that he was going deaf, killed himself with an overdose of the barbiturate veronal.[19] A desperate young Russian mother "left without means" threw herself in the Seine with her three-month-old son; a Russian taxi driver committed suicide, worn down by unemployment and hunger; stories such as these featured regularly in the French and émigré press.[20]

The sad end of Count Evgeniy Kobosky was one such. He was found dead from a gunshot wound on a park bench on the rue de la Chine in January 1929; once a diplomat fluent in six languages, after holding a post at the imperial court, he had led a miserable, lonely existence in Paris. Friends in London and New York who were better off than he had helped out when they could, and he received a few commissions for translation work; sometimes Russian neighbors in the colony shared their own meager meals with him. The count's one consolation was his old French governess, Blanche Gay, who lived in the Paris suburbs and whom he visited regularly. But then she fell sick and was taken to the Tenon Hospital in the 20th arrondissement. Kobosky became ever more despairing, ruminating in his tiny rented room over his former days of glory in imperial Russia, of a time when he was once noble and rich. The room contained little more than an iron bedstead, a little table, and a few engravings cut from illustrated magazines stuck on the walls, but not a single book or personal object. The death of his dearest friend, his governess, at Tenon had been the final unbearable chapter in his émigré life.[21]

Many suicides were clearly connected to economic hardship or emotional breakdown, but some were the result of years of exile burdened by the growing realization of never being able to go home. Some reached a point where they simply wanted to go home to die. During the 1930s, some of the émigrés started seriously pondering this possibility, even though in their hearts they realized that the Soviet Union they would go back to might not be the Russia that they had once known. As early as 1924, the Union for the Return to the Motherland had been set up to assist in this aspiration, but by 1937, when it became known as the Society of Friends of the Soviet Union, its underlying motive became only too clear—to encourage acceptance of the new communist regime and a return to Russia. Such an organization was, inevitably, controlled by agents of the NKVD, who actively propagandized among the Russian émigré community to go home right up till the fall of France in 1940.

Writers and poets, in particular, seemed to live on the edge of self-destruction, as Nina Berberova recalled of her chronically depressive partner, Khodasevich: she "couldn't leave him alone for more than an hour," she wrote, "He might jump out of the window, or turn on the gas . . . at such moments I saw him constructing his personal or private hell around himself."[22] Yet despite his anguish, Khodasevich could not go back to Russia, as he knew he would not be able to write there. In contrast, Alexey Tolstoy, author of epic historical novels, had seemed positively relieved to be one of the first Russian writers to return—as early as 1923. Ilya Ehrenburg explained that Tolstoy's return to Russia was prompted by his love of his people and his devotion to his art. "He sensed, rather than understood logically, that he would not be able to write outside Russia. And his love of Russia was so great that he broke not only with his friends but also with many things within himself: he believed in his people and believed that everything must take the course it did."[23] In the Soviet Union, Tolstoy was greeted like a returning hero and quickly reestablished himself by toeing the line of socialist realism and becoming a pillar of the literary establishment. He earned the highest awards and accolades that the Soviet Union could load on him, becoming an influential member of the Academy of Sciences and a winner of the 1943 Stalin Prize, for his enormous trilogy *The Road to Calvary*.[24] Tolstoy's success prompted a desperate and abject Bunin to write to him during the war begging his help in getting unpaid Russian royalties that he desperately needed, his Nobel Prize money long since having run out.[25]

Another literary émigré who returned to Russia was Alexander Kuprin, a master of the short story in prerevolutionary days, whose successful career had effectively ended the minute he left. Lacking the visible source of his inspiration—the Russian people—and unable to write about them from the distance of Paris, Kuprin never overcame that loss and had retreated in on himself. He earned very little from his writing in Paris, and he and his wife struggled with extreme poverty and debt: "I am left naked . . . and destitute as a homeless old dog," he had written to a friend. He sunk into alcoholism; then in the early 1930s his sight began to fail. In 1937 Kuprin resolved that his only option was to go back to Russia: "It's the duty of every true patriot to return there," he said, and certainly "it would be sweeter and easier to die there."[26] At least the socialist state would attend to his medical needs, for his health was rapidly fading. Upon his arrival in the Soviet Union, the Writer's Union allotted Kuprin a dacha in the writer's village at Golytsino at which to recuperate. With his wife and daughter, he then settled in Leningrad. But he now seemed to be in mental decline too; some sensed that he was going senile. But he at least had the pleasure of seeing his collected works republished, although people who met him in those final years thought Kuprin ill at ease in the new Soviet Russia. He resisted demands to turn out socialist realist literature: "Collective farm themes are not for me," he said, "there's no music to me in the sound of machines." The new work he had dreamed of being able to write once back home never materialized; and then Kuprin developed esophageal cancer. And so, as he himself had once said, "just like a wild animal in the forest that goes off to its lair to die," he did so within fourteen months of his return to his homeland, on August 25, 1938.[27]

Without doubt the most notable and tragic returnee—now acknowledged as one of Russia's greatest poets—was Marina Tsvetaeva. During her Paris exile she had been a domestic drudge, making sacrifices for her husband, Sergey (who suffered from TB and could not work), and their two children. She struggled to support them with her spasmodic literary earnings, supplemented by handouts from friends and well-wishers, but she always felt unappreciated and unthanked and was never left with enough time for her own work. "My people at home," she complained, were "interested in everything but me, for at home I'm [just] dishes, broom, cutlets." In the mid-1930s Sergey, who had now warmed to the Soviet Union, and their daughter Alya, who had been suffering intense homesickness, both tried to convince her that it was all right for them to return, especially with war rumbling in Europe. "There's nothing

for me to live on—alone—here," she said. "The émigré community *doesn't like* me."[28] Indeed, most of the Paris literary groups
rejected Tsvetaeva's modernist style and found her manner stand-
offish. Pale, thin, and intense with short, cropped hair, she lived for
her poetry. She was inordinately proud and did not mix easily, and
had a brilliant intellect that seemed incapable of listening to others.
"To talk, that is, to exchange ideas with her, was almost impossible," Vasily Yanovsky remembered. She was very shortsighted and
often failed to acknowledge people, which also offended.[29] Alexey
Remizov strongly disliked Tsvetaeva "for her posturings . . . and
for her extraordinary vanity." Bunin thought her a "psychopath"
with her "leaden eyes, gifted, but lacking in shame." More percep-
tively, Nina Berberova thought her a tragic misfit who "had faith in
dreams, trusted in certain fantasies" that made her a perpetual out-
cast in Paris: "she had no readers, there was no reaction to what she
wrote."[30] To be fair, Tsvetaeva had no interest in the Paris literary
colony either; she was dismissive of the work of the emigration's
rising star, Vladimir Nabokov, and had not admired Bunin's Nobel
win, although she grudgingly admitted that Boris Poplavsky had
been "a poet of some talent but a mixed-up, dissolute man."[31]

Unsurprisingly, therefore, Tsvetaeva felt completely isolated in
Paris, and her attempt to break into the French literary scene failed.
With little or no published work and perpetually on the brink of
poverty, she had had to resort to scavenging to survive. She "made
the rounds of the markets at closing time to get the cheapest unsold
remnants of fruit and vegetables," dressed in a threadbare skirt and
faded sweater with a shopping bag slung over her shoulder. Friends
like Hélène Iswolsky would fill her bag with gifts of food and
clothing; in the woods around the suburb of Meudon, she would
take her son, Mur, to forage for firewood and gather berries and
mushrooms—it reminded her of her beloved Russia.[32] In the émigré
community, her few friends formed an unofficial "Tsvetaeva Aid So-

ciety" and managed to get some of her work published and helped her pay the rent, but she always struggled.[33]

By 1935, Sergey Efron was determined to go back to Russia, even though he had fought for the Whites; Alya was anxious to go too, but still Marina hesitated: was the Russia she remembered still there? "Can one return to a / House which has been razed?" she asked in a poem.[34] She feared the old Russia was a mirage; yet she remained indifferent to her current surroundings in Paris — out of place, out of time, a wanderer who fitted in nowhere:

> *Homesickness! That long*
> *Exposed weariness!*
> *It's all the same to me now*
> *Where I am altogether lonely*
>
> *Or what stones I wander over*
> *Home with a shopping bag to*
> *A house that is no more mine*
> *Than a hospital or a barracks. . . .*[35]

Efron's mind was finally made up when a friend, the literary critic Dmitri Mirsky — now a convert to communism — abandoned his academic career in Paris and took the train back to Moscow, "like a postulant entering a religious community."* His return encouraged Efron, who meanwhile had taken a job with the Union for a Return to the Motherland and for the first time supported the family financially. But his manner changed; he became dogmatic and overtly pro-Soviet. The visa he was granted to return to the Soviet Union was in fact a trade-off for him becoming an NKVD agent. Efron

---

* It was a mistake. The NKVD arrested Mirsky in 1937 for supposedly deviating from the party line. He died in the Gulag two years later.

left for Russia in a hurry in September 1937 after being implicated in a couple of political assassinations in Paris (and possibly also the abduction of General Miller).[36] Alya had already returned in March. It was another two years before Tsvetaeva followed them, extremely reluctantly, capitulating to the insistence of her son, Mur, to whom she was devoted, that they do so.[37] She left on June 12, 1939, without saying goodbye to anyone and boarded the train for Le Havre and from there a ship to Poland and then the train to Moscow. She arrived at the height of the Stalinist Great Terror and the show trials. Two months later, in August, twenty-seven-year old Alya was arrested. The NKVD came for Sergey Efron soon after; Tsvetaeva never saw either of them again. Her husband was later shot, but the Soviets never clarified the precise date of his death—either 1939 or 1941.[38] It would seem that Alya had confessed, under torture in prison, that Sergey was a Trotskyite spy.

When she returned to Moscow, there was no warm welcome home for Tsvetaeva like that accorded to fellow writers Tolstoy and Kuprin before her. She arrived back in the hope that her poetry would be better understood and appreciated in her homeland, but the fact that she had fled in the first place meant she was always under suspicion. She was therefore consistently cold-shouldered by the Soviet literary establishment and not even allowed into the Union of Soviet Writers. The poet Boris Pasternak, who had warned her not to return, interceded and through his contacts obtained translation and editorial work for her, but it left no time for Tsvetaeva's own poetry.[39] When the Germans invaded Russia in 1941, Tsvetaeva managed to get herself and Mur six hundred miles east to a writers' colony in the Tatar town of Elabuga in the remote Volga-Kama region. She rented a cheap room, but the only work she could get was washing dishes. Rejected, desperate, and at the end of her strength she finally succumbed to the suicide she had long contemplated: "I do not want to *die*. I want *not to be*," she wrote; "Oh God, how insignificant I am, how little I can do! To live my life out is to chew bitter wormwood to the end." On August 31, 1941, Marina Tsvetaeva hanged herself in the grim little hut in which she was living and was buried in an unmarked common grave. Her suicide was not reported in the Soviet press.[40]*

There is no doubt that the shunning of Tsvetaeva by so many of her literary peers in the Paris community had contributed to her sense of rejection and her departure for Russia. But Yanovsky concluded that it ran deeper than that; Tsvetaeva had "killed in herself what had tortured her during her entire life and what would not let her find communion with the world"—a "luciferian pride."[41] Two days after she had left for Russia, the émigré community lost another of its writers with the death of Vladislav Khodasevich. Nina Berberova had separated from him in 1932, unable any longer to endure his neuroses. But in January 1939 he had become seriously ill with abdominal cancer. He suffered terribly and grew extremely thin; Berberova, who had remained close to him, visited regularly and witnessed his anguish. But an operation failed to save Khodasevich. His funeral was held at the Russian Catholic Church on rue François-Gerard. His many friends who attended marked the occasion by acknowledging Khodasevich's passion for bridge—his sole consolation in exile—and by going to their favorite café, the Murat, afterward for an impromptu game in his memory.[42]

Khodasevich's funeral had been attended by Vladimir Nabokov, who had seemed at that time to Nina Berberova to be the hope for the future of Russian writing in emigration—"a phoenix from the ashes of the Revolution and exile."[43] But on September 3, 1939, Britain and France declared war on Germany, and France capitulated to the invasion by German troops with alarming speed. The Hitler-Stalin

---

* Mur disappeared in the summer of 1944, reportedly killed in action. Alya was released from the Gulag in 1947 but rearrested in 1949. After her final release in 1955, she collected and published her mother's work during the post-Stalin thaw.

nonaggression pact of August 1939 had already prompted a new exodus of Russians, many of them utterly distraught to see their former
homeland—which had fought alongside France in World War I—
collaborating with the invading German forces. Russians were now
seen even more as pariahs in France and were victimized as enemies,
purely on grounds of their origins. People refused to get in a cab if
the driver was Russian; some Russian shop workers were dismissed;
others were refused work permits. Anti-Russian feeling grew after
the Soviets invaded Finland, even though some émigrés supported
Soviet Russia's right to regain territories it had once owned. As a
"tide of xenophobia" swept over France, the Nazis stormed their
way to the gates of Paris. In June 1940, emigrés described how a
thick cloud of smoke descended on the city, blackening the grass
and leaves on the trees. "Explosions could be heard from all sides—
gas tanks and factories being blown up."[44] As the Germans entered
Paris, they occupied the empty houses, for many had fled the city.
Russian socialist and Jewish émigrés were now in danger from Nazi
roundups and, if they could, fled to the unoccupied zone. It was a
dark and frightening time for the capital's émigré Russian population.[45] "Occupied Paris is extremely sad, one might say a dead city,"
wrote Olga Hendrikoff, who had once been a lady-in-waiting at the
imperial court:

> *Only the hammering of the cast iron soles of German boots*
> *and German cars roaring by at crazy speeds resonate in the*
> *empty streets. Most of the houses have their shutters closed.*
> *All the administration offices, ministries, and so on and the big*
> *hotels have been occupied by the Germans, as have the private*
> *mansions belonging to Jewish families.*[46]

With the German occupation, the Russian workers were squeezed
even harder. "The few French companies that have not been requisi-

tioned by the Germans naturally prefer to employ French people," Olga Hendrikoff noted in her diary, adding that this would mean émigrés would have to find employment in German-run businesses. No wonder so many were desperate to get away; those who were lucky enough to obtain "the USA serum"—a precious American visa—wept with relief.[47] For the United States was the preferred new destination of many in Paris's Russian colony, particularly Jews. Vladimir Nabokov and his wife, Vera, had managed to escape just before the Germans took Paris and settled in New York. Stravinsky had already left for the United States the previous September, despite having taken French citizenship in 1934 and setting up home in Paris. Both men subsequently enjoyed prosperity and success in their new American homes. Mark Chagall also wisely headed for the United States in 1941; he had already moved his canvases out of Paris to safety and had been living in rural Provence, but when the Gestapo started rounding up French Jews, he decided to get out while he could. He and his wife went south across the Spanish border to Madrid and from Lisbon sailed to New York on May 11, 1941. Most of the sixteen thousand Jews in his beloved homeland, the shtetl at Vitebsk, were murdered by the Nazis that October.

Of the original artists' colony of 1900s Montparnasse, Chagall's fellow Jew, Chaim Soutine, had remained in Paris, although he had had to go into hiding at Champigny-sur-Marne in the southeastern suburbs. Here he carried on painting, but he was plagued by spasms of terrible pain caused by serious ulcers. In July 1943 he was forced to seek medical help and was sent to the Maison de Santé in Paris for surgery but died on August 9, the day after an emergency operation, and was buried in Montparnasse, his funeral attended by Picasso and Cocteau.[48]

Kerensky was one of several of the editorial staff of the Russian émigré press in Paris who ended up in the United States after they had been forced to close down by the German invasion. Writers

Vasily Yanovsky, Mark Aldanov, and Andrey Sedykh also headed to
America during the war. Nina Berberova didn't leave until 1950, after which she enjoyed a distinguished writing and academic career at
Yale and Princeton. A few more Parisian Russians returned to the Soviet Union: the singer Alexander Vertinsky opted to go back in 1943
and toured extensively before his death in Leningrad in 1957. Irina
Odoevtseva proved that it was never too late to embrace the motherland again: having seen out the war in Biarritz till 1946, she stayed
on in France until 1987 and finally returned to Russia at the grand
old age of ninety-one—to a rapturous welcome and considerable acclaim. She published her best-selling memoirs of her émigré life, *Na
beregakh Seny* (On the Banks of the Seine) and attracted numerous
interviews as an interesting relic of the Paris emigration before dying
in Leningrad in 1990.

Many Russian émigrés, however, remained in France, if not in
Paris, during the German occupation, although others managed to
make their way to the unoccupied zone, such as Bunin, who went
south to Grasse. But it was a grim time, marked by extreme poverty
and hunger for most. Some were prevented from leaving by crippling
ill health. The poet Irina Knorring, debilitated by severe diabetes, died
at the age of thirty-seven of her condition in Paris in 1943, prompting
Anna Akhmatova to recall of her plight: "I forever pity the exile / A
prisoner, an invalid." Alexander Remizov was another prisoner of his
illness: in the spring of 1940, a bomb had hit the rue Boileau where he
lived, and unable to get to the air raid shelter, Remizov was hit by flying glass. He lived in terror of further raids, but his wife was too sick
to be moved. Serafima died not long after, leaving Remizov to live
on through the German occupation alone. He was rapidly losing his
eyesight and could no longer see what he was writing. But he had nowhere else to go. When his friend Andrey Sedykh visited him, he was
shocked to see how Remizov "had become decrepit, rooted in the

ground, and with the same look of horror I had seen after the bombing still in his eyes. He now looked completely like a gnome from an old fairy tale, was hunched and could not see anything but only make out indistinct shapes." A few compassionate Russian ladies came to clean his room, feed him, and read to him. They suggested he should return to Russia, but Remizov refused. How could he even cross his own street in Auteuil? he asked, let alone reacclimatize to the Soviet Union? And so he carried on scribbling his demonic and fantastical stories, illustrating them in his beautiful calligraphy, till his lonely and painful death in Paris in 1957.[49]

Dmitri Merezhkovsky and his partner, Zinaida Gippius, had spent the first days of the war in Biarritz and then returned to Paris, where he died of a brain hemorrhage in December 1941, worn down by the war, hunger, and money worries. He had also been abandoned by practically everyone in the Russian colony after having made a broadcast on German radio in June 1941 in support of Hitler's turnabout against the Soviet Union with the launching of Operation Barbarossa. As a virulent anticommunist, he celebrated the "heroic feat" of the German army against the Soviet Union.[50] Metropolitan Evlogii conducted Merezhkovsky's funeral service at rue Daru, to which forty or so elderly Russian émigrés turned up, thanks to a notice in *Paris-soir,* after which Merezhkovsky was buried at the Russian Orthodox Cemetery at Sainte-Geneviève-des-Bois. It is not surprising so few turned up for the funeral of one of Russian Paris's eminent intellectuals: the winter of 1941 was unusually cold, everyone was starving, preoccupied simply with surviving. Zinaida Gippius lingered on for a few more years, very deaf and losing her sight, and rudderless without her longtime companion. Once so luminously beautiful, she struck a gaunt but still elegant figure. She kept her suffering to herself and persisted with her long-planned biography of Merezhkovsky, but died on September 9,

1945—a painful, lingering death from a series of strokes that had left her semi-paralyzed.[51]

The last of the old guard of prerevolutionary writers to live on in France were Teffi and Bunin, who both died in Paris—Teffi not long after her eightieth birthday in 1952, of angina. Bunin, angry and disillusioned to the end, resentful of the poverty inflicted on him by his infrequent income from royalties, died aged eighty-three of asthma and pneumonia in 1953. No doubt the health of both had been worn down by the many privations they had had to endure in emigration; indeed, the pathologically morbid Bunin had anticipated his own death for some time and had been bedridden for his final year. The Paris community remembered both much-loved writers with respect and considerable grief at their funeral services at the Alexander Nevsky Cathedral. It was the end of an era, the last days of the first wave of the Russian emigration; some felt that with Teffi's death "a particle of our soul, of our distant Russian past, had departed."[52]

As for the aging aristocratic émigrés: some of the lucky ones lived out their days at the Maison Russe at Sainte-Geneviève-des-Bois, surrounded by mementos of their imperial Russian past, still holding out the plaintive hope for "The Day when the blood-red [Soviet] regime shall come to its appointed end."[53] Before his death in 1933, Sandro had remarked that "Had they known that they would never go back, possibly they would have preferred to brave the bullets and the ration cards" of the Soviet Union. Might they really have had a better life staying put in Russia?[54] Certainly not the Romanovs. Their ranks in Paris were increasingly diminished. By 1936 Grand Duke Dmitri Pavlovich's marriage to Audrey Emery was in trouble. They had led a rather unsettled life, commuting between France, the United States, and England, and Audrey had eventually met and fallen in love with a Georgian prince, Dimitri Djordjadze, and asked for a divorce. By now Dmitri Pavlovich was sickening with tuberculosis; he was also dismayed by the continuing divisions in the family over the line of accession to the throne. Luckily, unlike his cousins Boris and Andrey, who had to live on through the German occupation of Paris, he avoided that in Switzerland. But his condition rapidly worsened, and he died at a TB sanatorium in Davos at the age of only fifty in March 1942. His sister Maria Pavlovna, meanwhile, had left the United States in disgust in 1941 when it had joined Stalinist Russia in the war against the Germans. She traveled south to Argentina, where she lived in the Russian colony in Buenos Aires till 1949, and then in 1952 went to live in Munich, spending a great deal of time with her son Prince Lennart in Mainau. She died in Germany in 1958. She and Dmitri Pavlovich, whose remains Lennart had moved from Davos, are buried side by side in the family crypt at the palace church at Mainau.

The last days of Grand Duke Mikhail's widow, Natasha, marked the pitiful reduction to loneliness and poverty of a once wealthy Romanov. Running out of money in England, in 1927 she had moved to Paris. Grand Duke Kirill had granted her the honorary title of Princess Brassow, but it had not saved her from the misery of poverty after she had sold off her jewelry, piece by piece. The loss of her son George in a motor accident in 1931 left her with nothing to live for, but she struggled on, living in a poky room on the top floor of a house on the Left Bank, offered for free by a pitying Russian émigré. But in 1951 she developed breast cancer, and her host, not wishing to nurse her, asked her to leave. Natasha was taken to the ward of a charity hospital, where she died on January 23, 1952. The Paris community, most of whom had ignored her plight, nevertheless turned out for her funeral, as they did also for the last of the old imperial Russian guard, Felix Yusupov, and his wife, Irina, when they died in Paris in 1967 and 1970 respectively. Both coffins, like those of so many other members of the Russian aristocracy in Paris, wended their way to that little bit of Mother Russia at Sainte-Geneviève-des-Bois.

By August 1940 all the old émigré life of Russian Paris had been closed down with the enforced disbanding of cultural, educational, and charitable bodies, but Mother Maria Skobtsova had refused to abandon her philanthropic work. The only place she would leave for was home, she insisted: "I would prefer to perish in Russia," she said, "rather than starve to death in Paris."[55] She knew that her hostel would be even more badly needed in the coming winter, and so it was designated a "Cantine Municipale"—an official food-distribution point. During the German occupation, she worked tirelessly to protect her own Russian community—who were now being targeted by the Gestapo. In June 1941, a thousand Russians, including some of Mother Maria's close friends and colleagues, were arrested.[56] She also sought to protect Jews threatened with deportation by the Nazis; in 1942 they had begun turning up at her refuge in fear for their lives. Mother Maria provided them with false papers and baptismal certificates, putting them under the protection of her parish at rue Lourmel. When the mass roundup of Paris's Jewish population came in July 1942, she took food and water to the 6,900 deportees who were held for five days at the cycling stadium—the Vélodrome d'Hiver—and managed to persuade the rubbish collectors to help her smuggle several children out to safety in dustbins.[57]

But early in 1943 the Gestapo came and arrested Mother Maria, her son Yuri, and several of her staff. She was put in a cattle truck on a transport to the concentration camp at Ravensbrück, where she survived for two years, almost till the liberation. She spent her time there trying to buoy up the spirits of her fellow prisoners while hiding her own profound inner suffering. But sadly, on March 31, 1945, with the artillery fire of the approaching Russians in the distance, and now extremely frail and sick, she was sent to the gas chamber; it is said that she volunteered to take the place of another, Jewish, inmate.[58] In 2004 the Metropolitan of Constantinople declared Mother Maria a saint, along with her son Yuri, who also died in the camps, in 1944.[59]

By the end of the war there were only 55,000 Russians left in France; thanks to the slow but steady emigration of many in the diaspora to the United States, by the 1950s New York had supplanted Paris as the political and cultural capital of the emigration.[60] Of those émigrés who left Russia after the 1917 revolution, while we have a wealth of painful reflections on their predicament by writers and poets, so few voices of ordinary Russians have been recorded. But when they were, they were stoic and unself-pitying. They spoke most simply and eloquently of what they had left behind in Mother Russia. "What do I miss most about my old life?" mused taxi driver Sergey Rubakhin when interviewed:

> *It's no big thing, in truth. . . . A real winter, perhaps, a real Russian winter, with 35 degrees below zero. . . . Here the winter is a joke. . . . And then, there's the beautiful serenity of the Russian people . . . who accepted everything and never complained, even when in misery. "Why complain? God is so high, and the tsar is so far."*[61]*

The Russian emigration described by those who lived it as *Zarubezhnaya Rus*—Russia Abroad, or Russia Beyond the Border—was a concept that many had stubbornly looked upon as temporary. Their enclave in Paris was "like an island torn off by earthquake forces from the mainland and similar to the latter in its structure

---

* A popular Russian proverb expressing acceptance of the remoteness of God and central government from the interests of the Russian population at large.

and essence." But sooner or later, they hoped, the two would be re-united.[62] Meanwhile, sympathy for the old, inward-looking émigrés was rapidly fading as admiration grew for the economic, industrial, and military achievements of the new Soviet Union. The longer it endured, the greater its legitimacy in the eyes of the world. The new, younger generation of Paris-born Russians, who had never experienced their parents' homeland, largely saw it as a romanticized ideal with which they had nothing in common. They found their parents' talk of return wearisome, as they assimilated ever more into French life, language, and customs.[63] Henri Troyat, whose adopted French identity was confirmed by the award of the Prix Goncourt in 1938, saw the sentimentalism of the older generation and their grief over the loss of status as a funereal cult of the past, a desperate need to validate their existence in a world that no longer wanted them. Nina Berberova had seen the demise of the first-wave emigration during World War II almost as a blessing — "the shabby, unhappy provincial emigration was ending"; those who had not left were now growing old and dying; others went to Berlin to volunteer in the fight against Stalin's Soviet Union.[64] In the 1960s Sergey Rubakhin recalled how his children had now become thoroughly French, which he was sure was the best thing for them. He had long since accepted his life in France and had ceased to weep for "Sainted Russia." For years and years, he said, he and his fellow émigrés had vainly dreamed of an imminent return. "Like the Jews of the Diaspora, they said to us: 'Next year in Moscow.'" For a while the possibility had fueled their ability to endure. "But for a long time now, that hope has been buried with the rest."[65]

Acknowledgments

For various unexpected reasons, I shall undoubtedly recall the writing of this book more vividly than that of any of my others. This is because it was written, for the most part, in the self-isolation of lockdown during the Covid-19 pandemic of 2020. For this reason, *After the Romanovs* is likely to be one of hundreds, if not thousands, of "Covid books" affected by the widespread lockdown of libraries, archives, museums, and other resources upon which historians such as myself rely. I therefore count myself very lucky that I had already collated, downloaded, and brought together the vast majority of the research material for this book just a month or so before Covid struck. However, my research trip to Paris, to which I had greatly looked forward, was a casualty and one that I very much mourn. In consolation, I was able, as always, to draw on the help and moral support of numerous friends, who generously sent me source material from their own libraries, found digital material for me, and happily shared their expert knowledge of certain specialist areas of this story with which I was less familiar.

My Russophile friend Sue Woolmans, to whom this book is dedicated, should have been on the Eurostar with me to Paris in March

2020, but instead provided unlimited and generous moral support, sent scans and photocopies, and was, as she has been for so many of my other books, a much-valued cheerleader. From Finland, Rudy de Casseres helped me access difficult-to-find Russian sources; from New York, Nick Nicholson contributed his peerless expertise on all things Romanov and checked key parts of the text; from Swindon, Phil Tomaselli, an old and much-trusted advisor on all things relating to intelligence matters, checked a key chapter on ROVS and the OGPU; the Reverend Ed Hanson provided insightful comments on Grand Duke Dmitri Pavlovich; my good friend and balletomane Celia Brayfield advised on Diaghilev and ballet; Dr. Oleg Beyda at the University of Melbourne shared material on the White Russian Army and ROVS; fellow historian Susan Ronald loaned books and shared her knowledge of the Americans in Paris in the 1920s; and Alan Sergeant in Scotland did some valuable research for me in digital newspapers. Other friends, colleagues, and fellow historians shared information and their expert opinion: Doug Smith, Andrei Korliakov, Amy Ballard, Anna Erm, Anne Sebba, Caroline de Souza, Catherine Barr Windels, Christopher Hadley, Justine Picardie, Lesley Chamberlain, Michael Holman, Ricardo Javier Mateos Sainz de Medrano, Richard Davies, and Vanora Bennett. My thanks to Maria Rubin for her translation of the Adamovich poem in the epigraphs. I must also thank the many readers who share my passion for Russian history, who follow me on Twitter and Facebook, and who have kept me going through two lockdowns with their enthusiasm and support for my work. On an entirely personal level, my dear friend Lynne Hatwell has been an absolute rock and an indispensable lifeline for moral support, advice, and good cheer during some difficult days as I wrote this, as too my brother Chris and his wife, Sue, who live down the road and who—when social distancing permitted—provided wine and roast dinners to keep my spirits up. Separation from my daughters, grandchildren, and the rest of my family has been hard, but I am grateful for their love and support for my work.

It has not been easy writing a book in such strict isolation, and I have missed my trips from the West Country to London, to meetings with my agent and to speak at literature festivals, but I have, as always, had a wonderful publisher behind this latest project. My dear friend Charles Spicer at St. Martin's Press in New York has always been at hand to advise and offer support, as too associate editor Sarah Grill. I am grateful to my copy editor, Angela Gibson, for a restrained and judicious edit and deeply indebted to my hardworking picture researcher, Laura Hanifin, who went to exhaustive lengths in seeking out the best combination of affordable images for the photo insert. Throughout the writing of this book, I have as always benefited from the unfailing support of my tireless and muchtreasured friend and agent, Caroline Michel; her assistant, Laurie Robertson; and all the wonderful team at PFD who take such good care of me and my books.

Finally, it is always a pleasure being contacted by readers with new information, stories, and material relating to the subjects of my books and I would welcome hearing from anyone in this regard, via my website, www.helenrappaport.com or info@helenrappaport .com.

West Dorset, June 2021

Notes

ABBREVIATIONS:

Bunin 1   Marullo, *Russian Requiem*
Bunin 2   Marullo, *From the Other Shore*
Bunin 3   Marullo, *The Twilight of Emigré Russia*
Always   Alexander, *Always a Grand Duke*
Belle Époque   Zeisler, *Vivre la Belle Époque*
Elysian Fields   Yanovsky, *Elysian Fields*
Exile   Marie, Grand Duchess, *A Princess in Exile*
Flight   Perry and Pleshakov, *Flight of the Romanovs*
Grand Duke   Alexander, *Once a Grand Duke*
Homesick   Huntington, *The Homesick Million*
Italics   Berberova, *The Italics Are Mine*
Les Russes   Menegaldo, *Les Russes à Paris*
"New Mecca"   Johnston, *"New Mecca, New Babylon"*
Night Roads   Gaito Gazdanov, *Night Roads*
People and Life   Ilya Ehrenburg, *People and Life*
"Refugees"   Hassell, *"Russian Refugees"*
Things   Marie, Grand Duchess, *Things I Remember*

CHAPTER I: LA TOURNÉE DES GRANDS DUCS

1.   Pierre de Coulevain, *Sur la branche*, Paris: Calmann-Levy, 1903, 250.
2.   *Homesick*, 226.
3.   See *Les Russes*, 14–17.
4.   For an account of the Romanovs in Biarritz, see Alexandre de la Cerda, *La Tournée des grands ducs: Les Russes sur la Côte Atlantique*, Biarritz: Atlantica, 1999.

5.   Buxhoeveden, *The Life and Tragedy of Alexandra Fyodorovna*, London: Long-
        mans Green, 1928, 74; Helen Rappaport, *Four Sisters: The Lost Lives of the Ro-
        manov Grand Duchesses*, London: Macmillan, 2014, 41–42.

6.   www.theromanovfamily.com/romanov-family-in-paris-1896/.

7.   Skinner, *Elegant Wits and Grand Horizontals*, 225.

8.   See chapter 6, "The Grand Dukes' Tour," in Dominique Kalifa, *Vice, Crime, and
        Poverty: How the Western Imagination Invented the Underworld*, New York:
        Columbia UP, 2019; "A Paris, la tournée des grands-ducs," chapter 3 of Boulay,
        La France des Romanov.

9.   He was second in line after the death of Nicholas's brother George in 1899 until
        the birth of Alexey in 1904; Ular, *Russia from Within*, 74.

10.   See *Flight*, 39, and Chavchavadze, *Grand Dukes*, 114–15.

11.   Elizabeth Drexel Lehr, "*King Lehr" and the Gilded Age*, Philadelphia: J. B. Lip-
        pincott, 1935, 239; Marguerite Cunliffe-Owen, *Within Royal Palaces,* Philadel-
        phia: Enterprise Publishing, 1892, 286; E. A. Brayley Hodgetts, *The Court of
        Russia in the Nineteenth Century*, vol. II, London: Methuen & Co., 1908, 225.

12.   Ular, *Russia from Within*, 84.

13.   Gelardi, *From Splendor to Revolution*, 125; Sommerville Story, *Dining in Paris:
        A guide to Paris à la carte and table d'hôte*, New York: R. M. McBride, 1924, 85.

14.   Ular, *Russia from Within*, 82.

15.   Meriel Buchanan, *Victorian Gallery,* London: Cassell, 1956, 50. See also Princess
        Catherine Radziwill, *Memories of Forty Years*, New York: Funk & Wagnalls,
        1915, 228.

16.   James Laver, *Manner and Morals in the Age of Optimism, 1848–1914*, London:
        Weidenfeld & Nicolson, 1966, 238.

17.   Marcel Fouquier, *Jours heureux d'autrefois*, vol. 2, *A Travers l'Europe*, Paris: Al-
        bin Michel, 1944, 50, 142. Maurice Dekobra, *Rendez-vous chez Maxim's,* Paris:
        Presses de la Cité, 1970, 15.

18.   Skinner, *Elegant Wits*, 225; *Grand Duke*, 41, 137–38.

19.   Skinner, *Elegant Wits*, 225.

20.   Ibid.

21.   Ralph Neville, *Unconventional Memories: Europe—Persia—Japan,* London:
        Hutchinson, 1923, 283–84.

22.   Marie, *Story of My Life*, 84.

23.   Chavchavadze, *Grand Dukes*, 114.

24.   *Grand Duke*, 41.

25.   Ibid., 139; Chavchavadze, *Grand Dukes*, 115.

26.   Ular, *Russia from Within*, 83.

27.   *Grand Duke*, 151–52.

28.   See Ferran Canyameres, *L'homme de la Belle Époque*, Paris: Bellenand, 1946,
        80; Michel Souvais, *Moi, La Goulue de Toulouse-Lautrec: Les mémoires de mon
        aïeule*, Paris: Publibook, 2008, 90–91; Flanner, *Paris Was Yesterday*, 57.

29.   Skinner, *Elegant Wits*, 224.

30.   Ritz, *Cézar Ritz*, 239.

31.   *New York Herald*, November 22, 1899; see Ritz, *Cézar Ritz*, 239, 261–62, 264.

32.   *Belle Époque*, 29.

33. Kleinmichel, *Shipwrecked*, 152.
34. Edward J. Bing, *The Secret Letters of the Last Tsar*, New York: Longmans, Green & Co., 1938, 165.
35. Greg King, *The Court of the Last Tsar*, Hoboken, NJ: Wiley, 2006, 83.
36. Paléologue, *Three Critical Years*, 161.
37. See, for example, *St. James Gazette*, February 22, 1905.
38. Paléologue, *Three Critical Years*, 178.
39. *Evening Standard*, August 24, 1906.
40. *Belle Époque*, 43.
41. See Marcel Proust, *Time Regained*, London: Chatto & Windus, 1949, 189–90.
42. Widow of a Diplomat, *Intimacies of Court and Society: An Unconventional Narrative of Unofficial Days*, New York: Dodd, Mead, 1912, 29.
43. *Belle Époque*, 61.
44. Chavchavadze, *Grand Dukes*, 129; *Belle Époque*, 79.
45. *Le Figaro*, June 1, 1911.
46. See Francesca Brickell, *The Cartiers: The Untold Story of the Family behind the Jewelry Empire*, New York: Ballantine Books, 2019, 66 and note 555; *Belle Époque*, 167, 169. See *Belle Époque* for a fascinating account of Olga's spending habits, based on Wilfred Zeisler's firsthand research in her diaries and account books at GARF in Moscow, 67.
47. *Belle Époque*, 115–16, 149.
48. Ibid., 95, 167.
49. Charles de Chambrun, *Lettres à Marie: Pétersbourg–Petrograd, 1914–1918*, Paris: Plon, 1941, 223.
50. See *Belle Époque*, 67–68.
51. Julian Barnes, *The Man in the Red Coat*, London: Jonathan Cape, 2019, 124.
52. Kahan, *Music's Modern Muse*, 150.

CHAPTER 2: "WE REALLY DID STAGGER THE WORLD"

1. Diaghilev, letter to his stepmother. Quoted in Volkov, *Saint Petersburg*, 130.
2. Volkov, *Saint Petersburg*, 262.
3. Sjeng Scheijen, *Diaghilev*, 149.
4. Volkov, *Saint Petersburg*, 262.
5. See Benois, *Reminiscences*, 237–38.
6. Ibid., 239.
7. Volkov, *Saint Petersburg*, 262.
8. Kodicek, *Diaghilev*, 51–52. See 52 for details of the concert program.
9. *Gil Blas* [Parisian literary journal], May 18, 1907.
10. See, e.g., "Fédor Chaliapine à Paris," *Le Figaro*, May 14, 1907; *Belle Époque*, 105; Scheijen, *Diaghilev*, 160.
11. Kodicek, *Diaghilev*, 67.
12. Benois, *Reminiscences*, 299; Vassiliev, *Beauty in Exile*, 13.
13. Kodicek, *Diaghilev*, 67, 68.
14. Ibid., 71, quoting *La Liberté*.
15. Ibid, 57.

16. Kahan, *Music's Modern Muse*, 153–54; *Le Figaro*, June 4, 1908.

17. Kschessinska was *prima ballerina assoluta* at the Mariinsky at the time. She was also Nicholas II's former lover, and had angrily refused to take part in the Diaghilev season when offered only one role. She may have influenced the withdrawal of the subsidy as part of a court intrigue to send the Imperial Ballet rather than Diaghilev's Ballets Russes to Paris. See Kodicek, *Diaghilev*, 88.

18. Lifar, *Serge Diaghilev*, 156.

19. Benois, *Reminiscences*, 319.

20. Karsavina, *Theater Street*, 186; Kodicek, *Diaghilev*, 53.

21. Lifar, *Diaghilev*, 154.

22. Ibid.

23. Karsavina, *Theater Street*, 194.

24. Baxter, *The Golden Moments of Paris*, 29.

25. Alexander Schouvaloff, *The Art of Ballets Russes: The Serge Lifar Collection of Theater Designs, Costumes and Paintings at the Wadsworth Atheneum*, New Haven: Yale University Press, 1998, 36.

26. Benois, *Reminiscences*, 284–85.

27. Fokine, *Memoirs of a Ballet Master*, 147–48.

28. Benois, quoted in Kodicek, *Diaghilev*, 80.

29. Benois, *Reminiscences*, 284.

30. Karsavina, *Theater Street*, 151.

31. Benois, *Reminiscences*, 288.

32. Kschessinska, *Dancing in Petersburg*, 113.

33. Benois, *Reminiscences*, 294.

34. Lifar, *Serge Diaghilev*, 158.

35. Ibid., 219.

36. Fokine, *Memoirs of a Ballet Master*, 148.

37. Benois, *Reminiscences*, 285.

38. Vassiliev, *Beauty in Exile*, 21.

39. Baxter, *The Golden Moments of Paris*, 31–32; Scheijen, *Diaghilev*, 202.

40. Vassiliev, *Beauty in Exile*, 28.

41. Mary E. Davis, *Classic Chic: Music, Fashion and Modernism*, Berkeley: University of California Press, 2008, 22–23.

42. Vassiliev, *Beauty in Exile*, 28, 35.

43. Lifar, *Diaghilev*, 135; Scheijen, *Diaghilev*, 201.

44. Stravinsky interview, 1960s, www.youtube.com/watch?v=RZEsmbcwngY

45. Fokine, *Memoirs of a Ballet Master*, 158, 165.

46. Walsh, *Stravinsky*, 143.

47. Karsavina, *Theater Street*, 198.

48. Ibid., 199; Bronislava Nijinska, *Early Memoirs*, Durham, N.C.: Duke University Press, 1992, 273.

49. Karsavina, *Theater Street*, 200.

50. Lynn Garafola, *Diaghilev's Ballets Russes*, Oxford: Oxford University Press, 1989, xi.

51. Craft and Stravinsky, *Memories and Commentaries*, London: Faber, 1981, 38.

52. Kahan, *Music's Modern Muse*, 166.

53. Walsh, *Stravinsky*, 138.

54. Kodicek, *Diaghilev*, 84.
55. Scheijen, *Diaghilev*, 264.
56. Walsh, *Stravinsky*, 180; Puccini apparently also thought it "the stuff of a mad-man . . . sheer cacophony," Mosco Carner, *Puccini: A Critical Biography*, New York: Holmes & Meier, 1977, 173.
57. Scheijen, *Diaghilev*, 265.
58. Walsh, *Stravinsky*, 180–181.
59. Ibid., 179; Benois, *Reminiscences*, 346, 347.
60. Lifar, *Diaghilev*, 143.
61. Lopokova, *Dancing for Diaghilev*, 442.
62. Walsh, *Stravinsky*, 202–03.
63. James S. Williams, *Jean Cocteau*, London: Reaktion Books, 2008, 50, 51; Jann Pasler, *Writing Through Music: Essays on Music, Culture, and Politics*, Oxford: Oxford University Press, 2008, 147.
64. Walsh, *Stravinsky*, 203.
65. Davis, *Ballets Russes Style*, 94; see also Thomas Forrest Kelly, *First Nights: Five Musical Premieres*, New Haven: Yale University Press, 2000, chapter 5.
66. Davis, *Ballets Russes Style*, 94. Edith Wharton attended one of the performances, but probably not the first night. She found *The Rite of Spring*'s brutal primitivism "extraordinary," so much so that she went to see the production for a second time.
67. 1960s interview, quoted in Craft and Stravinsky, *Expositions and Developments*, 143.
68. Kahan, *Music's Modern Muse*, 185.
69. For an interesting assessment of the supposed "riot" at the premiere that sets the record straight, see https://notanothermusichistorycliche.blogspot.com/2018/06/did-stravinskys-rite-of-spring-incite.html.
70. Schiejen, *Diaghilev*, 272–73.
71. Lopokova, *Dancing for Diaghilev*, 42, 44.
72. Peter Hill, *Stravinsky: The Rite of Spring*, Cambridge: Cambridge University Press, 2008, 30.
73. Walsh, *Stravinsky*, 204.
74. Marie Rambert, *Quicksilver, The Autobiography of Marie Rambert*, London: Macmillan, 1972, 65.
75. Walsh, *Stravinsky*, 599.
76. Ibid., 206.
77. Salisbury, *Black Night, White Snow*, 217.
78. Benois, *Reminiscences*, 284.

CHAPTER 3: "PARIS TAUGHT ME, ENRICHED ME, BEGGARED ME, PUT ME ON MY FEET"

1. David C. Gordon, *French Language and National Identity (1930–1975)*, Berlin: De Gruyter Mouton, 1978, 35.
2. By 1872 almost half of France's Russian-Jewish population lived in Paris. See Nancy L. Green, *The Pletzl of Paris: Jewish Immigrant Workers in the Belle Époque*, Boulder, Colo.: Lynne Rienner Publishers, 1985.
3. Lenin's first apartment at rue Beaunier was grand and spacious but far too expensive at 840 francs a year plus 60 in taxes and as much again for the concierge.

Lenin moved to a cheaper two-room apartment at 4 rue Marie-Rose in July 1909. Trotsky, who came to Paris in November 1914, often went to the Rotonde and also the Baty restaurant; he was friendly with Diego Rivera and often seen with him in the Paris cafés.

4.   *People and Life,* 68, 69.

5.   Marevna, quoted in Obolensky, *Russians in Exile,* no page [unfortunately this useful POD book has no pagination]; *People and Life,* 69.

6.   Obolensky, *Russians in Exile,* np.

7.   Nina Gourfinkel, *Lenin,* New York: Grove Press, 1961, 82.

8.   Rappaport, *Conspirator,* 184. For Lenin's life in Paris, see chapter 12: "Why the Hell Did We Go to Paris?"

9.   Carter Elwood, *The Non-Geometric Lenin: Essays on the Development of the Bolshevik Party, 1910–1914,* London: Anthem Press, 2011, 129.

10.   *People and Life,* 75, 82.

11.   Crespelle, *Chagall,* 21.

12.   Kluver, *Kiki's Paris,* 63.

13.   Léon-Paul Fargue, *Le piéton de Paris,* Paris: Gallimard, 1998, 140–41.

14.   *People and Life,* 83.

15.   Ibid., 88.

16.   Ibid., 86.

17.   Ibid., 94.

18.   Drot, *Les heures chaudes,* 25.

19.   Klüver, *Kiki's Paris,* 59, 219.

20.   Drot, *Les heures chaudes,* 22.

21.   Klüver, *Kiki's Paris,* 59. La Ruche was saved from demolition in the 1960s, thanks to a campaign by Jean-Paul Sartre, Jean Renoir, and others. It was refurbished and still serves as studios for artists today.

22.   *Les Russes,* 68.

23.   Ibid., 70.

24.   Drot, *Les heures chaudes,* 26, 164; *Les Russes,* 68, 70.

25.   *The London Magazine,* 4:5, 1964; www.thelondonmagazine.org/archive-memories -of-modigliani-by-anna-akhmatova/.

26.   Anna Akhmatova, *My Half Century: Selected Prose,* Evanston: Northwestern University Press, 1992, 76.

27.   Amanda Haight, *Akhmatova: A Poetic Pilgrimage,* Oxford: Oxford University Press, 1976, 16; see also Lucy Davies, "Modigliani and the Russian Beauty: The Affair That Changed Him," *Telegraph,* April 15, 2015.

28.   See Tamara Eidelman, "Modigliani and Akhmatova in Paris," *Russian Life,* March 5, 2016.

29.   In 1963, during the thaw of the Khrushchev era, Akhmatova was finally allowed to publish a volume of her work. Entitled *The Flight of Time,* it appeared in a limited print run that quickly sold out. Akhmatova chose a drawing of herself by Modigliani from 1911 for the front cover. She wrote a beautiful study, "Memories of Modigliani," first published not long after her death in *The London Magazine* 4: 5, 1964.

30.   *Les Russes,* 70; Alexander, *Chagall,* 128.

31.   Klaus H. Karl, *Soutine,* New York: Parkstone International, 2015, 31.

32. Alexander, *Chagall*, 114–15.
33. Ibid., 102.
34. Crespelle, *Chagall*, 79.
35. Alexander, *Chagall*, 101.
36. Ibid., 114–15.
37. Wiser, *Crazy Years*, 96.
38. See Crespelle, *Chagall*, 35–40.
39. Alexander, *Chagall*, 122–23.
40. Karl, *Soutine*, 34.
41. Anglade, *La vie quotidienne*, 64.
42. *People and Life*, 99.
43. Alexander, *Chagall*, 112.
44. Rappaport, *Conspirator*, 174; Robert Service, *Lenin*, Cambridge: Harvard University Press, 2000, 189.
45. *Belle Époque*, 132, see figs. XVIII and XIX.
46. *Belle Époque*, 188–89. There were six francs to the dollar in 1912, making this $166, 667, which is around $4,435,000 today.
47. Muriel Delahaye, *Miss Daisy's Secret Russian Diary, 1916–1918*, Kibworth Beauchamp, Eng.: Matador, 2017, 184.
48. Anatoli Nekludoff, *Diplomatic Reminiscences Before and During the World War, 1911–1917*, London: Dutton, 1920, 222–23.
49. Ibid., 223.
50. Elisabeth Marbury, *My Crystal Ball: Reminiscences*, London: Hurst & Blackett, 1924, 229.
51. Irene Castle, *Castles in the Air*, New York: Doubleday, 1958, 80.
52. Ibid, 81–83.
53. Zinaida Gippius, "Dmitrii Merezhkovsky," in Buslakova, *Russkii Parizh*, 44–45. For Merezhkovsky and Gippius in Paris at this time, see also Salisbury, *Black Night, White Snow*, 216–19.
54. Crespelle, *Chagall*, 115.
55. By 1914 the Russian population of France was 30,000–40,000. See Durkheim, "Report on the Situation of Russians in France in 1916," 184. Durkheim was Chair of the Aliens Committee to French Minister of Interior at the time and conducted the report in response to the campaign against Russian aliens, especially Jews, who were accused of refusing to do their duty to Russia and France.
56. Durkhheim, "Report," 184.
57. *People and Life*, 161.
58. Durkheim, "Report," 190.
59. Ibid., 185.
60. See *People and Life*, 167–68; Durkheim, "Report," 185.
61. *People and Life*, 223.
62. Schiejen, *Diaghilev*, 331.
63. *People and Life*, 218–19.
64. *"New Mecca,"* 17–18.
65. *People and Life*, 220.
66. Ibid., 223.
67. Ibid.

CHAPTER 4: "WE HAD OUTLIVED OUR EPOCH AND WERE DOOMED"

1. *Exile,* 56.
2. Paléologue, *Ambassador's Memoirs,* 368.
3. Norman Stone, *The Eastern Front, 1914–1917,* London: Penguin, 1998, 261–62; Robert Cowley, *The Great War: Perspectives on the First World War,* London: Random House, 2004, 229.
4. Paléologue, *Ambassador's Memoirs,* 903; *Belle Époque,* 220.
5. Paléologue, *Ambassador's Memoirs,* 904.
6. *Things,* 302, 306.
7. Grand Duke Paul, quoted in Chavchavadze, *Grand Dukes,* 132.
8. Smith, *Former People,* 133.
9. See ibid., 76–79.
10. Brackman, *The Secret File of Joseph Stalin,* 125.
11. *Things,* 339.
12. Smith, *Former People,* 132–33.
13. For a description of Russian refugees in Kislovodsk at this time, see Ignatieff, *The Russian Album,* chapter 7.
14. Meriel Buchanan, *Victorian Gallery,* London: Cassell, 1956, 60.
15. Clarke, *Hidden Treasures,* 80.
16. Ibid., 89, 127.
17. Robien, *Diary of a Diplomat,* 153–54.
18. *Things,* 340.
19. Robien, *Diary of a Diplomat,* 153–54; *Things,* 341.
20. *Things,* 341.
21. Jevakhoff, *Les Russes blancs,* 59.
22. *Things,* 351.
23. Paley, *Memories of Russia,* chapter XIX; www.alexanderpalace.org/memoriesrussia /index.html; Smith, *Former People,* 326.
24. Nostitz, Countess, *Romance and Revolutions,* London: Hutchinson, 1937, 117.
25. Robien, *Diary of a Diplomat,* 225–26.
26. Gabriel, *Memories in the Marble Palace,* 316.
27. *Things,* 350.
28. Charlotte Zeepvat, *Romanov Autumn: The Last Century of Imperial Russia,* Stroud, UK: Sutton, 2006, 261–62.
29. *Things,* 356–57.
30. Ibid., 369.
31. Ibid., 373.
32. Ibid., 374.
33. Ibid., 382.
34. George, *Romanov Diary,* 232–33.
35. Ibid., 237.
36. *Exile,* 118.
37. George, *Romanov Diary,* 229; *Exile,* 118; Paley, *Memories* online, chapter XXXV.
38. Paley, *Memories* online, chapter XXV.
39. George, *Romanov Diary,* 233–34, 238.
40. Gabriel, *Memories in the Marble Palace,* 319.

41. Perry, *Flight*, 208; Cockfield, *White Crow*, 241.

42. Arkadi Vaksberg, *The Murder of Maxim Gorky: A Secret Execution,* New York: Enigma Books, 2007, 90.

43. Antonina Romanova, "Kak Byl Spasen Knyaz Gavriil Konstantinovich," 1934, 9: 14.

44. Gabriel, *Memories in the Marble Palace,* 339; Antonina Romanova, "Kak Byl Spasen Knyaz Gavriil Konstantinovich," 1934, 9: 15.

45. Iosif Leibovich Gerzoni was a doctor and gynecologist. See Vaksberg, *The Murder of Maxim Gorky,* 90–91.

46. Gabriel, *Memories in the Marble Palace,* 345–46; see also Antonina Romanova, no. 40, 20.

47. George, *Romanov Diary,* 238–39; Paley, *Memories* online, chapter XXXVII.

48. *Exile,* 117.

49. Cockfield, *White Crow,* 241.

50. See Brummer, "Les derniers jours," 264–66; George, *Romanov Diary,* 239; Marie, *Exile,* 118–22; *Flight,* 209.

51. Brummer, "Les derniers jours," 265–66; Cockfield, *White Crow,* 245. Many Russian websites now confirm the execution date as 30 January. See, e.g., http://deduhova.ru/statesman/velikij-knyaz-pavel-aleksandrovich/.

52. Brummer, "Les derniers jours," 265–66.

53. Cockfield, *White Crow,* 245; *Grand Duke,* 334; Janet Ashton et al., *The Other Grand Dukes: Sons and Grandsons of Russia's Grand Dukes,* Richmond Heights, CA: eurohistory.com, 2013, 132.

54. Van der Kiste and Hall, *Xenia,* 143; Cockfield, *White Crow,* 242; Lobashkova, *Knyaz imperatorskoi krovi Gavriill Konstantinovich,* 59.

55. Letter to Grand Duchess Xenia, February 19, 1919, in Van der Kiste and Hall, *Xenia,* 143.

56. *Belle Époque,* 226; *Exile,* 123; see Paley, *Memoirs* online, chapter XLII.

57. Mitterrand, *Mémoires d'exil,* 53.

58. *Belle Époque,* 227.

59. Frances Welch, *The Russian Court at Sea: The Last Days of a Great Dynasty,* London: Short Books, 2011, 25–26.

60. *Grand Duke,* 4.

61. *Always,* 3, 4.

62. *Grand Duke,* 6.

63. *Always,* 17.

64. Ibid., 28.

65. Ibid., 18.

66. Clarke, *Hidden Treasures,* 114–15.

67. Ibid.

68. Ibid., 115.

69. Kschessinska, *Dancing in Petersburg,* 200.

70. Clarke, *Hidden Treasures,* 117–18.

71. For a fascinating account of what happened to Grand Duchess Vladimir's jewels, see Clarke, *Hidden Treasures,* chapter 14. Unfortunately, Grand Duchess Vladimir failed to tell her family that in November 1918 she had also arranged for a confidant to smuggle some of her jewelry out to Sweden via the Swedish embassy in Petrograd. These items, including jewel-encrusted cuff links and

gold and silver Fabergé cigarette cases, were not discovered in the Swedish Foreign Ministry's storerooms in Stockholm until 2009: www.digitaljournal.com /article/278453.

72.   Obolensky, *Russians in Exile,* chapter 6, np.

CHAPTER 5: "I NEVER THOUGHT I WOULD HAVE TO DRAG OUT MY LIFE AS AN ÉMIGRÉ"

1.   *Always,* 66.
2.   Ibid., 39.
3.   See *Always,* 51–59.
4.   Bonsal, *Suitors and Supplicants,* 30: diary entry, February 24, 1919.
5.   Ibid., 24.
6.   Shakhovskaya, *Takov moy vek,* 54.
7.   *Homesick,* 7–8.
8.   Shakhovskaya, *Takov moy vek,* 54.
9.   *Homesick,* 15.
10.   Raymond and Jones, *Russian Diaspora,* 6.
11.   Cameron, *Goodbye Russia,* 88.
12.   See *Homesick,* 7–12.
13.   Teffi, *Memories: From Moscow to the Black Sea,* 311–12. The reference to her steamship is on 310, but Teffi was not specific about the date of her sailing to Constantinople.
14.   Don-Aminado, *Poezd na tretem puti,* 239.
15.   Ibid., 241.
16.   Ibid., 244–45.
17.   Troyat, *Un si long chemin,* 25, 26.
18.   Shakhovskaya, *Takov moy vek,* 54.
19.   Ibid., 72.
20.   Valentin Kataev writing in 1918, quoted in Bunin 1: 255.
21.   Bunin 1: 283.
22.   Ibid., 312–13.
23.   Vera Muromtseva diary, quoted in Bunin 1: 354, 355, 356.
24.   Ibid., 357, 358.
25.   Ibid., 359.
26.   Cameron, *Goodbye Russia,* 51–52.
27.   Ibid., 52, 53.
28.   Ibid., 57.
29.   Ibid., 59–62.
30.   Boris Alexandrovsky, *Iz perezhitogo v chuzhikh krayakh,* 1, www.litmir.me/br/ ?b=249356&p=1#section_3.
31.   Ross, *Aux sources de l'émigration,* 46.
32.   Vladimir Berg, *Prisoners of Bizerte,* quoted in Knorring, *Povest iz sobstvennoy zhizni,* http://az.lib.ru/k/knorring_i_n/text_1926_dnevnik.shtml.
33.   Alexandrovsky, *Iz perezhitogo v chuzhikh krayakh,* 3.
34.   Ibid., chapter 1.
35.   Melenevsky, *Les naufrages,* 166.

36. Alexandrovsky, *Iz perezhitogo v chuzhikh krayakh,* online, chapter 2; Marc Mikhailovich Wolff, "In the Crimea," in Glenny, *The Other Russia,* 151; *Near East Review,* November 27, 1920, 1; Knorring, *Povest iz sobstvennoy zhizni,* diary, November 26, 1920, http://az.lib.ru/k/knorring_i_n/text_1926_dnevnik.shtml.
37. Ross, *Aux sources de l'émigration,* 47; Melenevsky, *Les naufrages,* 168–69.
38. Alexandrovsky, *Iz perezhitogo v chuzhikh krayakh,* 4; Vertinsky, "Chetvert veka bez rodiny," 5, www.rulit.me/books/chetvert-veka-bez-rodiny-stranicy-minuvshego-read-394498-1.html.
39. Vertinsky, "Chetvert veka bez rodiny," 6.
40. Ibid., 5; Knorring, *Povest iz sobstvennoy zhizni,* diary, November 7/20, 1920, http://az.lib.ru/k/knorring_i_n/text_1926_dnevnik.shtm; see also Vassiliev, *Beauty in Exile,* 61.
41. Vertinsky, "Chetvert veka bez rodiny," 5.
42. Alexandrovsky, *Iz perezhitogo v chuzhikh krayakh,* 5.
43. *New Near East,* VI, April 1921, 13.
44. Charles King, *Midnight at the Pera Palace: The Birth of Modern Istanbul,* New York: Norton, 2014, 65.
45. Graham, *Europe—Whither Bound,* 38.
46. Ibid., 38–39.
47. Cameron, *Goodbye Russia,* 221.
48. Alexandrovsky, *Iz perezhitogo v chuzhikh krayakh,* 5.
49. Vertinsky, "Chetvert veka bez rodiny," 8.
50. Alexandrovsky, *Iz perezhitogo v chuzhikh krayakh,* 6; Roberts, "Drifting Leaves," 365.
51. *Homesick,* 13; Alexandrovsky, *Iz perezhitogo v chuzhikh krayakh,* 6.
52. See *"New Mecca,"* 13–15.
53. *Homesick,* 30; *"New Mecca,"* 25.
54. Cameron, *Goodbye Russia,* 231, 235.
55. *Literary Digest,* July 2, 1921, 33.
56. Vishniak, *Gody emigratsii,* 9, 10.

CHAPTER 6: "PARIS IS FULL OF RUSSIANS"

1. Jean-Michel Rabaté, *1922: Literature, Culture, Politics,* Cambridge: Cambridge University Press, 2015, 91.
2. Ernest Hemingway, "Paris Is Full of Russians," *Toronto Star,* February 25, 1922.
3. *Always,* 42.
4. *Exile,* 51.
5. Ibid., 51–52.
6. Ibid., 52–53.
7. Ibid., 54.
8. Ibid., 58–59.
9. Ibid., 49.
10. Ibid., 113.
11. Ibid., 126.
12. Meier, *The Lost Spy,* 159.

13.   "Russian Princess's Claim," *Dundee Courier*, November 27, 1928. For an account of Olga's legal action, see the epilogue to *Belle Époque*, 221–27.

14.   Mitterrand, *Mémoires d'exil*, 54–55.

15.   Ibid., 129.

16.   "Princess Paley," *Daily Mirror*, November 5, 1929.

17.   *Always*, 113–14.

18.   Woon, "Russian Nobles," *Bridgeport Telegram*, April 28, 1922.

19.   Vassiliev, *Beauty in Exile*, 163.

20.   Ibid., 130–31.

21.   Perry, *Flight of the Romanovs*, 127.

22.   Collins, *Woman's Home Companion*, 1922, 18; Collins, *This King Business*, 16.

23.   *Flight*, 260.

24.   Consuelo Vanderbilt, *The Glitter and the Gold*, London: Hodder & Stoughton, 2012, 169.

25.   *The Sketch*, December 17, 1919.

26.   "Newest Love Affair of Russia's Unhappiest Prince," *Philadelphia Inquirer*, October 10, 1920.

27.   See Collins, *This King Business*, 5, 8.

28.   Chaney, *Chanel*, 190; Garelick, *Mademoiselle*, 118.

29.   Dmitri Pavlovich diary, quoted in Anne De Courcy, *Chanel's Riviera*, London: Weidenfeld & Nicolson, 2019, 33; Caroline Young, *Living with Coco Chanel*, London: White Lion Publishing, 2019, 58.

30.   Wiser, *The Crazy Years*, 88.

31.   Hal Vaughan, *Sleeping with the Enemy: Coco Chanel's Secret War*, New York: Knopf, 2011, 25.

32.   Garelick, *Mademoiselle*, 118; Charlotte Zeepvat, "The Harsh Light of Day: Grand Duke Dmitri in Exile," *Royalty Digest*, IV: 3, September 1994, 66–70.

33.   See Eve Golden, *Vernon and Irene Castle's Ragtime Revolution*, Lexington: University Press of Kentucky, 2007, 61–62, for a brief account of this little-known affair between Dmitri Pavlovich and Irene Castle, Vernon's wife.

34.   Caroline Young, *Living with Coco Chanel*, London: White Lion Publishing 2019, 59.

35.   Boulay, *La France des Romanov*, 235.

36.   See Barbara Herman, *Scent and Subversion: Decoding a Century of Provocative Perfume*, 35; information from Rev. Ed Hanson.

37.   Chaney, *Chanel: An Intimate Life*; Picardie, *Chanel*, 130.

38.   Garelick, *Mademoiselle*, 118–19.

39.   Mitterrand, *Mémoires d'exil*, 131; Garelick, *Mademoiselle*, 120–22.

40.   Picardie, *Chanel*, 128–29.

41.   *Always*, 124.

42.   Picardie, *Chanel*, 137.

43.   Ibid., 311.

44.   Woon, "Russian Nobles Work and Play to Eat," *Bridgeport Telegram*, April 28, 1922.

45.   Ibid.

46.   Chaney, *Chanel*, 230; Garelick, *Mademoiselle*, 149–50.

47. King and Wilson, *Gilded Prism,* 188.
48. Before leaving Petrograd, Yusupov had hidden more jewels—including a diamond Cartier tiara and a dozen more of Irina's tiaras—behind a fake wall under a staircase. Unfortunately, these were later found by the Soviets. In 1924 Cartier sold the black pearls on Felix's behalf for $400,000 to an American heiress, Mathilde (Mrs. Peter) Goelet Gerry. She sold them and they were last heard of in 1936. https://girlinthetiara.com/yusupov-black-pearl-necklace/.
49. *Always,* 113.
50. Youssoupoff, *En exil,* 4–5.
51. Ibid., 13.
52. Collins, "What's Happened to Royalty?," 18.
53. Wood, *The Paris That's Not in the Guide Books,* 142.
54. Ibid; Collins, *This King Business,* 13.
55. Collins, "What's Happened to Royalty?," 18; Collins, *This King Business,* 16–17.
56. Woon, "Russian Nobles Work and Play to Eat."
57. Collins, "What's Happened to Royalty?," 17–18.
58. Ibid., 19–20, 122.
59. Ibid., 122.
60. Vassiliev, *Beauty in Exile,* 171.
61. Marcel Couland, "La grande-duchesse Marie brodeuse à Paris," *Le Journal,* March 26, 1926.
62. Vassiliev, *Beauty in Exile,* 234–36.
63. Ibid., 241.
64. Collins, "The City of Exiles," 12.
65. Boulay, *La France des Romanov,* 239; *Les Russes,* 118, 120.
66. Roberts, "Waifs of an Empire," 58; Collins, *This King Business,* 41. See also Boulay, *La France des Romanov,* 229–43.
67. Orwell, *Down and Out in Paris and London,* 6, 8.
68. Nin, *Diary of Anaïs Nin,* 123.
69. Jevakhoff, *Les Russes blancs,* 346–47.
70. *Homesick,* vi; Yusupov, *En exil,* 45; Boulay, *La France des Romanov,* 239.
71. *Tatler,* September 15, 1920.
72. Collins, *This King Business,* 58–59.
73. *Homesick,* 33.

CHAPTER 7: "HOW RUINED RUSSIANS EARN A LIVING"

1. Woon, "Russian Nobles Work and Play to Eat."
2. Collins, *This King Business,* 46–47.
3. Collins, *This King Business,* 47–48, 51; *The Mail* (Adelaide), September 22, 1923.
4. *Exile,* 134; Delage, *La Russie en exil,* 65.
5. Glenny and Stone, *The Other Russia,* 269–70.
6. No two sources agree on figures, but see especially Guichard, *Construction des nationalités,* 216; "*New Mecca,*" 22–25; Raeff, *Russia Abroad,* 24, 201–03.
7. *Homesick,* 74.
8. "*New Mecca,*" 76.

9.   Raymond Seris, "Les Réfugiés Russes à Paris," *Le Petit Journal,* March 6, 1922; *Les Russes,* 128.

10.   *Logansport Pharos Tribune,* September 11, 1920; See Ignatieff, *The Russian Album,* 150–52, which rather contradicts this, saying the Ignatieffs were managing a dairy farm in Hastings, Sussex, having moved to England from Paris. It is, of course, possible that the Garches venture was short-lived. It was reported in several papers.

11.   "Princess as a Cow Keeper. How Ruined Russians Earn a Living," *Perth Daily News,* October 12, 1920.

12.   *Galveston Tribune,* October 25, 1920.

13.   *Les Russes,* 158.

14.   Ibid.; *"New Mecca,"* 77.

15.   Excerpt from Catherine Guseff, *Russkaya emigratsiya vo Frantsii,* 146; "Taxi Drivers: Myth and Reality," https://daily.afisha.ru/archive/vozduh/books /russkaya-emigraciya-vo-francii-katrin-guseff/.

16.   *Les Russes,* 159.

17.   *Homesick,* 63.

18.   "Russkoe Taksi v Parizhe," https://paris1814.com/; see also *Homesick,* 62–65.

19.   "Refugees," 49.

20.   Grouix, *Russes de France,* 123; *Les Russes,* 158–59, 161; Kazansky, *Cabaret russe,* 209–10.

21.   *Homesick,* 61–62.

22.   www.leparisien.fr/info-paris-ile-de-france-oise/il-y-a-cent-ans-les-russes-blancs -trouvaient-refuge-a-billankoursk-03–11–2017–7371543.php.

23.   8,400 taxis were registered in Paris in 1920. "Les Russes blancs, chauffeurs de Taxi a Paris" below, cites a figure of 3,156 Russian taxi drivers in Paris, of whom 1,481 were in the city and 1,265 in the suburbs, www.lestaxis.fr/viewtopic.php?t=668.

24.   *Les Russes,* 171.

25.   Jevakhoff, *Les Russes blancs,* 407.

26.   Nin, *Diary of Anaïs Nin,* 122.

27.   Zinovieff, *Red Princess,* 150; Skipwith, *Sofka,* 89.

28.   Bryunelli's story is summarized in *"New Mecca,"* 79–80; additional detail can be found in Grouix, *Russes de France,* 158–60.

29.   *Night Roads,* 29, 39–41.

30.   Ibid., 33, 147.

31.   Ibid., 68, 72.

32.   See ibid., 150–57.

33.   Ibid., 76–77, 143.

34.   Ibid., 143.

35.   Ibid., 191, 218.

36.   Ibid., 226, 231; *Les Russes,* 170; *Night Roads,* 222.

37.   Gul, *Ya unes Rossiyu,* 22–23.

38.   Ibid., 25–26.

39.   "Refugees," 49; https://tanya-mass.livejournal.com/2128504.html.

40.   "From Purple and Plush to—Dish Washing and Screen 'Crowd' Parts," *People,* February 15, 1931; Berberova, *Billancourt Tales,* 22.

41.   Guseff, *Russkaya emigratsiya,* 143.

42. See the front-page article, Roger Valbelle, "Billancourt, Grand Quartier de l'Émigration Russe en France," in *Excelsior,* August 25, 1930. Also Charles Ledré, *Les émigrés russes en France,* Paris, 1930, 64; *Italics,* 329.
43. *Italics,* 326.
44. *Les Russes,* 135; "Refugees," 48; Gouix, *Russes de France,* 138–39.
45. *Les Russes,* 126.
46. Ibid., 127; Raymond, *Russian Diaspora,* 22.
47. Georges Suarez, "Les Russes à Paris: II, La colonie de Billancourt," *Le Petit Journal,* December 5, 1927; *Les Russes,* 130.
48. "Refugees," 49; Jevakhoff, *Les Russes blancs,* 342; Guseff, *Russkaya emigratsiya,* 141–42. It is impossible to find any two sources agreeing on the number of Russians working at Renault in the 1920s. Figures cited vary between five and ten thousand but these appear to be overestimates. It is probable that the total never exceeded four thousand. See *Les Russes,* 126. There are no accurate figures for Russian workers at Citroën, but it is likely to have been several hundred. The Zemgor had been instrumental in negotiating with Renault and Citroën on behalf of Russian émigrés stranded in Turkey, Bizerta, and elsewhere. *Les Russes,* 127.
49. Hassell, "Russian Refugees," 49.
50. Berberova, "Kolka and Luisenka," in *Billancourt Tales,* 155.
51. See ibid., 154, and "The Violin of Billancourt," 168.
52. *Italics,* 387.
53. Berberova, "Versts and Sleeping Cars," 102, and "Billancourt Manuscript," 126, in *Billancourt Tales.*
54. *Italics,* 328.
55. "Les Russes," in Anglade, *La vie quotidienne des immigrés en France,* 21.
56. Ibid., 21–22.
57. Teffi, "Que faire," in *Subtly Worded,* 139; see also Svetlana Maire, "La recherche de 'l'âme slave,'" 34.
58. Quoted in Haber, *Teffi,* 103.
59. "Paris," 1924, quoted in Haber, *Teffi,* 112.
60. *"New Mecca,"* 15.
61. Ibid., 21.

CHAPTER 8: "WE ARE NOT IN EXILE, WE ARE ON A MISSION"

1. Bunin 2: 42, 43.
2. Ibid., 52.
3. Ibid, 43, 44, 52.
4. *Italics,* 253.
5. Ibid., 241.
6. Nabokov, *Letters to Vera,* 194.
7. Teffi, "The Merezhkovskys," in *Rasputin and Other Ironies,* 171, 184.
8. *Elysian Fields,* 115; *Italics,* 239.
9. Odoevtseva, *Na beregakh Seny,* 51.
10. For a perceptive portrait of Gippius, see *Italics,* 239–46; a rather crueller portrait of her and Merezhkovsky can be found in *Elysian Fields,* 110–16, and in Odoevtseva's *Na beregakh Seny,* 49–68.

11. *Italics*, 260; Teffi, *Rasputin and Other Ironies*, 172, 173, 182.
12. Odoevtseva, *Na beregakh Seny*, 50.
13. "*New Mecca*," 48; Slobin, *Russians Abroad*, 55.
14. Gippius, quoted in Terras, *A Handbook of Russian Literature*, New Haven: Yale University Press, 1990, 193.
15. Pachmuss, *Between Paris and St. Petersburg*, 49, 50; *Elysian Fields*, 4.
16. *Elysian Fields*, 111.
17. Ibid., 112, 113, 115.
18. Ibid., 119.
19. Bunin 2: 62.
20. Bunin 2: 78; Graham, *Part of the Wonderful Scene*, 289.
21. Chavchavadze, *Grand Dukes*, 238.
22. Galya Diment, *Katherine Mansfield and Russia*, Edinburgh: Edinburgh University Press, 2017, 37.
23. Ibid.; Bunin 2: 81.
24. Ibid., 56.
25. Ehrenburg, *Memoirs, 1921–1941*, 22, 23, 58.
26. Bunin 2: 91.
27. Ehrenburg, *Memoirs*, 46; James Whitlark and Wendell M. Aycock, eds., *The Literature of Emigration and Exile*, Lubbock: Texas Tech University Press, 1992, 44.
28. Graham, *Part of the Wonderful Scene*, 290.
29. Ehrenburg, *Memoirs*, 44.
30. *Italics*, 261; *Elysian Fields*, 7; Ehrenburg, *Memoirs*, 22, 44, 45.
31. Graham, *Part of the Wonderful Scene*, 289, 290; *Italics*, 259.
32. *Elysian Fields*, 169.
33. Woon, *The Paris That's Not in the Guidebooks*, 237.
34. Ehrenburg, *Memoirs*, 90; Crespelle, *Chagall*, 176–77.
35. Crespelle, *Chagall*, 172–73.
36. Sedykh, *Dalekie, blizkie*, 258, 259; Crespelle, *Chagall*, 177.
37. For a fascinating account of the Caveau Caucasien and the restaurants and *cabarets russes* in Paris of the 1920s and 1930s, see Kazansky, *Cabaret russe*.
38. Michael Dregni, *Gypsy Jazz: In Search of Django Reinhardt and the Soul of Gypsy Swing*, New York: Oxford University Press, 2010, 165.
39. Kazansky, *Cabaret russe*, 289.
40. Orwell, *Down and Out in Paris and London*, 30.
41. Ibid., 31.
42. Ibid., 33.
43. Zinovieff, *A Princess Remembers*, 142. Obolensky later immigrated to the United States and taught at the Juilliard School of Music. He also became a professional backgammon player.
44. "Tolstoy's Son Becomes Entertainer," *Evening Telegram* (St. John's Newfoundland), 4 January 1923.
45. Krummenacker, "La mode des cabarets russes," 17.
46. Vassiliev, *Beauty in Exile*, 198–99, 211–12.
47. Vaill, *Everybody Was So Young*, 117–18.
48. Bunin 2: 115–16.
49. Ibid., 125.

50. Ibid., 125, 126.

51. Ibid., 131.

52. Dominique Hoffman, "Without Nostalgia: Nina Berberova's Short Fiction of the 1930s," 2011, thesis, University of North Carolina at Chapel Hill, 159; the quotation is often misattributed to Gippius or Merezhkovsky.

53. *Italics*, 210.

54. Ibid., 212–14.

55. Karlinsky, *Bitter Air of Exile*, 64.

56. *Italics,* 242.

57. Ibid., 214, 215.

58. Ibid., 215–16, 218, 220, 281.

59. Ibid., 221.

60. *Elysian Fields,* 96, 98.

61. Author's translation; Karlinsky, *Bitter Air of Exile*, 65.

62. Obolensky, *Russians in Exile,* np.

63. Quoted in Figes, *Natasha's Dance,* 535.

64. *Elysian Fields,* 199.

65. Odoevtseva, *Na beregakh Seny,* 6.

66. Sedykh, *Dalekie, blizkie,* 76, 87.

67. Karetnyk, *Russian Short Stories*, 5.

CHAPTER 9: "EMPEROR KIRILL OF ALL THE RUSSIAS"

1. See, e.g., *Auckland Star,* December 28, 1923; "New Czar. Secret Crowning. Pathetic Scene in French Village," *Evening News* (Sydney), December 26, 1923; "Pathos of Secret Ceremony in Paris Suburb," *Sheffield Independent,* December 28, 1923.

2. As confirmed by *The Bystander,* December 19, 1923, 884.

3. "Waiters and Valets Hold Court," *Southern Morning Herald,* December 28, 1923.

4. "Czar of All the Russias. Secretly Crowned in Paris," *Western Mail,* December 28, 1923; Maxwell, "Shuttered Room," 392–93.

5. *The Times,* 10, August 18, 1922.

6. *Daily Herald,* August 23, 1922.

7. Robinson, *Grand Duke Nikolai Nikolaevich,* 324.

8. *Exile,* 237, 238.

9. www.russianlegitimit.org/who-shall-be-the-emperor-of-russia.

10. Grand Duke Cyril, *My Life in Russia's Service,* 222.

11. *Exile,* 238.

12. Jevakhoff, *Les Russes blancs,* 389; see also Nicholas Nicholson, "How Lovely a Country This Is," part II, note 15, http://nicholsonadvisory.com/how-lovely-a -country-this-is-part-ii.

13. Robinson, *Grand Duke Nikolai Nikolaevich*, 315–16.

14. H. G. Graf, *In the Service of the Imperial House of Russia, 1917–1941,* Hagerstown: V. Graf, 1998, 184–85; Beatrice de Holguin, *Tales of Palm Beach,* Palm Beach: Vantage Press, 1968, 146–47.

15. Crawford, *Michael and Natasha,* 387.

16. *Evening Journal,* January 26, 1925.

17.   Kirill's letter of October 11, 1924 is quoted in full in Olga Romanoff, *Princess Olga, A Wild and Barefoot Princess,* London: Shepheard-Walwyn, 2017, 151.

18.   *Always,* 126.

19.   Ibid., 126–27.

20.   Ibid., 127.

21.   Karina Urbach, *Go-Betweens for Hitler,* Oxford: Oxford University Press, 2015, 135; for an account of Victoria Melita's U.S. tour, see Nicholas Nicholson, "How Lovely a Country This Is," http://nicholsonadvisory.com/how-lovely-a-country-this-is-part-i.

22.   *Exile,* 237; *Homesick,* 164.

23.   See *Always,* chapter 7, "Cyril and His Invisible Empire."

24.   Gleb Botkin, *The Real Romanovs,* New York: Flemming H. Revell, 1931, 265.

25.   Peter Kurth, *Anastasia,* London: Pimlico, 1995, 205; Greg King and Penny Wilson, *Resurrection of the Romanovs,* New York: Wiley, 2010, 208–09.

26.   *Western Mail,* February 10, 1928; *Nottingham Evening Post,* February 10, 1928.

27.   Letter to Grand Duke Andrey, September 19, 1927; Kurth, *Anastasia,* 186.

28.   Basily, *Memoirs of a Lost World,* 222.

29.   Letter to Yusupov, February 29, 1928, quoted in Coutau-Bégarie Catalog, Lot 89, www.coutaubegarie.com/lot/21555/4392055?npp=150&.

30.   Youssoupoff, *En exil,* 121.

31.   Vertinsky, "Chetvert veka bez rodiny," 41.

32.   Beucler, *Russes de France,* 887.

33.   Vertinsky, "Chetvert veka bez rodiny," 41.

34.   *"New Mecca,"* 43, 46.

35.   Pachmuss, *Between Paris and St. Petersburg,* 148; "Refugees," 44.

36.   Lesley Blanch, "Cuckoo in the Nest," *The Times Saturday Review,* August 17, 1968, 15.

37.   "Refugees," 42.

38.   Chamberlain, *The Philosophy Steamer,* 238.

39.   *"New Mecca,"* 44.

40.   Ibid., 46.

41.   Jevakhoff, *Les Russes blancs,* 564; "Refugees," 68.

42.   "Refugees," 68; Nostitz, *Romance and Revolutions,* 132–33.

43.   "Refugees," 68; Mitterrand, *Mémoires d'exil,* 209.

44.   Delage, *La Russie en exil,* 34.

45.   Ibid., 36–7; Rappaport, *Four Sisters,* 379–80. Her grave can be seen here: www.findagrave.com/memorial/82441701/elizaveta-alexeevna-naryshkina.

46.   According to Lesley Chamberlain, *The Philosophy Steamer,* 235, 242. Unfortunately nothing more can be found about Florence West's funding. She also gifted Berdyaev the rented house that he lived in in the suburb of Clamart.

47.   *Exile,* 137.

48.   Mary Britnieva, *A Stranger in Your Midst,* London: Arthur Barker, 1936, 146; "Refugees," 73.

49.   Roberts, "Waifs of an Empire," 54.

50.   For an account of the school, see Olga Efimovsky, *Il était une fois . . . Brunoy . . . Quincy . . .* Paris: O. Efimovsky, 1991.

51.   Meier, *The Lost Spy,* 158–9.

CHAPTER 10: "UBIQUITOUS INTRIGUERS," SPIES, AND ASSASSINS

1. The National Archives [TNA] FO 371/9370, June 15, 1923.
2. Ibid.
3. Miller, *Shanghai on the Métro*, 143.
4. Perry, *Flight of the Romanovs*, 279, 280.
5. Ibid., 281.
6. Résumé of email discussions and research notes from Phil Tomaselli, an expert on Soviet and anti-Soviet intelligence of the 1920s; information from Reilly expert Professor Rick Spence.
7. Perry, *Flight of the Romanovs*, 279.
8. Ibid., 282.
9. Ibid., 284–7.
10. Ibid., 285, 286.
11. Bailey, *Conspirators* 77–9; *The Times*, April 9, 1927; Jonathan Haslam, *Near and Distant Neighbors: A New History of Soviet Intelligence*, Cambridge: Cambridge University Press, 2015, 36.
12. Bailey, *Conspirators*, 99; *Flight*, 291–2; *The Times*, July 11, 1928.
13. Bailey, *Conspirators*, 89.
14. Vera Bunina, diary, January 6, 1929, quoted in Robinson, *Grand Duke Nikolay Nikolaevich*, 346.
15. Perry, *Flight.* 293; Robinson, *Grand Duke Nikolay Nikolaevich*, 345–6.
16. Huntington, *Homesick Millions*, 245.
17. https://scepsis.net/library/id_2157.html#a6: quoting M. V. Kolytsov, *Izbrannye proizvedeniya*, vol. 2, "Zarubezhnye ocherki," 176–87.
18. https://scepsis.net/library/id_2157.html#a6 : "Beloemigrantskii aktivizm," chapter III part 2 of Leonid Shkarenkov, *The Agony of the White Emigration*, Moscow: Mysl, 1987.
19. Bailey, *Conspirators*, 101; Grouix, *Russes de France*, 143; Brackman, *Secret File of Joseph Stalin*, 188.
20. Iswolsky, *No Time to Grieve*, 175; Brackman, *Stalin*, 188.
21. Brackman, *Stalin*, 189, who claims that Kutepov was brought back to Moscow alive in February 1930 and later executed in the Lyubyanka prison; Hassell, "Russian Refugees," 51.
22. Bailey, *Conspirators*, 110–11.
23. Struve, *Soixante-dix ans*, 177; *Flight*, 295. For a comprehensive account of the known facts see Bailey, *Conspirators*, chapter 5, 89–117.
24. Bailey, *Conspirators*, 258; Miller, *Shanghai on the Metro*, 143; Raymond, *Russian Diaspora*, 155.
25. Brackman, *Stalin*, 250; "Refugees," 52.
26. Brackman, *Stalin*, 250.
27. Vladislav I. Goldin and John W. Long, "Resistance and Retribution: The Life and Fate of General E.K. Miller," *Revolutionary Russia*, 12:2 (1999), 19–40. See also Brackman, *Stalin*, 251, who argues that Miller was shot in December 1938.

28.   www.russianlegitimist.org/grand-duke-dmitri-pavlovich-of-russia; *Flight,* 301. Another useful account of Mladrossi can be found here: www.foiaresearch.net /organization/mladorossi.

29.   Judith Keene, *Fighting for Franco: International Volunteers in Nationalist Spain,* London: Continuum, 2007, 188–9.

30.   Ibid., 209–11; see also: https://www.rbth.com/history/328778-soviet-in-spanish -civil-war.

31.   *Homesick,* 169–72.

32.   See *Le Figaro,* November 6, 1921; *Daily Telegraph,* September 7, 1921.

33.   *Homesick,* 174.

34.   See Helen Rappaport, *The Race to Save the Romanovs: The Truth behind the Secret Plans to Rescue Russia's Imperial Family,* London: Hutchinson, 2018, 270–1.

35.   *Homesick,* 177.

36.   Ibid., 177, 179.

37.   Sedykh, *Dalekie, blizkie,* 145.

38.   "*New Mecca,*" 35.

39.   *Homesick,* 204.

40.   Sedykh, *Dalekie, blizkie,* 147–8.

41.   See "*New Mecca,*" 49–51.

42.   *Homesick,* 202–3.

43.   Ibid., 199.

44.   *Homesick,* 198–9.

45.   Ehrenburg, *Memoirs 1921–1941,* 219; see also *The Times,* May 18, 1932.

46.   "M. Doumer's Assassin: an Anti-Bolshevik Fanatic," *Manchester Guardian,* May 9, 1932.

47.   Ibid.

48.   Ibid.

49.   Ibid.; Ehrenburg, *Memoirs, 1921–1941,* 218–19.

50.   Ehrenburg, *Memoirs, 1921–1941,* 217.

51.   *Elysian Fields,* 16.

52.   "*New Mecca,*" 109.

53.   *The Times,* July 26, 1932.

54.   Rubins, *Russian Montparnasse,* 249, 250.

55.   *Italics,* 355.

56.   "*New Mecca,*" 105.

57.   *Italics,* 355.

58.   https://en.topwar.ru/138854-ubeyte-menya-kak-vy-ubili-moyu-stranu.html; *The Times,* May 18, 1932.

59.   *Elysian Fields,* 17. There was extensive coverage in the French press on September 14 and 15. See e.g. *Le Matin, Excelsior, L'Intransigeant, Le Petit Journal, L'Echo de Paris,* which can be consulted on Gallica, https://gallica.bnf.fr/.

60.   The Mary Knight account of Gorgulov's execution was widely syndicated; see e.g., *Jefferson City Post-Tribune,* September 14, 1932.

61.   George Fetherling, *The Book of Assassins,* New York: Wiley, 2001, 168.

62.   "*New Mecca,*" 106, 108.

63.   Ibid., 105.

64.   Ibid., 109.

CHAPTER II: "A FAR VIOLIN AMONG NEAR BALALAIKAS"

1.   Bunin 2: 146, 147.
2.   Ibid., 230, 228–9.
3.   Ibid., 230.
4.   Graham, *Part of the Wonderful Scene*, 289.
5.   Bunin 2: 73.
6.   Ibid., 242–3, 250.
7.   Ibid., 255–6.
8.   Ibid., 256; Slobin, *Russians Abroad*, 159.
9.   Bunin 2: 266.
10. www.nobelprize.org/prizes/literature/1933/summary.
11. Bunin 2: 282.
12. Ibid., 270–2.
13. As said to writer Andrey Sedykh, Bunin 2: 293; ibid., 297.
14. Ibid., 270–1.
15. *Elysian Fields*, 123.
16. Bunin 2: 271, 284, 298.
17. Ibid., 283, 284, 301.
18. Haber, *Teffi*, 146; Bunin 2: 285.
19. *Poslednie novosti*, November 24, 1929; *Homesick*, 29.
20. *Elysian*, xiv.
21. Oldenbourg, *Visages d'un autobiographie*, 256.
22. Ibid., 255, 327, 328.
23. Delage, *La Russie en exil*, 25; "New Mecca," 205.
24. "New Mecca," 70, 74.
25. Orwell, *Down and Out in Paris and London*, 39.
26. Ibid., 41.
27. Ibid., 136.
28. Glenny, *The Other Russia*, 284.
29. Raeff, *Russia Abroad*, 38.
30. "New Mecca," 144.
31. Haber, *Teffi*, 158–59.
32. Ibid., 134.
33. Ibid., 145.
34. Troyat, *Un si long chemin*, 36.
35. *Homesick*, 165; interview in *Weekly Journal*, 11, 1930, quoted in Engberg, *Maria*, 223.
36. Vassiliev, *Beauty in Exile*, 173.
37. Engberg, *Maria*, 226–27; Vassiliev, *Beauty in Exile*, 177–78.
38. Engberg, *Maria*, 236, 237.
39. Vassiliev, *Beauty in Exile*, 196–97.
40. Ibid., 242, 257.
41. Ibid., 272–74.
42. Ibid., 280.
43. Ibid., 333.
44. Walsh, *Stravinsky*, 484.

45. Mackrell, *Flappers: Six Women of a Dangerous Generation,* London: Macmillan, 2013, 333.
46. Vaill, *Everybody Was So Young,* 196.
47. Mary Jo Tate, *Critical Companion to F. Scott Fitzgerald: A Literary Reference to His Life and Work,* New York: Facts on File, 2007, 292.
48. Kschessinska, *Dancing in Petersburg,* 222–23.
49. Ibid., 231.
50. Vertinsky, "Chetvert veka bez rodiny," 30.
51. Karsavina, *Theater Street,* 295.
52. Knorring, "Okno v stolovoy," https://biography.wikireading.ru/256099.
53. Odeovtseva, *Na beregakh Seny,* 294, 300; *Elysian,* 7; *Italics,* 269.
54. Karlinsky, *Bitter Air of Exile,* 321.
55. Obolensky, *Russians in Exile,* np.; *Elysian Fields,* 10.
56. *Elysian Fields,* 18; Karlinsky, *Bitter Air of Exile,* 329.
57. Karlinsky, *Bitter Air of Exile,* 277.
58. Livak, *How It Was Done in Paris,* 86.
59. Karlinsky, *Bitter Air of Exile,* 329.
60. Ibid., 324–25. *Poslednie novosti* reported on Poplavsky's death at length in their issue on October 11, 1935.
61. *Italics,* 268.
62. Karlinsky, *Bitter Air of Exile,* 276.
63. Ibid., 333; Nabokov, *Speak, Memory,* 225; Karlinsky, *Bitter Air of Exile,* 331.
64. Nabokov, *Speak, Memory,* 215.
65. Chaliapin, *Man and Mask: Forty Years in the Life of a Singer,* London: Victor Gollancz, 1932, 304, 310.
66. Sedykh, *Dalekie, blizkie,* 123, 125.
67. Ibid., 125, 128.
68. Ibid., 140.
69. Bunin 2: 282.
70. Haber, *Teffi,* 131.
71. *Italics,* 282; Chamberlain, *Philosophy Steamer,* 253.

CHAPTER 12: "I FOREVER PITY THE EXILE, A PRISONER, AN INVALID"

1. Forest, "Mother Maria of Paris," 14–15.
2. *Elysian Fields,* 153; T. Stratton Smith, *Rebel Nun,* Springfield, Ill.: Templegate, 1965, 135.
3. John Witte, Jr., *The Teachings of Modern Orthodox Christianity,* New York: Columbia University Press, 2007, 294.
4. Hackel, *Pearl of Great Price,* 36; *Elysian Fields,* 157.
5. Schmemann, in a radio talk, quoted in Michael P. Plekon, *The World as Sacrament,* Collegeville, Minn.: Liturgical Press, 2017, 38; Hackel, *Pearl of Great Price,* 35.
6. Iswolsky, *No Time to Grieve,* 191.
7. Ibid., 208; James H. Forest, *Silent as a Stone: Mother Maria of Paris and the Trash Can Rescue.* New York: St. Vladimir's Seminary Press, 2007.
8. *Elysian Fields,* 158.

9.   Plekon, *The World as Sacrament*, 38.

10.   Hackel, *Pearl of Great Price*, 52.

11.   Ibid., 36.

12.   Ibid., 37.

13.   Ibid., 39.

14.   *Elysian Fields*, 154.

15.   "*New Mecca*," 52.

16.   *Homesick*, 288–89.

17.   Hassell, "Refugees," 45.

18.   Vassiliev, *Beauty in Exile*, 414–18, https://beautifulrus.com/miss-russia-winners
       -1929–1939/; Haber, *Teffi*, 130.

19.   Khodasevich, *Necropolis*, 3, 15; *Elysian Fields*, 165.

20.   "Refugees," 29.

21.   Yves Krier, "La vie et la mort du comte Kobosky, émigré russe, triste et misérable,"
       Paris-midi, 28 January 1929.

22.   *Italics*, 263.

23.   *People and Life*, 138.

24.   Ibid., 131, 138.

25.   Bunin 3: 142.

26.   http://kuprin.gatchina3000.ru/19_luker_kuprin10.htm.

27.   Sedykh, *Dalekie, blizkie*, 7; http://kuprin.gatchina3000.ru/19_luker_kuprin11
       .htm.

28.   Karlinsky, *Bitter Air of Exile*, 178; Simon Karlinsky, *Freedom from Violence: Essays on Russian Poetry and Music*, Boston: Academic Studies Press, 2013, 180.

29.   *Elysian Fields*, 199.

30.   Karlinsky, *Tsvetaeva*, 223; *Italics*, 202.

31.   Karlinsky, *Tsvetaeva*, 206.

32.   Iswolsky, *No Time to Grieve*, 197.

33.   Ibid., 199.

34.   Quoted in Figes, *Natasha's Dance*, 532.

35.   Translated by Elaine Feinstein, in Yevgeny Yevtushenko, ed. *Twentieth-Century Russian Poetry*, London: Fourth Estate, 1993, 234.

36.   Iswolsky, *No Time to Grieve*, 201.

37.   Karlinsky, *Tsvetaeva*, 224–25.

38.   Ibid., 230.

39.   Ibid., 232.

40.   Ibid., 236, 245.

41.   *Elysian Fields*, 199.

42.   Ibid., 101–02

43.   Figes, *Natasha's Dance*, 547.

44.   Hendrikoff, *Countess in Limbo*, 112.

45.   "*New Mecca*," 157; see also 158–60.

46.   Hendrikoff, *Countess in Limbo*, 117.

47.   Ibid., 162.

48.   See Stanley Meisler, *Shocking Paris: Soutine, Chagall and the Outsiders of Montparnasse*, New York: St. Martin's Press, 2015, 185–88.

49.   See Sedykh, *Dalekie, blizkie*, 116–20.

50.   Bunin 3: 166.
51.   Terapiano, *Vstrechi*, 40.
52.   Haber, *Teffi*, 224.
53.   "White Russia Waits for 'The Day' in Paris," *The Tatler*, March 6, 1940.
54.   *Always*, 66.
55.   Hackel, *Pearl of Great Price*, 98–99.
56.   Ibid., 102–03.
57.   Hackel, *Pearl of Great Price*, 53; see Forest, "Mother Maria of Paris," in *Mother Maria Skobtsova: Essential Writings*, Maryknoll, N.Y.: Orbis, 34.
58.   Hackel, *Pearl of Great Price*, 148.
59.   https://incommunion.org/2004/10/18/saint-of-the-open-door/.
60.   *"New Mecca,"* 182.
61.   Anglade, *La vie quotidienne des immigrés*, 26.
62.   *Homesick*, 289–90.
63.   For a useful overview, see Bunin 3: 4–10.
64.   Jevakhoff, *Les Russes blancs*, 397–98; Bunin 3:18.
65.   Anglade, *La vie quotidienne*, 26.

Bibliography

ELECTRONIC NEWSPAPER AND MAGAZINE ARCHIVES:

British Library Newspaper Archive
Gallica BnF (French newspapers)
Illyustrirovannaya Rossiya online at Ghent University Library
Newspaperarchive.com
Newspapers.com
Persee.fr
The Times Archive

ELECTRONIC BOOKS ONLINE:

www.alexanderpalace.org
archive.org
az.lib.ru
hathitrust.org
litmir.me
rulit.me

PUBLISHED BOOKS AND ARTICLES:

In order to facilitate the most user-friendly listing of sources, these are grouped by language rather than primary and secondary sources.

I. ENGLISH SOURCES

Alexander, Grand Duke of Russia, *Once a Grand Duke*, Garden City, NY: Garden City Publishing, 1932.

——*Always a Grand Duke*, New York: Farrar & Rinehart, 1933.

Alexander, Sidney, *Marc Chagall: An Intimate Biography*, London: Cassell, 1978.

Bailey, Geoffrey, *The Conspirators*, London: Gollancz, 1961.

Basily, Lascelle Meserve de, *Memoirs of a Lost World*, Stanford: Hoover Institution Press, 1975.

Basily, Nicolas de, *Memoirs: Diplomat of Imperial Russia*, Stanford: Hoover Institution Press, 1973.

Baxter, John, *The Golden Moments of Paris: A Guide to the Paris of the 1920s*, New York: Museyon Guides, 2014.

Bennett, Vanora, *The White Russian*, London: Century, 2014.

Benois, Alexandre, *Reminiscences of the Russian Ballet*, London: Putnam, 1947.

Berberova, Nina, *The Italics Are Mine*, London: Vintage, 1993.

——*Billancourt Tales*, New York: New Directions Publishing, 2002.

——*The Tattered Cloak and Other Novels*, New York: Knopf, 1991.

Bethea, David M., *Khodasevich: His Life and Art*, Princeton: Princeton University Press, 1983.

Bonsal, Stephen, *Suitors and Suppliants: The Little Nations at Versailles*, New York: Prentice Hall, 1946.

Boyd, Brian, *Vladimir Nabokov: The Russian Years*, Princeton: Princeton University Press, 1990.

Brackman, Roman, *The Secret File of Joseph Stalin: A Hidden Life*, London: Frank Cass, 2001.

Bunin, Ivan, "The Late Hour," "In Paris" in Karetnyk, *Russian Émigré Short Stories*

——*Life of Arseniev*, Evanston, IL: Northwestern University Press, 1994.

Cameron, Evan P., *Goodbye Russia: Adventures of HM Transport Rio Negro*, London: Hodder & Stoughton, 1934.

Cantacuzene, Princess, "How the Russian Refugees Are Making Good in Europe," *Ladies' Home Journal* 43, 1926: 18, 193, 258.

——"Exiles Are Reviving Russian Handicrafts," *Ladies' Home Journal* 38, 1921, 122.

Chamberlain, Lesley, *The Philosophy Steamer: Lenin and the Exile of the Intelligentsia*, London: Atlantic Books, 2006.

Chavchavadze, David, *The Grand Dukes*, New York: Atlantic International Publications, 1990.

Claflin, Davis, C., "Refugees," chapter VI, 201–26, in Clarence R. Johnson, ed., *Constantinople To-day; or, The Pathfinder Survey of Constantinople*, London: Macmillan, 1922.

Clarke, William, *Hidden Treasures of the Romanovs: Saving the Royal Jewels*, Edinburgh: National Museums of Scotland, 2009.

Cockfield, Jamie, *White Crow: The Life and Times of the Grand Duke Nicholas Mikhailovich Romanov, 1859–1919*, Westport, Conn.: Praeger, 2002.

Collins, Frederik L., *Woman's Home Companion* 49, December 1922, Part I: "What's Happened to Royalty?": 17, 18, 119, 120, 122; 50, January 1923, Part II: "The City of Exiles": 12, 13, 17, 66.

——*This King Business: Intimate Accounts of Royalty as a Going Concern*, London: T. Werner Laurie, 1923.

Craft, Robert and Igor Stravinsky, *Memories and Commentaries*, Berkeley: University of California Press, 1992.

Crawford, Rosemary and Michael, *Michael and Natasha*, London: Weidenfeld & Nicolson, 1997.

Crespelle, Jean-Paul, *Chagall*, New York: Coward-McCann, 1970.

"Cruel Fate of the Russian Refugees," *Literary Digest* 107, October–December 1930, 27.

Cyril, Grand Duke, *My Life in Russia's Service, Then and Now*, London: Selwyn & Blount, 1939.

Davis, Mary E., *Ballets Russes Style: Diaghilev's Dancers and Paris Fashion*, London: Reaktion Books, 2010.

Dewar, Hugo, *Assassins at Large*, chapter 1: www.marxists.org/archive/dewar/assassins/index.htm.

Durkheim, Émile, "Report on the Situation of Russians in France in 1916," in Martins, Herminio and William Pickering, *Debating Durkheim*, London: Routledge, 1994.

Ehrenburg, Ilya, *People and Life: Memoirs, 1891–1917*, London: MacGibbon & Kee, 1961.

—— *Memoirs, 1921–1941*, Cleveland: World Publishing Company, 1964.

—— *Julio Jurenito*, London: MacGibbon & Kee, 1958.

Engberg, Magnus, *Maria, Swedish Princess* [*Maria: Sveriges ryska priinsessa*], Sweden: Magnus Engberg Kulturproduktion, 2018.

Figes, Orlando, *Natasha's Dance: A Cultural History of Russia*, London: Allen Lane, 2002.

Fitzgerald, Zelda, *Save Me the Waltz*, London: Vintage Classics, 2001.

Flanner, Janet, *Paris Was Yesterday, 1925–1939*, London: Virago, 2003.

Fokine, Michel, *Memoirs of a Ballet Master*, New York: Little, Brown & Co., 1961.

Forest, Jim, "Mother Maria of Paris," in *Mother Maria Skobtsova: Essential Writings*, Maryknoll, NY: Orbis, 2003.

Gabriel Constantinovich, Grand Duke, *Memories in the Marble Palace*, Ontario: Gilbert's Books, 2009.

Garelick, Rhonda K., *Mademoiselle: Coco Chanel and the Pulse of History*, New York: Penguin Random House, 2015.

Gazdanov, Gaito, *Night Roads*, Evanston, IL: Northwestern University Press, 2009.

Gelardi, Julia, *From Splendor to Revolution: The Romanov Women, 1847–1928*, New York: St. Martin's Press, 2011.

Glenny, Michael and Norman Stone, eds., *The Other Russia*, London: Faber, 1991.

Graham, Stephen, *Part of the Wonderful Scene: An Autobiography*, London: Collins, 1964.

—— *Europe—Whither Bound?*, chapter II, "From Constantinople," Toronto: Ryerson Press, 1921.

Graves, Charles, "Russian Royalties in Exile," *Britannia & Eve*, March 1, 1933, 22–23, 122–24.

Gray, Pauline, *The Grand Duke's Woman*, London: Macdonald and Janes, 1976.

Griffin, Peter, *Less Than a Treason: Hemingway in Paris*, Cary, N.C.: Oxford University Press, 1990.

Hackel, Sergei, *Pearl of Great Price: The Life of Mother Maria Skobtsova, 1891–1945*, London: Darton, Longman & Todd, 1981.

Hall, Coryne, *Imperial Dancer*, Stroud, UK: Sutton Publishing, 2006.

Hassell, James E., "Russian Refugees in France and the United States between the World Wars," Philadelphia: American Philosophical Society, 1991.

Hemingway, *A Moveable Feast*, London: Arrow Books, 1994.

Hendrikoff, Olga, *A Countess in Limbo: Diaries in War and Revolution*, Vancouver: Inklight, 2016.

Huddleston, Sisley, *Bohemian Literary and Social Life in Paris*, London: George G. Harrap & Co., 1928.

"Humble Jobs of Former Russian Aristocrats," *Literary Digest* 78, July 21, 1923, 46, 48, 50, 51.

Huntingdon, William Chapin, *The Homesick Million: Russia-out-of-Russia*, Boston, Mass.: Stratford Co., 1933.

Ignatieff, Michael, *The Russian Album*, Penguin: London, 1987.

Iswolsky, Hélène, *No Time to Grieve: An Autobiographical Journey*, Philadelphia: Winchell Company, 1985.

Johnston, Robert H., *"New Mecca, New Babylon": Paris and the Russian Exiles, 1920–1945*, Kingston, Ont.: McGill-Queen's University Press, 1988.

Jordan, Pamela A., *Stalin's Singing Spy: The Life and Exile of Nadezhda Plevitskaya*, Lanham, Md., Rowman & Littlefield, 2016.

Kahan, Sylvia, *Music's Modern Muse: A Life of Winnaretta Singer*, Rochester: University of Rochester Press, 2009.

Karetnyk, Brian, ed., *Russian Émigré Short Stories from Bunin to Yanovsky*, London: Penguin Random House, 2017.

Karl, Klaus H., *Soutine*, New York: Parkstone International, 2015.

Karlinsky, Simon, *Marina Tsvetaeva: The Woman, Her World, and Her Poetry*, Cambridge: Cambridge University Press, 2009.

——"In Search of Boris Poplavsky" in *Bitter Air of Exile*, 311–33.

——and Alfred Apple, *The Bitter Air of Exile: Russian Writers in the West, 1922–1972*, Berkeley: University of California Press, 1992.

Karsavina, Tamara, *Theater Street: The Reminiscences of Tamara Karsavina*, London: Constable, 1982.

Kessel, Joseph, *Princes of the Night*, New York: Macaulay Co., 1928.

Khodasevich, Vladislav, *Selected Poems*, London: Angel Classics, 2013.

——*Necropolis*, New York: Columbia University Press, 2019.

King, Greg and Penny Wilson, *Gilded Prism: The Konstantinovichi Grand Dukes and the Last Years of the Romanov Dynasty*, Richmond Heights, Calif.: Eurohistory, 2006.

Kleinmichel, Countess, *Memories of a Shipwrecked World*, New York: Brentano's, 1923.

Klüver, Billy and Julie Martin, *Kiki's Paris: Artists and Lovers, 1900–1930*, New York: Harry N. Abrams, 1994.

Kodicek, Ann, ed., *Diaghilev: Creator of the Ballets Russes: Art, Music, Dance*, London: Lund Humphries Publishers, 1996.

Kschessinska, Mathilde, *Dancing in Petersburg*, New York: Doubleday, 1961.

Lifar, Serge, *Serge Diaghilev, His Life, His Work, His Legend: An Intimate Biography*, New York: G. P. Putnam's Sons, 1940.

Livak, Leonid, *Russian Émigrés in the Intellectual and Literary Life of Interwar France*, Ontario: McGill-Queen's University Press, 2010.

Lopokova, Lydia, *Dancing for Diaghilev*, London: John Murray, 1960.

Marie, Grand Duchess of Russia, *Things I Remember*, London: Cassell, 1930. [NB: published in New York as *Education of a Princess*]

——*A Princess in Exile*, London: Macmillan, 1932.

Marie, Queen of Roumania, *The Story of My Life*, New York: Charles Scribner's Sons, 1934.

Marullo, Thomas Gaiton, ed., *Ivan Bunin, A Portrait from Letters, Diaries, and Fiction:* 1 *Russian Requiem, 1885–1920,* Chicago: Ivan R. Dee, 1993.

——2 *From the Other Shore, 1920–1933,* Chicago: Ivan R. Dee, 1995.

——3 *The Twilight of Emigré Russia, 1934–1953,* Chicago: Ivan R. Dee, 2002.

Maxwell, W. T., "The House with Shuttered Windows," *London Magazine* 50: 152, June 1923, 392–96.

Meier, Andrew, *The Lost Spy: An American in Stalin's Secret Service,* New York: W. W. Norton & Company, 2008.

Miller, Michael, *Shanghai on the Métro: Spies, Intrigue, and the French between the Wars,* Berkeley: University of California Press, 1995.

Nabokov, Vladimir, *Speak, Memory,* London: Everyman's Library, 1999.

——*Letters to Vera,* New York: Knopf, 2015.

Nadelhoffer, Hans, *Cartier,* London: Thames & Hudson, 2007.

Némirovsky, Irène, *Le Bal and Snow in Autumn,* London: Vintage Books, 2007.

Nin, Anaïs, *Diary of Anaïs Nin, 1939–1944,* New York: Harcourt Brace Jovanovich, 1971.

Obolensky, Valerian, *Russians in Exile: The History of a Diaspora,* CreateSpace Independent Publishing Platform, 2016. [NB: this book has no pagination]

Odoevtseva, Irina, *Isolde,* London: Pushkin Press, 1929.

Orwell, George, *Down and Out in Paris and London,* London: Victor Gollancz, 1933.

Pachmuss, Temira, *Betweeen Paris and St. Petersburg: Selected Diaries of Zinaida Hippius.* Urbana: University of Illinois Press, 1975.

Paléologue, Maurice, *Three Critical Years, 1904, 1905, 1906,* New York: Robert Speller & Sons, 1957.

——*An Ambassador's Memoirs: 1914–1917,* London: Hutchinson, 1973.

Paley, Princess, *Memories of Russia: 1916–1919,* Urbana: University of Illinois Press, 1975, http://www.alexanderpalace.org/memoriesrussia/index.html.

Peak, Mayme Ober, "Former Ladies of Russian Royalty Working as Paris Dressmaking Models," *Boston Sunday Globe Magazine,* February 19, 1922.

Perry, John Curtis and Constantine Pleshakov, *The Flight of the Romanovs: A Family Saga,* New York: Basic Books, 2001.

Phillips, Alastair, *City of Darkness, City of Light: Émigré Filmmakers in Paris, 1929–1939,* Amsterdam: Amsterdam University Press, 2014.

Picardie, Justine, *Chanel: The Legend and the Life,* London: HarperCollins, 2017.

Plekon, Michael, *Uncommon Prayer: Prayer in Everyday Experience,* Notre Dame, Ind.: University of Notre Dame Press, 2016.

Radziwill, Princess Catherine, "The Broken Heart of the Exiled Princess Paley," *Moline Daily Dispatch,* February 7, 1920.

Raeff, Marc, *Russia Abroad: A Cultural History of the Russian Emigration, 1919–1939,* Oxford: Oxford University Press, 1990.

Rappaport, Helen, *Conspirator: Lenin in Exile,* London: Hutchinson, 2009.

——*Four Sisters: The Lost Lives of the Romanov Grand Duchesses,* London: Macmillan, 2014.

Raymond, Boris and David R. Jones, *The Russian Diaspora: 1917–1941,* Lanham, Md.: Scarecrow Press, 2000.

Ritz, Marie Louise, *César Ritz: Host to the World,* London: George Harrap, 1938.

Roberts, Kenneth L., "Waifs of an Empire," *Saturday Evening Post* 194, July–September 1921, 14, 15, 49, 52, 54, 57, 58, 61.

——"Drifting Leaves," *Harper's* 144, February 1922, 364–72.

Robien, Louis de, *The Diary of a Diplomat in Russia: 1917–1918,* New York: Praeger, 1970.

Robinson, Paul, *Grand Duke Nikolai Nikolaevich: Supreme Commander of the Russian Army,* Ithaca, N.Y.: Cornell University Press, 2016.

——*The White Russian Army in Exile 1920–1941,* Oxford: Oxford University Press, 2002.

Ronald, Susan, *A Dangerous Woman: The Life of Florence Gould,* New York: St. Martin's Press, 2018.

Rood, Karen Lane, *American Writers in Paris, 1920–1939,* vol. 4 of *Dictionary of Literary Biography,* Detroit: Gale Research Company, 1980.

"Royalty Yields to Romance," *Woman's Home Companion* 51, 1924, 7–12, 25–26, 106.

Rubins, Maria, *Russian Montparnasse: Transnational Writing in Interwar Paris,* London: Palgrave Macmillan, 2015.

Russian Paris, 1910–1960, exhibition catalog, St. Petersburg: State Russian Museum, 2003.

Salisbury, Harrison E., *Black Night, White Snow,* New York: Doubleday, 1978.

Scheijen, Sjeng, *Diaghilev,* London: Profile Books, 2010.

Schouvaloff, Alexander, *The Art of Ballets Russes: The Serge Lifar Collection of Theater Designs, Costumes, and Paintings at the Wadsworth Atheneum,* New Haven: Yale University Press, 1998.

Skinner, Cornelia Otis, *Elegant Wits and Grand Horizontals: Paris, La Belle Époque,* London: Michael Joseph, 1963.

Skipwith, Sofka, *Sofka, the Autobiography of a Princess,* London: Hart-Davis, 1968.

Slobin, Greta, *Russians Abroad: Literary and Cultural Politics of Diaspora, 1919–1939,* Brighton, Mass.: Academic Studies Press, 2013.

Smith, Douglas, *Former People: The Destruction of the Russian Aristocracy,* London: Macmillan, 2012.

Starostina, Natalia, "On Nostalgia and Courage: Russian Émigré Experience in Interwar Paris through the Eyes of Nadezhda Teffi," in *Diasporas: Circulations, Migrations, Histoire* 22, 2013, 38–53, https://journals.openedition.org/diasporas/.

Teffi, *Memories: From Moscow to the Black Sea,* London: Penguin, 2016.

——*Subtly Worded,* London: Pushkin Press, 2014.

——*Rasputin and Other Ironies,* London: Pushkin Press, 2014.

——*Gorodok / Little Town,* 1927, translated by Edythe Haber, 1982, http://az.lib.ru/t/teffi/text_1927_gorodok.shtml.

Tsvetaeva, Marina, *After Russia (Paris 1928): The First Notebook,* Swindon, UK: Shearsman Books, 2017.

Ular, Adam, *Russia from Within,* London: Heinemann, 1905.

Vaill, Amanda, *Everybody Was So Young,* London: Warner Books, 1999.

Van der Kiste, John, *Princess Victoria Melita: Grand Duchess Cyril of Russia, 1876–1936,* Stroud, UK: Sutton, 1991.

——and Coryne Hall, *Once a Grand Duchess: Xenia, Sister of Nicholas II,* Stroud, UK: Sutton Publishing, 2004.

Vassiliev, Alexandre, *Beauty in Exile: The Artists, Models, and Nobility Who Fled the Russian Revolution and Influenced the World of Fashion,* New York: Harry N. Abrams, 2000.

Volkov, Solomon, *Saint Petersburg: A Cultural History,* London: Sinclair-Stevenson, 1996.

Walsh, Stephen, *Stravinsky*, vol. 1, *A Creative Spring: Russia and France, 1882–1934*, London: Pimlico, 2002.

Wiser, William, *The Crazy Years: Paris in the Twenties*, New York: Atheneum, 1983.

Woon, Basil D., "Russian Nobles Work and Play to Eat," *Bridgeport Telegram*, April 28, 1922.

——*The Paris That's Not in the Guide Books*, New York: Robert McBride & Co., 1931.

Yanovsky, V. S., *Elysian Fields: A Book of Memory*, Ithaca, N.Y.: Cornell University Press, 1987.

Zinovieff, Elizabeth, *A Princess Remembers: A Russian Life, 1892–1982*, New York: Y. N. Galitzine & J. Ferrand, 1997.

Zinovieff, Sofka, *Red Princess: A Revolutionary Life*, London: Granta Books, 2007.

2. FRENCH SOURCES

Anglade, Jean, *La vie quotidienne des immigrés en France de 1919 à nos jours*, Paris: Hachette Littératures, 1976.

Beucler, André, "Russes de France," *Revue de Paris* 44: 2, April 15, 1937, 866–96.

Boulay, Cyrille, *La France des Romanov: De la villégiature à l'exil*, Paris: Perrin, 2010.

Brummer, General C., "Les derniers jours du Grand Duc Nicholas Mikhailovitch," *Revue de deux mondes*, November 15, 1921.

Bucamp, Philippe, and Martine Mouchy, *Guide de la Russie à Paris*, Paris: Parigramme, 2000.

Collin, Lucien, "La Nation Dans La Ville: Les 'Jeunes pousses' des Russes à Paris," *Intransigeant*, November 10, 1921; "Princesses X . . . et Z . . . Robes et Manteaux," November 11, 1921.

Coulaud, Marcel, "La Russie d'hier refugiée à Paris: Portraits et Confiances," *Le Journal*, March 23, 1926; "La grande-duchesse Marie, brodeuse à Paris," March 24, 1926; "Princesses et comtesses devenues couturiers," March 26, 1926.

Crespelle, Jean-Paul, *La vie quotidienne à Montparnasse à la grande époque, 1905–1920*, Paris: Hachette, 1976.

Delage, Jean, *La Russie en exil*, Paris: Paul Brodard, 1930.

——"L'affreuse misère de l'émigration russe," *Echo de Paris*, July 11, 1935.

Drot, Jean-Marie, *Les heures chaudes de Montparnasse*, Paris: Editions Hazan, 1995.

Ferrand, Jacques, *Le Grand-Duc Paul Alexandrovitch de Russie, sa famille, sa descendance: Chronique et photographies*, Paris, 1993.

Franklin-Marquet, Henry, *Ceux qui ont tué Doumer. La Vérité sur l'affaire Gorgoulov*. Paris: Bureau Editions, 1932.

Gippius, Zinaida, *Dmitry Merezhkovsky*, Paris, 1951.

Gorboff, Marina, *La Russie fantôme: L'émigration russe de 1920 à 1950*, Paris: L'Âge d'homme, 1995.

Gouix, Pierre, *Russes de France: D'hier à aujourd'hui*, Paris: Le Rocher, 2007.

Gray, Marina, *Le général meurt à minuit: L'enlèvement des généraux Koutiépov et Miller*, Paris: Plon, 1981.

Guillou, Olivier le, "Eléments de Recherche sur l'Émigration russe en France. Les Russes de Boulogne-Billancourt en 1926," in Guichard, Éric and Gérard Noiriel, *Construction des nationalités et immigration dans la France contemporaine*, Paris: Presses de l'École normale supérieure, 2002.

Jevakhoff, Alexandre, *Les Russes blancs*, Paris: Tallandier, 2001.

Kazansky, Konstantin, *Cabaret russe,* Paris: Olivier Orban, 1978.

Kessel, J., "De quoi se compose Paris?—Les Russes," *Paris-soir,* April 13, 1924.

Korliakov, Andrei, *Histoire illustrée de l'émigration russe, 1917–1947,* rev. ed., Paris: YMCA-Press, 2020.

Krummenacker, Carolyne, "La mode des cabarets russes à Montmartre," *Le Vieux Montmartre,* Société d'Histoire et d'Archéologie des IX et XVIII Arrondissements Fondée en 1886, 2003. 12–19.

Ledré, Charles, *Les émigrés russes en France, Ce qu'ils sont, ce qu'ils font, ce qu'ils pensent,* Paris: Editions Specs, 1930.

"L'Émigration russe à Paris," *Echo de Paris,* November 10, 1929–January 28, 1930.

Léon-Martin, Louis, "Montmartre Russes, choses vues," *Candide,* April 24, 1924.

"Les Russes blancs, chauffeurs de Taxis à Paris," www.lestaxis.fr/viewtopic.php?t=668.

Liaut, Jean-Noël, *Natalie Paley: Une princesse déchirée / princesse en exil,* Paris, Filipacchi, 1996.

Maire, Svetlana, "La recherche de l'âme slave' chez les émigrés russes de la première vague en France," www.persee.fr/doc/russe_1161–0557_2011_num_36_1_2442?q=Teffi.

Marevna (Marevna Vorobieff), *Mémoires d'une nomade,* Paris: Encre Editions, 1979.

Melenevsky, Natalia, *Les naufrages de la mer noire: Historie de Malia, jeune fille russe,* Paris: Fayard, 1978.

Menegaldo, Hélène, *Les Russes à Paris 1919–1939,* Paris: Editions Autrement, 1998.

Mitterrand, Frédéric, *Mémoires d'exil,* Paris: Robert Laffont, 1999.

Oldenbourg, Zoé, *Visages d'un autoportrait,* Paris: Gallimard, 1977.

Raynaud, E., "Paris Capitale de l'exil—II Les Émigrés russes," *Le Petit Journal,* February 14, 1930.

Ross, Nicolas, *De Koutiepov à Miller. Le combat des russes blancs, 1930–1940,* Paris: Syrtes, 2017.

——*Aux sources de l'émigration russe blanche: Gallipoli, Lemnos, Bizerte, 1920–1921, mémoire de l'émigration blanche,* Geneva: Editions des Syrtes, 2011.

Schor, Ralph, *L'opinion française et les étrangers, 1919–39,* Paris: Publications de la Sorbonne, 1985.

——"Les Russes blancs devant l'opinion française (1919–1939)," *Cahiers de la Méditerranée,* 1994, 48, 211–24.

Seris, Raymond, "Les Réfugiés russes à Paris," *Le Petit Journal,* March 6, 1922.

Struve, Nikita, *Soixante-dix ans d'émigration russe, 1919–1989,* Paris: Fayard, 1996.

Suarez, Georges, "Les Enquêtes du *Petit Journal*: Les Russes à Paris." 10-part series of articles: December 4–10, 12–14, 1927.

Troyat, Henri, *Un si long chemin: Conversations avec Maurice Chavardès,* Paris: Stock, 1987.

——*Marina Tsvetaeva, l'éternelle insurgée,* Paris: B. Grasset, 2001.

Valbelle, Roger, "Les Émigrés russes en France. Une enquête." *Excelsior,* August 11–25, 1930.

Youssupoff (Yusupov), Prince Felix, *En exil,* Paris: Plon, 1954.

Zeisler, Wilfried, *Vivre la belle époque à Paris: Olga Paley et Paul de Russie,* Paris: Mare et Martin, 2018.

3. RUSSIAN SOURCES

Alexandrovsky, Boris, *Iz perezhitogo v chuzhikh krayakh,* Moscow: Mysl, 1969.

Alexinskaya, T., "Russkaya emigratsiya 1920–1939 gg," in *Russkii Parizh.*

Annenkov, Georges, *Dnevnik Moikh Vstrech, Tsikl tragedii.* 2 vols., Moscow: Inter-Language Literary Associates, 1966.

Buslakova, T. P., *Russkii Parizh*, Moscow: Izdatelstvo Moskovkogo Universiteta, 1998.

Damanskaya, A., "Na Ekrane moei pamyati," *Litsa: Biograficheskii almanakh*, Moscow: Feniks, 1996.

Don-Aminado, *Poezd na tretem puti*, Moscow: Proza, 2018.

Dumin, S. V., *Romanovy. Imperatorskii Dom v izgnanii. Semeinaia khronika*, Moscow: Zakharov, 1998.

Ehrenburg, Ilya and El Lissitzky, *Moi Parizh*, Gottingen: Steidl, 2005.

Gul, Roman, *Ya unes Rossiyu: Apologiya russkoy emigratsii*, vol. 2: *Rossiya vo Frantsii*, www.dk1868.ru/history/gul_ogl.htm.

Guseff, Katrin, *Russkaya emigratsiya vo Frantsii*, Moscow: Novoe Literaturnoe Obozrenie, 2014.

Knorring, Irina, *Povest iz sobstvennoy zhizni: Dnevnik*, vol. 2, Moscow: Agraf, 2009.

———*O chem poyut vody Salgira: bezhenskiy dnevnik, stikhi o Rossii*, Moscow: Krug, 2012

Kovalevsky, Petr, *Paskhalnyyi svet na ulitse Daryu: Dnevniki, 1937–1948,* Nizhniy Novgorod: Izdatelstvo "Kristianskaya Biblioteka," 2014.

Lobashkova, T. A., *Knyaz Imperatorskoy krovy Gavriil Konstantinovich 1887–1955, Biografiya i dokumenty.* Moscow: Bumagi Konstantinovichey Doma Romanovykh, 2016.

Lyubimov, Lev, "Na Chuzhbine," *Novyi Mir*, 1957, nos. 2, 3, 4.

Manukhina, T. I., *Puteshestvie iz Peterburga v Parizh v 1921 godu . . . Po materialam Bakhmetevskogo arkhiva*, ed. O. O. R. Demidova, Wilhemshorst: F. K. Göpfert, 1996.

Meisner, Dmitrii, *Mirazhy i deistvitelnost: Zapiski emigrant*, Moscow: Izd. Agentsva Pechati Novosti, 1966.

Obolensky, Pyotr, "Na chuzhoi storone," *Moskva*, 1965, 8, 209–12.

Obolensky, V. A. and B. M. Sarach, *Russkiy Almanakh*, Paris: B M Sarach, 1931.

Odoevtseva, Irina, *Na beregakh Seny*, St. Petersburg: Azbuka-Klassika, 1983.

Romanova, Knyagina Antonina, "Kak Byl Spasen Gavriil Konstantinovich," *Illyustrirovannaya Rossiya*, 1934, 35: 10–12, 36: 6–7; 37: 414–15, 18; 38: 6–7; 39: 14–15; 40: 18–20.

"Russkie emigranty. Shofery taksi: mif i realnost," https://tanya-mass.livejournal.com /2128504.html.

"Russkoe Taksi v Parizhe," https://paris1814.com/.

Sedykh, Andrey, *Dalekie, blizkie*, New York: Novoe Russkoe Slovo, 1962.

———*Tam, gde byla Rossiya*, Paris: Izd. Ya Povolotskago, 1930.

Shakhovskaya, Zinaida, *Otrazhenie*, Paris: YMCA-Press, 1975.

———*Takov moy vek*, Moscow: Russkii put, 2008.

Shkarenkov, L. K. "Belaya emigratsiya: agoniya kontrrevolyutsii," *Voprosy istorii*, 1976, no. 55, 100–20.

Stark, Archpriest Boris, "Po Stranitsam Sinoda," *Rossisskii Arkhiv: Istoriya Otechestva v svidetelstvakh i dokymentakh XVIII-XX vv. Almanakh*, V, 1994, 565–647.

Terapiano, Yuri, *Vstrechi*, New York: Izdatelstvo Imeni Chekhova, 1953.

Uritskaya, R. L. *Oni lyubili svoyu stranu. Sudba russkoi emigratsii vo Frantsii 1933–1948*, St. Petersburg: Dmitriy Bulanin, 2010.

Uspenskiy, V. V., "Vospominaniya parizhskogo shofera taksi," in V. Alloi, T. Pritykina, ed., *Diaspora: novye materialy*, vol. I, Athenaeum, Feniks, Paris, Saint Petersburg, 2001, 7–30.

Varshavsky, Vladimir, *Nezamechennoe pokolenie*, Moscow: Dom Russkogo Zarubezhya Imeni Aleksandra Solzhenitsyna, 2010.

Vertinsky, A., "Chetvert veka bez rodiny," *Moskva*, 1962, nos. 3: 211–20, 4: 205–20, 5: 9–20, 6: 212–19; www.rulit.me/books/chetvert-veka-bez-rodiny-stranicy-minuvshego-read -394498-1.html.

Vishniak, Mark, *Gody emigratsii: Parizh–Nyu Iork 1919–1969*, Stanford: Hoover Institution, 1970.

—— *"Sovremennye zapiski," Vospominaniya redaktora*, Bloomington, 1957, in Buslakova, *Russkii Parizh*.

Volkonskaya, Sofya, *Gore pobezhdennym bezhentsy: Vae Victis*, Moscow: Gosudarstvennaya publichnaya istoricheskaya biblioteka Rossii, 2017.

Yuniverg, Leonid, "'Illyustrirovannaya Rossiya' kak zerkalo emigrantskoy zhizni 20–30 godov," https://artrz.ru/download/1804913147/1805172601/1.

Index